D0592660

HIGH DAMS AND SLACK WATERS

HIGH DAMS AND SLACK WATERS

TVA Rebuilds a River

WILMON HENRY DROZE

LOUISIANA STATE UNIVERSITY PRESS / Baton Rouge

333.9109768
D793h

Copyright 1965 by
Louisiana State University Press
Library of Congress Catalog Card Number: 65-14533

Manufactured in the United States of America by
Kingsport Press, Inc., Kingsport, Tenn.
Designed by Jules B. McKee

188512

PREFACE

Creation of the Tennessee Valley Authority in 1933 officially committed the federal government to a policy of multipurpose development of the Tennessee River. For more than a century prior to that, federal and state efforts to make the river commercially usable had resulted in failure or, at best, piecemeal improvements. This study seeks to determine how well the TVA carried out its congressional mandate to develop maximum navigability of the river and how navigation improvement fared in the new scheme of comprehensive river-basin management. It also attempts to assess the impact of the new commercial artery on economic life in the valley and its hinterland.

The story of the evolution of the Tennessee River from a dangerous, erratic, sometimes useful stream to a safe and dependable artery of commerce is a testimonial to what man can do if motivation, circumstances, and wisdom exist in the proper relationship. The history of navigation improvement on the Tennessee falls into two distinct periods. The first era encompasses most of the nineteenth century and three decades of the twentieth century. The last period is that time from the creation of the TVA in 1933 to the present. The first era is only briefly treated; the history of the second is the theme of this work.

When the Authority was established by Congress little attention was given to the agency's navigation function, in spite of the fact that it was the "constitutional peg" on which the whole structure rested. In time, however, various factors compelled the TVA to give greater attention to its navigation assignment. As the main-river dams were built and the channel was extended and deepened, TVA's staff discovered how important river transportation could be to its overall goal of social and economic rehabilitation of the basin area. This recognition led the Authority to pursue its navigation objective to the utmost and ultimately to develop one of the nation's most modern waterways.

TVA's navigation program and project and the utilization of the waterway by both the Authority and private enterprisers is to many persons an entirely unfamiliar subject. Its role as a developer of one of the country's major rivers for navigation, a task usually assigned to the Corps of Engineers, has been far less controversial than its generation and sale of electric power. The importance of the new waterway in the development of the economy of the Southeast is not written in newspaper headlines, nor does one see a continual stream of towboats and barges moving on the river as vehicles rush along on a modern freeway. Nevertheless, grain barged from the upper Mississippi River region permits the southern farmer to raise his standard of living, and oil tows from the Gulf Coast bring to the city dweller a cheaper gallon of gasoline. The newly born industries along the riverfront furnish jobs for an ever increasing number of workers. Navigation, which was scoffed at by the skeptics in 1933, is a multimillion-dollar operation in 1964.

This story of the improvement of the Tennessee River for barge transportation is the product of the author but his debts are manifold. I owe much to Professors Dewey W. Grantham and Herbert Weaver of Vanderbilt University for their friendly counsel, their patience, and their encouragement, which they so generously gave as directors of this work when it was in the doctoral dissertation stage. I especially appreciate the cooperation of Mr. J. Porter Taylor, Director of the Division of Navigation of the TVA, his associates therein, and Mr. Bernard Foy of the TVA Technical Library in permitting me to utilize their materials and to borrow from their vast store of knowledge about the development of the Tennessee River for navigation. I am grateful to Dean Raleigh A. Suarez, McNeese

State College, Lake Charles, Louisiana, for reading the manuscript in its entirety and offering many valuable suggestions.

I am indebted to the following institutions, organizations, and individuals for their assistance at various stages of the manuscript's progress: Joint University Library, Nashville, Tennessee; Technical Library, Tennessee Valley Authority, Knoxville, Tennessee; Water Freight Bureau of the Interstate Commerce Commission, Washington, D.C.; Corps of Engineers, District Office, Nashville, Tennessee; East Central State College, Ada, Oklahoma; Ford Foundation; and the Southern Fellowship Fund. I would also like to thank Misses Barbara Luttrell and Janet LaCasse, students at McNeese State College, for their assistance in typing the manuscript.

Finally, I want to pay tribute to my wife, Carolyn Jung Droze, who offered many critical judgments on styling and who proofread innumerable pages of composition as the work progressed from an idea to a completed manuscript. I am additionally indebted to her for cheerfully granting to me long periods of solitary contemplation about boats, barges, and the river. To her—and to numerous others —I am most grateful.

McNeese State College
Lake Charles, Louisiana

WILMON H. DROZE

CONTENTS

HIGH DAMS AND SLACK WATERS

1

THE OLD RIVER DEFIES IMPROVEMENT, 1779–1930

The Tennessee River gathers the waters from a 40,900 square-mile area of the southeastern United States. The river originates in the Southern Appalachian Highlands, a region of low mountains with a heavy annual rainfall. The runoff from this massive rainfall has cut a number of tortuous, boulder-strewn streams which empty into the Tennessee at various places as it makes its way southwestwardly across East Tennessee. Four miles above Knoxville the waters of two of these streams, the Holston and the French Broad, wed to form the controversial Tennessee. Even the source of this mighty river was subject to controversy until a federal statute declared in 1890 that the juncture of the Holston and the French Broad was the head of the stream.[1]

From its head to its mouth the Tennessee is an illogical river. It traverses a distance of 652 miles and at one time or another flows in almost every direction. In its serpentine wanderings from Knoxville to Paducah, Kentucky, where it empties into the Ohio, the Tennessee bends southwestwardly across the eastern part of Tennessee into Alabama, westwardly across northern Alabama, northwardly between Alabama and Mississippi, and finally moves directly north through western Tennessee and Kentucky. As it rambles it falls .77 of a foot per mile, with a total decline of five hundred feet between its head and its mouth. The amount of its water flow in its natural state was as irregular as its course. At Florence, Alabama, midpoint of the river, the winter discharge was twenty times greater than that in summer.[2]

Before any improvements were undertaken the Tennessee consisted of three distinct sections, each having its own obstructions to navigation. The lower portion of the stream, which extends from the mouth to Florence, Alabama, was least hazardous to navigate. Major obstructions in this stretch were snags, sand bars, and two series of shoals. The middle portion of the river, from Florence to Chattanooga, contained the most serious impediments to navigation. In the lower part of this section were the famous Muscle Shoals, in reality four series of shoals, which constituted the major obstruction to river transportation throughout the entire watercourse. Above the Muscle Shoals, less formidable shoals existed. The upper part of the middle sector, which cut through the mountain gorges south of Chattanooga, contained The Narrows. The peculiar rock formations in the stream bed and the narrow width of the river in this 20-mile stretch created rapid currents and eddies, thus earning such names as The Frying Pan, The Boiling Pot, The Suck, and The Tumbling Shoals. In the upper part of the stream, numerous rock reefs and gravel bars were present. To make matters worse, the descent of the river, sometimes even and sometimes rapid, created changes in the velocity of the current from place to place. Finally, the seasonal nature of the Tennessee's water flow, much greater in winter and spring than in summer and fall, further limited the river's utility for transportation purposes.

In spite of its limitations the Tennessee has played a vital role in serving the people who have lived along its shores. The Cherokees found it especially useful in solving their problems of logistics in war and food in peace. When Virginia traders, French *Coureurs de bois,* and Carolina fur-seekers penetrated the region in the seventeenth and eighteenth centuries, the area became a pawn in the struggle for the vast interior of North America. The French and Indian War eliminated the French, and English control of the river and its hinterland for the remainder of the colonial period was assured.

Permanent agricultural settlement soon followed the westward march of British colors. Within a decade following the British conquest, the Watauga settlements were established. The Tennessee and its tributaries, though swift, dangerous, and often of uncertain depths for navigation, provided the settler with a means of transporting his family and goods. The dramatic episode of the Donelson party in 1779, when a group of settlers led by John Donelson journeyed from the Watauga colony in East Tennessee down the entire distance of the Tennessee, up the Ohio, thence up the Cumberland to settle finally at the present site of Nashville, vividly illustrates the importance of the river as an avenue to the West. More and more as the upper portions of the stream were settled and as the Tennessee frontier advanced westward, the river was put to work to serve the growing communities.

The conquest of the Tennessee country was not without its difficulties. In addition to the hardships involved in developing a frontier homestead, there were the problems of Indian warfare and, after the American Revolution ended British control of the area, of troubles with Spain, who sought to check American expansion during the formative years of the new republic. In spite of such obstacles to the occupation and control of the Tennessee territory, the area was brought under the influence of the American pioneers. In time, western commercial demands sparked diplomatic efforts to dislodge Spain from the mouth of the Mississippi, which ultimately controlled the outbound flow of goods from the Tennessee. Diplomacy, aided by European rivalry, assured a final settlement of political control over the gateway to the western waters when, in 1803, the United States purchased New Orleans and the Louisiana Territory.

Spanish control of the Mississippi River did not preclude the use of the Tennessee for local freight and passengers. The dugout canoe, the raft, the flatboat, and the keelboat were in turn put to work to carry the produce of the western farmer. Much of this early commerce was one-way, downstream traffic, since natural hazards and obstacles to upstream transport prevented the westerner from receiving his supplies from New Orleans via the Mississippi, the Ohio, and the Tennessee. A lively two-way commerce did develop on a local basis when the keelboat made upstream movements possible.[3]

The settlers of East Tennessee had to await the steamboat and river improvements before they could make more extensive use of the river. The flatboat-keelboat age restricted the use of the stream to men of substance, since the cost of transporting goods was beyond the means of the average landholder.[4] Moreover, the natural state of the river with its numerous shoals and seasonal low water levels limited rich and poor alike in utilizing the water artery. The inaccessibility of markets for the region of the river above the Muscle Shoals restricted the economic development of East Tennessee, where economic life tended to develop on a subsistence basis.[5]

While the eastern Tennessee region remained economically isolated by mountain barriers to the east and an unnavigable river to the west, the Great Bend section of the Tennessee was rapidly being brought under the plow. As Donald Davidson has written, the settlement of the Muscle Shoals region "was not the slow, steady infiltration of the older pioneering. It was a stampede." [6] Great riches from cotton production lured the horde to North Alabama. These would-be cotton aristocrats, drunk with visions of quickly accumulated wealth, foresaw little difficulty in producing bounteous crops and shipping the harvest down-river to New Orleans. The generosity of virgin land supported their dreams of princely yields, but the mighty Muscle Shoals and low water in the river at harvest time made the marketing of the crop expensive and hazardous. The conquest of the Tennessee was still a century away, but the advent of a new era on the Tennessee was at hand.

As the agricultural advance brought statehood to Tennessee and later to Alabama, pressure soon mounted for a legislative program of stream improvements. In Tennessee the first response came in the form of prohibitory legislation. Laws were passed to prevent the obstruction of rivers by persons engaged in fishing and milling. Fish traps and mill dams proved to be serious obstacles to pioneer flatboatmen.[7]

Although man-made impediments to navigation were a serious problem to river users, they in no way equalled the natural obstructions in the river. In time, as the inhabitants of the Tennessee country began to produce a surplus, more and more demands were made upon the legislature to adopt a positive program of river improvements. Since the state treasury was impoverished and funds were unavailable, these demands were met by encouraging navigation companies to incorporate in order that they might carry out programs of river improvement. These organizations were allowed to raise funds by stock subscriptions, lotteries, and other means. The collection of tolls provided the companies with revenue. Further, local governments were permitted to levy special taxes for similar projects. In the final analysis, this method of solving the problem of river betterment proved too costly and accomplished little.[8] The fruitlessness of these efforts spawned demands for direct appropriations for improving the state's rivers.

In 1817 a board was created by the legislature to supervise the improvement of the Holston and Tennessee rivers. Money was allocated to the board from interest payments due the state from land purchases.[9] This means of river development appeared at first to be the answer to local demands for state aid, but the panic of 1819 forced the state to abandon this policy. Its curtailment resulted from the legislature's increased interest in relief legislation and from its unwillingness to speculate on anticipated revenues from land sales.[10] A final consideration which helped to terminate the policy was the growing feeling by state leaders that the federal government was ready to initiate an internal improvements program.[11]

While the struggle over direct federal aid to river development was being fought in the early nineteenth century, the steamboat found its way to the Tennessee. In 1821 the *Osage*, first steamboat on the Tennessee, arrived at Florence, just below the Muscle Shoals, with a cargo of lead, coffee, nails, sugar, tea, molasses, mackerel, white lead, bar iron, and "Scotch bagging" from New Orleans.[12] During the following year regular service was initiated on the lower river between Florence and the Ohio River.

Steamboat service along the lower river left much to be desired. Its operations were plagued by natural obstacles and low water levels. During the dry months of the summer, loads were lightened by storage or transferred to keelboats so that the steamboats could navigate shallow stretches of the stream. These problems, occurring at the time of the cotton harvest, forced producers to rely on more costly land transportation. Nashville became the leading cotton shipping port of Tennessee and northern Alabama. Wagons brought the crop to Nashville; from there it was shipped by boat via the Cumberland, the Ohio, and the Mississippi rivers to New Orleans. During high water season Florence enjoyed a competitive trade relationship with Nashville.[13]

The partially successful use of the steamboat on the lower river stimulated the interest of East Tennesseans in procuring steamboat service for the river above Florence. The lack of capital in private hands precluded any river improvement program; [14] the hope of East Tennessee and North Alabama appeared to be in the development of lighter draft vessels which could navigate the river in its natural state.[15] Although it was recognized that the shoals region constituted an almost impossible barrier to the passage of the steamboat during the summer and fall, it was thought that keelboats of shallow draft could be utilized to connect an upper and lower river steamboat service during periods of low water.

The desire to initiate steamboat transportation above the shoals resulted in an intense promotional campaign by Knoxvillians and others to induce a dauntless captain to navigate the entire length of the river. A substantial sum of prize money attracted a candidate in the late 1820's. The *Atlas,* a small side-wheeler, fought shoals, narrows, and shallow water and arrived in Knoxville on March 3, 1828. The feat was celebrated with vigor. Speeches, toasts, and dinners were the order of the day. Captain S. D. Conner, the vessel's master, collected the prize of $640 and confidently observed that the "river from Brown's Ferry to Knoxville would be navigable nine months of the year." [16] A few discerning citizens viewed the visit of the *Atlas* more judiciously. Dr. James G. M. Ramsey, a leading citizen and promoter of East Tennessee, voiced the opinion that the salvation of the region rested on the building of public roads and railroads rather than on improved water transport. He felt that the area should develop connections with the Atlantic Coast instead of the Gulf, for the latter link would result in the exploitation of the region's resources without bringing in comparable benefits. Such admonitions provoked angry criticism from the jubilant celebrators,[17] but Ramsey's judgment proved to be sound. During the next decade only eight boats were able to conquer the shoals and participate in the upper Tennessee trade.

Neither early state efforts to eliminate the physical obstructions to navigation nor private attempts to use lighter draft vessels made significant progress toward more efficient use of the river. The propulsion problem of upstream sailing had been overcome by the steamboat, but the barriers nature placed in the stream remained. Moreover, the hope of direct and immediate federal aid in improving the river was ended by President Andrew Jackson's veto of the Maysville Road bill in 1830. These reverses led the advocates of river developments to turn again to the state for improvement funds.

The national movement of state aid to internal improvements was reflected in Tennessee by a new enthusiasm among the people for state assistance, not only for waterways but for turnpikes and railroads as well. Indeed, the rise of newer, more competitive means of transport boded ill for the proponents of river improvements, for now all three groups demanded a portion of state funds. Since the geography of the state varied so radically, each section proposed different solutions to its transportation problems. West Tennessee favored developing her river connections with the Mississippi, while Middle Tennessee preferred building turnpikes radiating from Nashville. Only the East Tennessee region clung to its long-standing dream of improving the Tennessee River. The railroad advocates were still in the minority.[18]

In January, 1830, Tennessee initiated a significant program of state aid to internal improvements. Opposition to such a policy was negligible, but the measure was delayed somewhat by disagreements among the three sections over the division of the funds, the method of spending the money, and the supervision of expenditures. Ultimately, a sum of $150,000 was appropriated and divided apparently on the basis of the political strength of each region. East and Middle Tennessee each received $60,000, and West Tennessee was allocated $30,000. A single board for the whole state was created to administer the program. Steamboat interests in Knoxville quickly grew impatient with the board's apparent inactivity and demanded more energetic action or a separate board. The legislature responded in 1831 and created a "Board of Internal Improvements for East Tennessee." This agency was directed to use the funds appropriated in 1830 for the betterment of the Holston and Tennessee rivers.[19]

The East Tennessee board began in January, 1832, to determine the needs of navigation on the Tennessee and the Holston. It secured from President Jackson, without cost, the services of Colonel Stephen H. Long of the United States engineers. Long surveyed the river and proposed a plan of development which involved the deepening of the channel and the provision of "warping" facilities where the current was too swift for upstream navigation. He estimated that such improvements would cost about $60,000. The board had already expended a portion of its original appropriation, and it was unable to finance the entire proposal. It petitioned the legislature for additional funds but was refused. During the next three years, 1832 to 1835, its remaining funds were utilized to improve those places between the Alabama line and Knoxville where the most serious obstructions to navigation existed. Though the amount of funds was limited, these improvements enabled the steamboats to operate for a longer portion of the year.[20] The Long survey was a precedent, for it marked the first major federal expenditure for navigation improvement of the

Tennessee. In addition, it pointed the way to the need for channel development as the key to more dependable steamboat service on the river.

The meager successes of the early 1830's heartened the supporters of river development and led them to demand greater legislative assistance. Their efforts bore little fruit. The state authorized the issuance of $300,000 in bonds in 1838 for improvement of the state's rivers, but the bonds could not be marketed in the midst of a depression which was bankrupting business and government. Even if the securities had been sold, the funds would have been used for the improvement of the tributaries of the Tennessee since the 1830 appropriations had gone to develop the main river. Thus, as the 1837 depression lingered, the issue remained dormant and no funds for river improvement were available.[21]

In 1841 a congressional decision to distribute money from public land sales to the states rekindled interest in the dormant bond issue. After much bickering among the three sections of the state, the legislature decided, in 1842, to redeem the securities and make outright appropriations of $100,000 to both East and West Tennessee from the anticipated federal funds.[22] During the next ten years the money was expended by each section on tributary improvements. The feeder streams were not greatly improved, for the funds were spent on too many small projects. The most important contribution of the 1842 law was that it stimulated traffic on the tributaries, which acted as feeder arteries for the main river.[23]

This increase in traffic brought demands that the federal government adopt a program for improving the Tennessee. The prolonged efforts of the state to develop the Tennessee for navigation brought little success,[24] but the agitation for state aid kept the issue alive until a more generous benefactor could be convinced of the importance of a navigable Tennessee.

While Tennesseans were struggling to improve their sections of the river, the people of North Alabama began to focus their attention on the problems of water transport in the region of the Great Bend. In that section lay the Muscle Shoals,[25] "a steamboatman's hell of agony and danger." [26] Prior to statehood in 1819, Alabama was unable to raise money for river improvement, because its people were heavily indebted for land purchases and its population was still shifting. When Alabama entered the Union, a greater interest in waterway improvement developed, for agricultural production was rapidly becoming commercialized and outlets to markets were essential.

The natural flow of goods from North Alabama was down the Tennessee, Ohio, and Mississippi to New Orleans and abroad. This access, however, was blocked by the seemingly unconquerable Muscle Shoals. Moreover, public officials in Alabama showed more interest in developing a system of canals to link the northern and southern parts of the state in order to prevent sectional rivalry and to foster the growth of the port of Mobile rather than improve the Tennessee which would benefit New Orleans. Several schemes for linking the Tennessee to Alabama's south-flowing rivers which emptied into the Gulf of Mexico were examined. In 1823 a navigation company chartered by the legislature was authorized to issue stock as a means of raising funds for a canal project. Public failure to purchase the stock ended this venture. Other companies organized for similar purposes met the same fate. Thus, the people of North Alabama, in the early years of statehood, continued to be economically isolated by the failure of the canal programs and by the Muscle Shoals obstructions in the Tennessee.[27]

As Alabama's canal fever subsided, interest in the Tennessee River as a commerical artery heightened. Also, the immensity of the Muscle Shoals barrier attracted the interest of the federal government since the shoals effectively blocked water transport on one of the nation's major rivers. Unlike Tennessee, then, Alabama was able very early to secure federal aid in the improvement of its portion of the waterway. In 1827 a congressional appropriation of $200 was made to conduct a survey of the shoals region. A year later the state was granted 400,000 acres of federal lands within its borders which were sold to finance navigation improvements at the shoals. The grant required that plans of the project had to receive presidential approval and that tolls could not be collected in the improved sections without congressional sanction. In spite of such a generous offer, Alabama waited almost two years before taking action on the proposition.[28]

In January, 1830, the General Assembly accepted title to the land grant and set up the Board of Tennessee Canal Commissioners to administer the project. Upon the advice of the United States Board of Internal Improvements, the commissioners decided that the shoals navigation problems could best be solved by building a lateral canal around the obstructions, which would link the upper and lower portions of the river. Work on the canal was begun in 1831, but immediately the project was beset with difficulties. Land sales were slow and revenues were inadequate to complete the original plan of bypassing all of the shoals.[29] Congressional approval was sought and obtained to shorten the canal so as to circumvent only the "Big Muscle Shoals." The 14-mile canal was finally completed in 1836 at a cost of $644,594.[30]

The project was a failure before it was completed, for obstructions to navigation still existed above and below the artificial waterway. To overcome these obstacles, Alabama once again appealed to the federal government for aid. In 1836 Congress allowed the state to levy tolls on river traffic to obtain revenues for carrying out the original plans. Of course, no traffic resulted in no revenue. The lack of funds led the board of commissioners to seek outright appropriations from both Congress and the state legislature during the next two years. The appeal was unanswered, for the panic of 1837 brought about a retrenchment in expenditures of both governments. Moreover, it is doubtful that the Congress would have inaugurated such a program of direct aid in view of the Jacksonian efforts to divorce government and business.[31]

The isolated canal soon fell victim to disrepair and disuse. The waterway began to fill with silt carried by streams which emptied into it. The alteration of the original plans had resulted in placing the depth of the channel lower than was first planned without any provision for preventing the discharge of water and silt into the canal by small streams and creeks. The continued existence of shoals above and below the canal effectively blocked traffic. In 1868 William B. Gaw, an engineer employed by the War Department to survey the Tennessee for navigation purposes, appraised the project accordingly: "At the present time it is simply a monument of misdirected energies and of a foolish expenditure of money." [32] The state of Alabama apparently thought likewise, for it showed little interest in making further waterway improvements in the Great Bend of the river. It focused its attention on developing its north-south waterway network and then turned to railroad construction as the solution to the state's transportation problems.[33]

By the mid-1840's, the panic of 1837 and its destructive effects on state-aid programs of river improvements, the rise of steamboating, the increasing influence of the Whig party in Tennessee, and the decreasing support of Jacksonian constitutionalism persuaded the people of Tennessee and North Alabama that direct federal aid for improving the Tennessee was desirable. Petitions, memorials, and resolutions in large numbers were sent to Congress from Tennessee and Alabama by local groups and the state legislatures asking for federal support.[34] The historian Philip Hamer observed that "in their desire for governmental aid, the first tendency of Tennesseans was to turn to the government of the United States."[35] In 1852, after several years of constant pressure by river improvement advocates, these efforts were rewarded by congressional designation of Knoxville and Chattanooga as ports of entry of the United States.[36] Thus began a new era in the development of the Tennessee for navigation.

The first direct federal appropriation for improving the river followed immediately after the naming of the two Tennessee cities as ports of entry. In the Rivers and Harbors Act of 1852, a sum of $50,000 was provided for open-river development between Knoxville and Kelley's Ferry, some twenty miles below Chattanooga. A minimum channel depth of two feet was to be obtained by the removal of sand bars, snags, boulders, and rock obstructions.[37] The initial attempt by federal engineers to tame the upper Tennessee was of little aid to steamboat operators, for a year-round 2-foot depth was never attained. The appropriation was much too small for such a large project, and no provisions were made to maintain the channel after its improvement.[38] Moreover, it is doubtful that a 2-foot minimum depth would have provided adequate water for most vessels.

Beginning in 1868, after a sixteen-year lapse, the central government inaugurated a more concerted program to provide a navigation channel. For the first time obstructions throughout the entire river were considered, and an improvement plan designed to provide navigation from Knoxville to the mouth of the river was developed. Federal engineers divided the waterway into three sections according to its physical nature: Knoxville to Chattanooga, Chattanooga to Riverton, Alabama, and Riverton to the mouth.[39] This division was necessitated by the differing nature of the obstructions to traffic in each section.

The upper portion of the river above Chattanooga, where only a small amount of local freighting was done, was to be deepened to three feet and the channel maintained accordingly. The excavation of rock and gravel and the construction of water contraction devices were to be the means of assuring the minimum depth. Once again the goal eluded the planners. The lack of success, however, did not seem to dishearten the War Department's engineers, for in 1894, 1912, and 1930 even more ambitious plans for improving the upper river were drawn and approved by the Congress.[40]

The 1894 statute provided for the continuance of old methods, but in 1912 the engineers changed their strategy. The new approach sought to eliminate the more serious obstructions by the building of low-lift locks and dams which would have impounded water to a depth of six feet. Additionally, rock excavation, dredging, and contraction works were to be developed at those places where a 3-foot depth could be attained. Under the 1912 statute a low dam was authorized at Caney Creek Shoals upstream from Chattanooga, but Congress failed to provide funds for the project. Again in 1930, a more ambitious plan for developing the river for navigation was proposed by the War Department and authorized by Congress. At that time, a project depth of nine feet was planned, but nothing of note was ever accomplished.[41] When the Tennessee Valley Authority (TVA) was assigned the task of developing the river, the upper portion was still an undeveloped waterway. Dependable depths in this section throughout the year were only 1.3 feet. During high-water season, from January to June, a 3-foot depth existed.[42] Since modern river transportation equipment was requiring deeper and deeper water, the shallow water of the upper Tennessee held out no inducement to barge traffic, and Knoxville, at the head of the river, was a port of entry only in fiction.

The middle part of the river, from Chattanooga to Riverton, Alabama, a distance of 237.4 miles, received the greatest attention and the largest amount of federal funds in the pre-TVA era.[43] Since the physical features of this stretch varied so greatly, the army engineers subdivided it into three sections for improvement purposes. The first part, a distance of 171 miles, reached from Chattanooga to Brown's Island, an island just above the Elk River, a tributary of the Tennessee. The next section was only 37 miles, but it contained the treacherous Muscle Shoals. It extended from Brown's Island to Florence. The last subdivision, from Florence to Riverton, was not quite so difficult to navigate as the immediate region above, but it was impassable at low water and did contain the Colbert and Bee Tree Shoals where steamboats incurred some danger from boulders and swift water. Altogether, the middle portion of the river, with its rapid currents just below Chattanooga and the numerous shoals between Brown's Island and Riverton, effectively divided the upper and lower river and thus prevented navigation of the river except for local hauls.[44]

Between 1868 and 1871 the Corps of Engineers worked out a twofold scheme for the improvement of the middle portion of the Tennessee. The engineers proposed to develop a 3-foot controlling depth from Chattanooga to Decatur, Alabama, by blasting and dredging, in order to eliminate boulders, snags, and gravel. Below Decatur, where the shoals precluded such open-channel work, a series of canals bypassing the obstructions was projected. A 5-foot depth at low water was fixed as the minimum navigation depth in the canals.[45]

Efforts to improve this section of the river by open-channel work came to naught. In the first place, the seasonal problem of low water remained unsolved, and the swift currents, just below Chattanooga where the Tennessee cuts its way through the Cumberland Plateau, continued to be dangerous to steamboats. The low-water problem could only be solved by a reservoir system on the tributaries of the Tennessee, but water-control technology of this type was apparently unknown by the engineers or too bold for Congress to finance. Since greater depth of water appeared to be the only alternative for making the stream useful, Congress approved an engineer plan in 1907 which called for an additional 2-foot depth.[46] Another decade of dredging and removing snags and boulders followed, but a 5-foot channel was not achieved.

In 1905 private interests, seeking to develop the power possibilities of the Tennessee in the Chattanooga area, came to the aid of the engineers. Between 1905 and 1913 a moderately high power dam and navigation lock was constructed on the Hales Bar site, approximately thirty-three miles downstream from Chattanooga. This impoundment created slack-water navigation of six feet from the dam to the Tennessee city. The lake formed by the dam eliminated the rapid whirls which for a century had created agony for steamboat operators as they neared Chattanooga. By 1916 the Corps of Engineers turned to dam construction as the only feasible way to provide navigation in the remainder of the middle section of the river above the shoals. The Rivers and Harbors Acts of 1916 authorized two such dams with locks and authorized the Secretary of War to select the sites and the kinds of dams necessary to provide a 5-foot navigation depth. The first of these dams, located at Widow's Bar, some twenty-three miles below the Hales Bar Dam, was finally completed in 1925 after a five-year construction period. The second dam, which was planned for

Bellefonte Island some seventeen miles below the Widow's Bar Dam, was never built because of Congress' refusal to appropriate funds for the project. Open-channel work was continued in the section from the Widow's Bar Dam to Brown's Island. In spite of the frustrating efforts by the Corps of Engineers to provide adequate navigation depths in the upper portion of the middle section of the river, little was accomplished. On the eve of the creation of the TVA, a 115-mile stretch of this portion had only an average navigable depth of 1.25 feet throughout the year. A lack of boldness in planning by the engineers and the meager funds provided by Congress for river improvement prevented successful development of the stream for navigation.[47]

The engineers were more successful in attacking the problems of navigation in the shoals section of the stretch from Chattanooga to Riverton. Navigation in this area was to be provided by the construction of a canal around the major shoals and open-channel work between the shoals. In 1871, almost forty years after the old Muscle Shoals Canal of 1831 had been abandoned, the Corps of Engineers under the direction of Congress began to canalize the river throughout the shoals region. Work was begun in 1875 but progress was slow, for the rivers and harbors committees of Congress provided a minimum of money for the undertaking. Finally, in 1890, two canals were completed around the Elk River and Big Muscle Shoals. Through the use of locks, a depth of five feet was obtained in the canals.[48]

The building of the two bypass canals only partially solved the problem of navigation in the shoals region. Another thirty-seven years would elapse before the conquest would be complete. Between 1916 and 1927 the shoals obstructions were eliminated by the construction of the massive Wilson Dam and a low dam,[49] 2.5 miles below that structure. These dams raised the water level well above the obstructions which formerly prevented navigation. The lower section of the middle part of the river was not forgotten as the shoals section was being improved. Beginning in 1868 the engineers commenced open-channel work in the area from Florence to Riverton. In 1890 a lateral canal 8.06 miles long and 112 feet wide was authorized around the Colbert and Bee Tree shoals located in this section. The project, completed in 1911, established a 7-foot depth at minimum low water which served the needs of navigation well for a time.[50]

Federal aid in developing the lower section of the Tennessee was less costly, and the problem of improvement was less complex. In this part of the stream, from Riverton to Paducah, a stretch of 225 miles, open-channel work and annual maintenance gave the desired channel depth until more modern waterway equipment necessitated deeper water. This section of the river was utilized more extensively than any other; thus Congress was less niggardly in providing funds for its improvement. River acts of 1868, 1890, 1894, 1899, and 1912 contained appropriations for dredging and removing obstructions in the lower river. By 1930, a 4.5-foot depth had been achieved from Riverton to Paducah, where the Tennessee empties into the Ohio River.[51]

The extended efforts of the War Department's engineers to develop the Tennessee for navigation in the pre-TVA era were far from successful. The work was costly,[52] slow, and wasteful, and navigation of the entire river was impractical except during the season of high-water flow. Under ideal conditions on the stream, navigable depths varied from three feet between Knoxville and Chattanooga to six feet for the remainder of the waterway, except for a short distance above the Wilson Dam. Even when these meager results were accomplished, the Tennessee River was an outmoded waterway when compared with channel development on other rivers of comparable importance.[53] In spite of the clamor of river improvement conventions in the first decade of the twentieth century for—"water, more water, and deeper water," the Corps of Engineers was forced to admit in 1930 that "under such conditions [referring to channel depths in existence if all projects then underway had been completed] navigation cannot be developed, and the money which is being expended does not accomplish any material good toward furthering water transportation." [54] Major General Lytle Brown, Chief of Engineers, endorsed this view when he reported to the Secretary of War in 1930 that "in its present condition, the river is not well adapted to navigation on a modern scale and the completion of the existing projects would not provide a satisfactory waterway." [55]

Several million dollars of federal and state funds and almost a century of effort were expended in the attempt to make the Tennessee a navigable river. Why had the local, state, and federal governments achieved such insignificant results? Lack of vision and unsound use of available funds account in part for the limited success of the engineers. But, the major responsibility for the piecemeal results must be assigned to other factors. Congressional appropriations were always too small and often uncertain. The limited amount of money had to be spread too thinly among projects throughout the entire river, which precluded substantial improvements in any given sector of the long, winding waterway. Moreover, the numerous obstructions to navigation of the Tennessee were more expensive to eliminate than those on most rivers because of the many shoals. Congress, it appears, doled out its funds without real concern for the task which had to be done, but rather on a "pork-barrel" basis.

Still other factors were responsible for the failure of single-purpose development of the river. Heavy construction machinery and a greater knowledge of construction materials were needed by the engineers to build with rapidity and boldness such structures as were built in the 1930's.[56] The conquest of this river, with its more than normal share of obstacles, required men of vision. Its conquerors would have to have the generous support of Congress. The nation would have to demand that its government chart untried courses in solving these problems. Until such a situation came into being in 1933, the old river defied improvement. The factors that converged to create the proper climate in which such an ambitious undertaking could be launched had their roots deep in the past. The story of the growth of these factors and how they finally merged in May, 1933, to produce a new concept of waterway development—the Tennessee Valley Authority—which would solve the navigation problems of the Tennessee River is told in the pages that follow.

2

NAVIGATION, PLANNING, AND POLITICS

Initial efforts by private enterprise, state governments, and the federal government to improve the Tennessee River had a single objective—navigation. But these endeavors bore little fruit, and after a century of trial the problem of making the river navigable remained unsolved. Single-purpose development of the stream could have provided 9-foot navigation, but by the time the Corps of Engineers and Congress produced such a developmental plan single-purpose river improvement was already outmoded. By 1930, when the engineers completed their plans for a modern navigation system on the Tennessee, multipurpose stream improvement methods were being utilized to develop some of the nation's rivers. The expense of instituting such a bold plan for the Tennessee prohibited its implementation until 1933. In that year, several forces converged to produce the Tennessee Valley Authority,[1] a depression-born federal agency which would in less than a decade transform the unruly river into a series of slack-water lakes providing 9-foot navigation, flood control, and water for power generation.

In May, 1933, the statute creating the TVA officially committed the federal government to a policy of comprehensive development of the river. The agency that was established to carry out the act was "a corporation clothed with the power of government but possessed of the flexibility and initiative of a private enterprise."[2] When its three-man board of directors met for the first time on June 16, 1933, in a bare Washington hotel room with fruit crates for chairs, the final effort to "tame" the Tennessee was about to begin. The corporation was directed to develop a river to serve several purposes, but the method and extent of this development was left to the ingenuity of the TVA board of directors.

The TVA statute was remarkably vague concerning the navigation assignment of the agency. It was directed to improve the navigability of the stream and empowered to construct navigation projects; but the Corps of Engineers was made responsible for the operation of the navigation locks, lifts, and other such facilities. The details of planning, building, and operating the water control system for a 650-mile channel were left to TVA. The failure of Congress to spell out TVA's navigation assignment in a more specific manner indicates that the improvement of the river for water transportation was of secondary importance to a Congress burdened with problems of nation-wide unemployment and recently enlightened about the widespread fraudulent practices of private utility corporations.

The important question at this point is how navigation would fit into the new scheme of comprehensive development. No member of the board was a river transportation specialist.[3] Fortunately for the harried planners, the mandate to build Cove Creek Dam[4] and an executive order[5] to provide employment by beginning the construction of Dam No. 3 left little time for planning the improvement of the entire river watershed. Moreover, the TVA board had inherited the Corps of Engineers' developmental plan of 1930, which was regarded as a "thorough and exhaustive study" of the river.[6] This plan, the last of seventeen surveys made of the stream, would be a guide for the new developmental agency. Another limitation that prevented any neglect of navigation by the directors was the existence of two high dams on the river, the Wilson Dam at Muscle Shoals and the Hales Bar Dam just downstream from Chattanooga. These structures would figure prominently in any scheme for providing a navigable waterway. Finally, concrete structures cannot be erased or repealed readily; and their permanence probably helped to prevent any hasty decisions on the location of dams which, if improperly located or designed, might have worked to the disadvantage of navigation. In brief, to a large degree the TVA board's plans for navigation were circumscribed by previous efforts to develop the river for water transportation. But, at the same time, the Authority was now the director of navigation planning, and its thinking would govern the manner in which the channel would be developed.

TVA's attitude toward its navigation assignment was voiced by Director David E. Lilienthal in the fall of 1933 when he told the Chattanooga Chamber of Commerce that the development of navigation was "not an immediate thing"[7] with the TVA. Lilienthal's remark aroused the river transportation enthusiasts of that city, and these dissenters ultimately helped to bring about more emphasis on the role of navigation in the TVA program. The corporation's apparent lack of concern with navigation stemmed from its dedication to its role as a public power "yardstick"; further responsible for TVA's slight interest in navigation were the urgency of initiating the massive construction program which had been assigned to it by the TVA Act and the President and the attitude of board chairman Arthur E. Morgan that river transportation was of dubious economic feasibility.[8]

By executive order the Authority became a construction organization. The building of Norris Dam on the Clinch River was ordered by the President. A short time later Roosevelt requested the organization to initiate the building of Wheeler Dam just above Wilson Dam where the Corps of Engineers had already begun a high-lift navigation lock. The construction of the Wheeler structure was urged as a relief project. Norris Dam would fit in well as a part of the plan for setting up the "yardstick" and would provide storage water to be released when navigation conditions demanded more water; but the building of the Wheeler Dam, the TVA argued, would upset its proposed utility-rate formula. Why build a dam if its power cannot be marketed? In other words, if rates were to be based on the cost of producing power, then the additional expense of constructing Wheeler Dam would force the Authority to increase its rates just when the agency was desperately seeking outlets for its Wilson Dam power. Rate making lost out to pump priming, and the TVA began the construction of its first main-river dam.[9]

The first two dams begun by TVA resulted from congressional direction and executive order, respectively. What did TVA intend to do about improving the remaining 520 miles of the Tennessee River which varied in navigable depths from one to four feet during periods of minimum flow in summer and fall? Was it economically feasible to improve the undeveloped portions of the river? The Corps of Engineers and Congress had reasoned affirmatively in 1930, but did these actions obligate the Authority to continue such a policy? It would seem that they did, but earlier thinking about navigation was confined to single-purpose development. Now that navigation was to be a part of a multipurpose program, was it still to enjoy a prime role in the new improvement scheme? This was TVA's responsibility; and no decision was forthcoming until the agency had collected, analyzed, and studied a vast amount of technical data on which to base its decision.

Engineering facts pointed to the wisdom of a high-dam system. Such a development would provide an excellent channel for barge transportation. The same dams would also provide flood storage space and house generators for the production of hydroelectric power. It was calculated that a high-dam scheme would be more economical to build than three separate systems. Finally, the TVA planners concluded that slack-water navigation would be far more efficient than that which would have been developed by the low-dam system proposed by the Corps of Engineers in 1930.[11]

Once the question of how the river was to be developed was answered, the Authority got busy building those dams already authorized and deciding upon the time and sequence of later projects. These were all important decisions, for if the construction of a dam was to be geared to the potentiality of a power market, as the TVA argued in its opposition to the early building of the Wheeler Dam, there might result a disconnected channel—a principal weakness in previous attempts to improve the river for navigation. Moreover, if navigation were "not an immediate thing" in the agency's program, then it might never be developed throughout the entire river; unforeseen circumstances might limit the developmental scheme to only a few dams when many would be needed to provide a navigable channel from Knoxville to Paducah.

Chairman Arthur E. Morgan revealed TVA's plans for its dam construction program in May, 1934, when he appeared before the House Appropriations Committee to inform Congress of the agency's proposed use of its allotment from the Emergency Appropriation Bill for the fiscal year 1935. Morgan related that the TVA planned to construct two main-river dams between Wilson Dam and the mouth of the river and two dams on tributaries of the Tennessee. The tributary dams would be located on the Little Tennessee and Hiwassee rivers, and the main-river structures would be at the sites of Aurora and Pickwick landings. The main-river dams were to contain navigation locks, but the other two would be storage reservoirs only. The cost of the program, including the dams already under construction, was estimated to be $330,000,000. Morgan pointed out that the TVA had planned a "crash program" because of the national economic situation and that if the unemployment factor had been excluded, some of the dams could have been delayed for another two years. The chairman reasoned that the plan would be a five-year undertaking. As for future building, the chief director told the committee that it might be a generation or more before all the potential dam sites were utilized.[12]

Despite the fact that it was to be a five-year program, the House Appropriations Committee was shaken by the expense and the immensity of the project. One member of the committee inquired about the navigation potential of the stream. Morgan dutifully recited the predictions made by the Corps of Engineers in 1930 that traffic would have amounted to 17,800,000 tons in 1950 if the river had been opened to navigation in 1930.[13] The committee was relieved of any decision, for the lump sum appropriation was divided by the President among several relief agencies. The TVA was later alloted $25,000,000 for its construction program in the next fiscal year.[14]

If the TVA had been able to carry out its original plans, what would have been the consequences for navigation of the river? A channel from the mouth of the river to Guntersville, Alabama, would have been commercially useful, but the major cities on the river, Knoxville and Chattanooga, would not have had water connections for five years or possibly for more than a generation. The Corps of Engineers had estimated that over half of the anticipated traffic on the river would originate or terminate in the region of the valley between the two major cities. Transportation savings, the difference in charges to the shipper for water transportation compared with the cost of the next-cheapest method of transport, would have been $13,200,000 less than the total savings expected if the waterway had been improved only to Chattanooga.[15] The Authority, in essence, was neglecting to provide navigation for that sector of the river which was expected to generate the bulk of the freight for the barge lines and restricting the use of the stream to the less populated regions.

By the fall of 1934 the TVA was ready to initiate its multipurpose plan for developing the Tennessee. On November 19 of that year the agency authorized the construction of the Pickwick Landing Dam. This dam was ideally suited to the multipurpose scheme. It would submerge the last remaining obstructions to navigation in the Muscle Shoals region and would provide several hundred thousand acre-feet of flood control storage. Its impounded waters would create slack-water navigation for fifty miles upstream to Dam No. 1, a low-navigation dam situated a mile below the Wilson Dam, and would eliminate the necessity of releasing large amounts of water from Wilson Dam for navigation requirements on the lower river. This requirement lessened the value of Wilson Dam power by one million dollars annually, because the water could not be stored for power head.[16] Navigation considerations were not overlooked in the design and construction of the dam, for an Ohio River-size lock, 600 feet long and 110 feet wide, was properly placed in the dam to allow vessels to pass.

Authorization of the Pickwick Landing project by the TVA resulted from engineering logic. The agency's engineers felt that each project should be initiated at a time when weather, low water, men, money, and materials could best be utilized at a given location. According to the Authority's assistant chief engineer, Harry Wiersema, the agency's engineering staff "planned to build alternately a storage dam, and a run-of-the river dam: Norris was a storage dam, Wheeler a run-of-the river dam, Hiwassee a storage, Pickwick a run-of-the river, and so on. This alternation would result in securing maximum benefits at the earliest dates."[17] Further, the engineering planners envisioned a long-term building program which would not be subjected to outside political pressures. The construction program would be kept in balance, and sizable economies of construction would be effected.

Undoubtedly, the alternate building scheme offered greater economy in building; it also would have enabled the Authority to gear its developmental program to the region's power needs. But, would not such a division of effort considerably delay the improvement of the main river for navigation? Obviously so, for only two main-river dams were to be built in the immediate future, both below the Wilson Dam. This would have limited main-stream navigation to Guntersville, Alabama. Water releases from the tributary dams would have aided navigation in the upper river, but vessels of 9-foot draft would have had to restrict their activities to the region below Guntersville. In other words, only about one half of the river would have been suitable for navigation under the proposed plan of development. Apparently navigation was being forced to play a secondary role in the integrated scheme, for it is almost certain that an alternate system of dam construction would have delayed or postponed for several years the building of those structures necessary to provide 9-foot navigation for the entire length of the river.

TVA's reluctance to build primarily for navigation is understandable. The immediate roots of TVA made it an experiment in public power development. Moreover, the previous efforts by the engineers to develop the Tennessee for navigation had been largely confined to the lower and middle portions of the stream, though the Corps of Engineers had belatedly predicted in 1930 that the upper part would supply most of the river freight. Then, too, only a few dams would be needed to set up the public power "yardstick" experiment. Add to this the severe economic situation in the 1930's which formerly had meant retrenchment in government expenditure, and one can sympathize with the director's view that it might be more than a generation before the river would be fully developed for multiple purposes. Who in 1933 would have ventured the opinion that the federal government would spend $2,098,365,462 in the Tennessee Valley region over the next twenty-five years when in the past "pork-barrel" funds had been spread so thinly? Regardless of the apparently limited consideration given to the full development of navigation on the river in TVA's early planning, a successful beginning in establishing a commercially useful channel was at last underway as construction progressed on the Norris, Wheeler, and Pickwick Landing dams and as foundation explorations proceeded at the Aurora and Hiwassee sites.

After the authorization of the Pickwick Landing Dam in November, 1934, the TVA began to lose a large measure of control over its planning and construction program. From the beginning certain elements in Congress and local pressure groups had sought to share in TVA's decisions concerning the time, sequence, and scope of the developmental plan. Both groups had been stymied in their efforts for a year and a half because the Authority's funds came directly from the President, and Roosevelt had assumed a personal responsibility for the agency. In the fall of 1934, when the question of TVA's constitutionality was raised in the Ashwander case, even presidential influence could not prevent other forces from sharing in the Authority's decision-making relative to the overall river improvement plan. To be sure, the corporation continued to supply engineering data and to make those determinations which only qualified engineers were capable of making, but major policy decisions involving the dam-building program were largely formulated thereafter by Congress. The struggle for control over which dams should be constructed first, when the building of a structure should be initiated, and the number of dams which should be built was waged at the local level and in Congress; and the results of the struggle were exceedingly important to the navigation phase of TVA's comprehensive developmental scheme.

Running the gauntlet of local discordants was the agency's first fight to retain its ability to make independent decisions. Local discontent stemmed from two factors. One was the Authority's seeming inactivity during the first few months of its life when its basic organization was being perfected. This dissatisfaction subsided for the most part when construction of the Norris and Wheeler dams was begun. Much of this early criticism was of TVA's own making, for its directors in numerous speeches overemphasized the planning and experimental aspects of the agency's assignment. A typical reaction to TVA's visionary attitude was expressed in this fashion: "A kindergarten for Appalachian hill-billies may be a fine objective, but it is hardly what the people of the Tennessee Valley had in mind." [18] An editor from the eastern portion of the valley said, "The grandiose ideas of the Authority have induced a little weariness." [19] All down the valley a vigorous press condemned the TVA for delaying its construction program.

Another basis of local criticism was the inability of several municipalities to persuade the TVA to build a dam in their vicinities. The engineer's report of 1930 had determined the general location of the more feasible dam sites for navigation, flood control, and power generation. Since these places on the main river were virtually fixed because of the navigation requirements, the river-port cities were in the best position to demand priority for projects in their areas. Long motor caravans from valley cities to Knoxville, TVA's headquarters, were very common in the early months of the agency's life. Each river city began to advance arguments for undertaking a project nearby. Chattanooga, a city long interested in a water transportation connection, took the lead in arguing that the Authority must not slight its navigation assignment. Other cities demanded dams for public relief purposes.[20]

Criticism had begun to subside by December, 1933, except in the lower Tennessee River region and in the Chattanooga area. As construction activity got underway at the Norris and Wheeler dams, local critics turned their barks into praise. The New York *Times* reported in March, 1934, that "concrete action by TVA is chasing gloom from the valley with more harmony among discordant elements."[21] An Alabama newspaper editor likened TVA to Santa Claus and added, "Today we have not only the entire Ford Plan coming into reality but more, much more, besides. This should be the happiest Christmas the District has ever known."[22] A Chattanooga editor begrudgingly admitted that TVA criticism appeared to be waning.[23]

While criticism from Chattanooga appeared to be decreasing, pressure was being shifted from Knoxville to Washington in order to force the TVA to build the Chickamauga Dam. An alliance composed of Chattanooga business interests and Tennessee congressmen was forming.[24] Senator Kenneth D. McKellar and Representative Sam D. McReynolds were expected to play the key roles in Congress. The coalition was powerful, for McKellar was second in seniority only to Virginia's Senator Carter Glass, chairman of the Senate Appropriations Committee. Since funds allocated to the Authority by the President were being expended rapidly for its Norris, Wheeler, and Pickwick Landing dams, it soon became apparent that the TVA would have to utilize its bond-issuing authority or Congress would have to appropriate additional money for the completion of these dams and other proposed structures. For several reasons the first course was not chosen,[25] and the agency would now be compelled to come before Congress each year for an appropriation. When, in 1935, the Authority came before the appropriations committees of Congress for its first direct appropriation, the TVA found that the senior senator from Tennessee was not only anxious but in a strong position to exercise a large degree of control over its building program. In later years McKellar and the Tennessee Valley Authority were often in conflict over funds and their use.[26] At this point in the agency's history and for the navigation program, his actions were of the utmost importance.

In December, 1933, a delegation of Chattanooga citizens made an attempt to get President Roosevelt to order the Authority to begin construction of the Chickamauga Dam. The President refused to see the group and announced that he preferred that the decision be made by the TVA board. The boosters then sought the aid of Senator McKellar. The Tennessee senator declared, "I'll take you to the President of the United States the first week in January [1934], with the entire Tennessee congressional delegation, and we'll do the best that lies within us to get Chickamauga Dam built." [27] The best at that time was not good enough, for the order to construct the dam was not issued. Nevertheless, in the future these efforts would be fruitful.

Although these early attempts to influence the Authority were unsuccessful, the pressure was continued. Throughout 1934 the Chattanooga dailies advanced arguments for immediately undertaking the project. The editor of a newspaper in Rossville, Georgia, a sister-city of the Tennessee municipality, accused the TVA of having made a deal with the Commonwealth and Southern Corporation, the private utility holding company that supplied the area with electricity, not to build the Chickamauga Dam. This accusation was groundless, of course, but it indicates the intensity of the campaign that was waged to coerce the Authority into undertaking the project.[28] With the initiation of the Ashwander proceedings in the fall of 1934, the proponents of early construction of the Chickamauga Dam obtained an unsought ally.

While powerful politicos in Congress were being urged by local interests to force an expansion of the Tennessee Valley Authority program, another equally influential development was emerging. In the summer of 1934 several coal and ice concerns located in Alabama and Tennessee raised the question of the TVA's constitutional status. These firms, sponsored by the Edison Electric Institute,[29] challenged the validity of the TVA statute and attempted to obtain an injuction from the United States District Court for the Northern District of Alabama that would curtail the construction and power generation programs of the Authority. The complainants were unable to establish standing to sue and eventually abandoned the suit. Failure to prosecute the suit further probably resulted from the institution of the Ashwander proceedings in September, 1934, which "offered a better vehicle for obtaining a decision of TVA's constitutionality." [30]

The Ashwander case grew out of TVA's attempt to market its surplus power. On January 4, 1934, the Authority entered into a contract with the Alabama Power Company in order to prevent wasteful duplication of facilities in the Wilson Dam transmission area and in order to serve municipalities in that area which had long sought to obtain power at the dam. The contract called for the sale of TVA power to the power companies, for an interchange of hydroelectric energy, for the purchase of certain transmission and distribution facilities by the Authority and local agencies, and for mutual restrictions as to the areas which would be served by the contracting parties. In September, 1934, George Ashwander and thirteen other holders of preferred stock in the Alabama Power Company, fearing that the contract would be injurious to their interests, sought to have the contract annulled. Having failed to secure company cooperation prior to the institution of the suit, the stockholders turned to the courts and "sought an injunction forbidding performance of the contract of January 4, 1934, and a judicial declaration that the Authority's program 'for the sale or distribution of energy created at the Wilson Dam or at any other Federal project in the Tennessee Basin' transcended the constitutional powers of the Federal government."[31]

The case was tried in the United States District Court for the Northern District of Alabama in the latter months of 1934. William I. Grubb, the presiding judge, rejected TVA's contention that the complainants were without standing to sue but accepted the Authority's argument that the major question before it involved only the validity of TVA's generation and sale of Wilson Dam power and not that of the entire TVA power program. Having limited the issue, the court then ruled in favor of the stockholders of the power company. Judge Grubb reasoned that the contract was in aid of an unconstitutional attempt by the federal government to manufacture electric power. On February 26, 1935, a decree and opinion were filed enjoining performance of the contract.[32]

The TVA was in serious trouble. To be sure, the issue had been limited to the power produced at the Wilson Dam, and the construction of that project for defense purposes had not been found invalid; but the definition given to "surplus power," if it should be upheld by the higher courts, would destroy the TVA's power-marketing program. The district court held that the TVA Act, "in directing the sale of 'surplus power' produced at Wilson Dam, must be interpreted as authorizing the sale only of so much excess power as was *unavoidably* produced in an effort to supply the government's own needs in the operation of the Muscle Shoals properties and the Wilson Dam lock, and that if construed otherwise the provision was unconstitutional."[33] The Authority lodged an appeal with the U.S. Circuit Court of Appeals for the Fifth Circuit on April 1, 1935. In the meantime, an ominous threat of unconstitutionality hovered over the TVA; even if the circuit court ruled in favor of the Authority, it was almost certain that the case would be appealed to the Supreme Court where chances of a favorable decision appeared to be dim indeed.[34]

The Grubb decision with the accompanying injunction had important effects on the navigation program. In the first place, it brought about a reevaluation of the integrated scheme of river development. Since navigation and flood control in a high-dam system are made economically feasible by the income from power sales, any restriction or curtailment of the power program might limit the economic benefits that could accrue from a unified plan of development. If the Grubb decision had been allowed to stand, it is doubtful that the unified river improvement program would have been completed. One can assume that Congress would not have approved such a vast spending program as was ultimately necessary to develop the river unless the prospects were good that the project would amortize itself. Only three high dams had been started at this time, and if others had not been constructed a useful commercial channel would not have been provided by existing structures. A system of low dams might have been built to provide a 9-foot channel, but such a waterway would have been inferior to that which resulted from the construction of high dams.[35]

The Grubb decision and the possibility of a Supreme Court affirmation of the lower court ruling produced a second effect, which is seen in the activities of Congress and the TVA to strengthen the agency's constitutional base. Two courses of action were taken. Congress went to work to revise the TVA statute by rewriting the navigation provisions of the act, and the Authority began to alter its plans so as to concentrate first on its navigation assignment.

In March, 1935, one month after the district court decision, the House Military Affairs Committee began hearings on amendments to the Tennessee Valley Authority Act. The Authority gave its assistance and approval to the proposed changes in the basic law. Since the district court had not questioned the power of the national government to improve the nation's streams for navigation under the "commerce power" of the Constitution, the law had to be securely grounded on this accepted area of federal responsibility. Changing the act was far from easy since it reopened the old issue of private versus public development of power generation sites.

A bitter battle took place in the House Military Affairs Committee over the proposed TVA amendments. The committee, after two months of hearings, rejected the TVA-sponsored amendments and by a vote of thirteen to twelve recommended a series of changes in the basic law which would have seriously limited the activities of the Authority. Representative John J. McSwain of South Carolina, the committee chairman and floor leader for the pro-TVA amendments, found himself in a peculiar position. He had to submit a committee report with which he disagreed. For two months, from May to July, 1935, a heated debate on the changes in the law took place in the House.[36]

The old issue of public versus private power was clearly the dividing line between the opposing sides. Representatives of other interest groups who had found reasons to oppose the agency since its establishment joined the advocates of private power development. Coal district representatives and railroad spokesmen supported the private utility devotees. The coalition gained added strength from the Republican party's position on the principle of government operation of business enterprises. A pro-TVA House of Representatives resolved the problem by dealing with the amendments in the committee of the whole. The amendments proposed by the House Military Affairs Committee were rejected. Representative Lister Hill of Alabama, a staunch supporter of the TVA, offered a series of amendments similar to those originally proposed by pro-TVA committee members. By a vote of 279 to 99, the House accepted Representative Hill's proposals.[37]

In the Senate the amendments escaped a committee fight but ran into strong opposition on the floor. Senator George W. Norris guided the Authority-sponsored measures through the upper chamber. The familiar accusations that the "power trust" was furnishing the opposition were made by the Nebraska senator. Norris charged that Senator Warren R. Austin of Vermont, the leader of the opposition to the changes in the 1933 statute, was a tool of the New England Power Association, a private utility league. Several anti-TVA amendments to the Norris-sponsored proposals were offered, but the Senate refused to alter the changes advocated by the Tennessee Valley Authority, the administration, and Senator Norris. Opposition forces were able to gather only nineteen votes out of a total of seventy-five. After House and Senate conferees worked out the differences between the Hill and Norris measures, the Senate bill was substituted for that of the House; and, on August 31, 1935, the 1933 statute was officially amended so as to make navigation and flood control the primary objectives of the Tennessee Valley Authority project.[38]

Three changes in the original act affected the status of navigation in the Authority's program. Whereas the 1933 statute gave only a vague statement of the agency's duty to improve the river for navigation, the 1935 amendment specifically declared that the river must be developed in such a way as to provide a 9-foot channel from Knoxville to the mouth of the stream. The act stipulated that the Authority

> shall have power to construct such dams, and reservoirs, in the Tennessee River and its tributaries, as in conjunction with Wilson Dam, and Norris, Wheeler, and Pickwick Landing, now under construction, will provide a nine-foot channel in the said river and maintain a water supply for the same, from Knoxville to its mouth, and will best serve to promote navigation on the Tennessee River and its tributaries. . . . The directors of the Authority are hereby directed to report to the Congress their recommendations not later than April 1, 1936, for the unified development of the Tennessee River system.[39]

The last provision was placed in the act at the insistence of those critics who claimed that the Authority was not informing Congress of its plans.[40]

To ensure that navigation and flood control received primary attention in the construction and operation of the system, the board was directed accordingly:

> . . . in the operation of any dam or reservoir in its possession and control to regulate the stream flow primarily for the purposes of promoting navigation and controlling floods. So far as may be consistent with other purposes, the board is authorized to provide and operate facilities for the generation of electric energy at any such dam for the use of the Corporation and for the use of the United States. . . .[41]

Thus, the Tennessee Valley Authority assignment was made to conform to traditional federal activity in the realm of stream improvement. Electrical power generation, according to the letter of the law, was to be an incidental result of obtaining navigation and flood control. Power was to be generated as a by-product to aid in the liquidation of the cost of the unified program.

One other amendment of importance to the integrated plan of development was made in 1935. The TVA was authorized to veto the construction of all subsequently proposed works upon the Tennessee River or any of its tributaries. This change was urged by the Authority because various organizations had sought, and in some instances obtained, power sites which the TVA expected to develop. The Authority felt that private ownership and development of key sites would seriously hinder its plans for a coordinated water control system. Furthermore, TVA hoped to prevent the construction of unwisely planned structures which might later require alteration. Of special importance to navigation was the fact that any future construction of bridges, river terminals, docks, and the like could be fitted into the whole scheme for river transportation.

The new amendments were probably essential to the survival of the Authority. The enacting law said nothing of the Rivers and Harbors Act of 1930 which had provided for a 9-foot channel by low or high dams or a combination of both. Nor did the basic law charge the TVA with the responsibility of completing the navigation project as begun by the Corps of Engineers.[42] The litigation begun in 1934 forced Congress to reexamine the basic statute in order to bring the TVA into line with accepted areas of federal activity such as navigation and flood control. As a former legal authority for the TVA has written: "In 1935, Congress . . . strongly buttressed its [TVA's] constitutional position in the legal battles which lay ahead."[43] Charges made by opponents of the amendments that champions of the Authority were trying to patch up the act to make it legal cannot be lightly regarded, even though their criticism had a subsurface motive.[44]

The TVA very early recognized the threatening nature of the Ashwander suit. Before Congress went into action to bolster the enacting statute by rewriting the navigation assignment of the agency, the Authority began to show greater concern over its so-called "constitutional peg." Several events between the initiation of the suits which questioned TVA's constitutional status and Judge Grubb's decision in February, 1935, indicate a renewed interest in the navigation program by the Authority. The high-dam system as proposed by the Corps of Engineers in its 1930 report must have received a great deal of study in those hectic days as the TVA sought to defend itself against the threat of unconstitutionality. When the directors were called to testify before the committees studying the proposed changes in the law in March, 1935, a more precise plan for improving the entire river for navigation was reported by TVA's policy-makers than had been offered nine months earlier.[45] The new plan conformed substantially to the Corps of Engineers' 1930 recommendation. The engineers had proposed seven high dams in addition to the Wilson and Hales Bar dams on the main river between Knoxville and the mouth of the stream.[46] The TVA, with but little change, now began to initiate such a program.

In September, 1934, the Authority wrote the district engineer's office in Nashville, requesting information concerning the number, size, and the arrangement of locks in future dams on the upper and middle sections of the river.[47] About a month later, on October 9, David E. Lilienthal formulated a series of principles to guide the Authority in its dam construction program. The first principle deserves attention: "The control of navigable waters in the interests of navigation and flood control form the constitutional basis for the expenditure of Federal funds in the construction of dams. Accordingly, navigation and flood control are first considerations in the construction of dams." [48] This important policy declaration just after the Ashwander proceedings were begun apparently was drawn up to bolster TVA's position in the court battle ahead.

Ten days after this declaration Lilienthal, in a speech before the Shelby County Democratic Club in Memphis, outlined the three major objectives of the Authority and carefully relegated the power part of TVA's program to a secondary or incidental position. He told his audience that the Tennessee Valley Authority had "in mind a navigable channel pretty much the full course of the river." [49] Obviously, Lilienthal had changed his attitude about navigation's importance since his Chattanooga speech of September, 1933. In November, 1934, the Pickwick Landing Dam was authorized for construction by the TVA board. Its value in the extension of the navigation channel has already been indicated.

Shortly before the Grubb decision was announced, the Authority began engineering surveys to determine the feasibility of two more dams on the main river. Carl A. Bock, chief engineering assistant to Arthur E. Morgan, told the press, "My preliminary consideration of conditions in the Tennessee River has led me to believe that in the interest of improving the river for commercial navigation intensive surveys of these proposed dams [Guntersville and Chickamauga] should be carried forward at once." [50] The Bock press release indicates that the TVA was committing itself to immediately improving the river for navigation from Knoxville to the mouth, since the Chickamauga Dam would provide a 9-foot channel for fifty-nine miles or one third of the distance from Chattanooga to Knoxville. The TVA's renewed interest in its navigation assignment on the eve of the district court's decision implies that the Authority had abandoned its earlier position that engineering and economic considerations should govern the time, sequence, and scope of its construction program. The agency was now determined to improve the river for navigation even though it felt that the establishment of a channel above Chattanooga was not feasible "as an immediate proposition." [51]

The succession of events between September, 1934, when the Ashwander case was instituted, and February, 1935, when the Grubb decision was rendered, clearly imply that the TVA was rapidly changing its thinking about the navigation part of its program. The apparent need for greater emphasis upon the navigation assignment which was engendered by the possibility of an adverse court decision pushed river improvement for navigation to the fore in the TVA's multiple-purpose planning scheme. When the change occurred, it put the Authority in a vulnerable position, for it would be unable to resist outside influence which it previously had been able to overcome. Decisions concerning its construction program, which TVA preferred to make on the basis of economic and engineering data, were no longer to be freely made. After two years of relatively unrestricted action, the Authority now found it necessary to accept a greater measure of legislative control. As Congress began to appropriate directly for the agency's program, it also began to exercise a guiding hand in the TVA's use of public funds.

By 1935 the national legislature had become less inclined to make blanket appropriations for executive dispensation. It will be recalled that during the first two years of its life the Authority had been allocated its funds by the President from vast sums appropriated by Congress for emergency purposes. The bitter controversy between the President and Congress over the 1935 Deficiency Appropriations Bill hardly needs retelling here, but its significance for the Tennessee Valley Authority was considerable. In the first place, a changed climate of opinion in Congress meant that appropriation committees would henceforth give greater attention to the disbursement of public funds for the TVA. In the second place, it strengthened the position of those members of Congress who sought to control the agency's developmental program. The congressional renaissance ended the authorization of dams by the President and TVA and placed the responsibility of determining such matters as the time and sequence of dam construction in the hands of Congress. Senator McKellar's exalted position on the Senate Committee on Appropriations would now have a telling effect on the Tennessee Valley Authority's plans for developing the river.

Thus in February, 1935, the Authority found itself faced with a hostile court opinion and a Congress which was determined to assert greater control over the expenditure of public funds. This formidable combination of circumstances encouraged compromise. In the period from January to August, 1935, the Authority apparently bowed to the requirements of the situation. As decisions were made to enlarge the dam construction program, it became obvious to the TVA that navigation had to be given more consideration in its thinking. Old arguments that had staved off many efforts to force it into a more extensive building program [52] were no longer looked upon with favor by Congress. The story of the agency's capitulation to Congress can be read in the history of the second Deficiency Appropriations Bill for 1935.

The President's budget for the fiscal year 1936 provided for an allocation of $56,785,152 to the Tennessee Valley Authority. It was presented to the Seventy-fourth Congress on January 3, 1935. At this early date the Authority did not envision a greatly enlarged program, but it hoped to begin the construction of two additional dams. Evidently these projects were to be the Hiwassee and Aurora dams since no other sites had received intensive engineering and economic surveys.[53] It will be recalled that extensive explorations of the Guntersville and Chickamauga locations were not begun until late February, 1935, shortly before the Grubb decision was announced. The Hiwassee and Aurora projects had been proposed by Arthur E. Morgan in his testimony before the House Appropriations Committee in May, 1934. They fitted in well with the TVA's building scheme of constructing alternately a storage dam and a run-of-river project. So, when TVA presented its building plans for 1936 to the President, it did so without pressure from proponents of an enlarged construction program.[54]

Between the date of the President's budget presentation in January, 1935, and the House Appropriations Committee hearings in May, 1935, the TVA revised the original program submitted several months earlier. Appropriations totaling $42,305,192 were now requested to begin the construction of two main-river dams, one at Guntersville, Alabama, and another at Chickamauga Creek, near the city of Chattanooga. The Authority strongly urged that funds be granted for the building of the Hiwassee Dam and that a limited amount of money be appropriated for continuing foundation studies at other dam sites. The House Appropriations Committee was not in as generous a mood as the Authority had hoped, and TVA's request was reduced by $7,630,000, leaving a recommended sum of $34,675,192. The Committee refused TVA's appeal for funds to begin the Hiwassee project. The House report on the appropriation for the Tennessee Valley Authority stated: "In providing for the commencement of construction of the Guntersville Dam . . . and the Chickamauga Dam . . . and the postponement of the Hiwassee Dam . . . the committee is actuated by a desire to provide the projects in the program which seem to them to be most beneficial to flood control and navigation." [55]

The committee exacted a gentlemen's agreement from the agency that it would use appropriations only for those projects outlined in its budget requests.[56] The committee's refusal to supply funds for the construction of the Hiwassee Dam indicates the use of congressional authority to control the TVA's building program. The unwillingness of the committee to appropriate for the Hiwassee project apparently stemmed from the Grubb decision. The committee report, as cited previously, clearly implied that public funds should not be appropriated for projects which did not definitely aid navigation and flood control. Since the Supreme Court had not reached a decision in the Ashwander case when the appropriations committee made its recommendations to the House and since the high court in several cases had ruled adversely on New Deal legislation, the House committee was dubious about allowing the TVA to initiate a project which might be declared an illegal undertaking. The litigation thus forced the expenditure of funds for main-river dams at a much earlier date than would have been likely had all planning been left to the TVA. The committee-sponsored appropriation had little difficulty on the House floor, and the bill was passed and sent to the Senate for further action.[57]

When the measure reached the Senate Appropriations Committee, it was subjected to several changes. Three of these were of major importance. The first of note was the amendment proposed by Senator McKellar. He asked that the House bill be amended to read as follows:

> . . . that for the purpose of securing uninterrupted navigation on the Tennessee River from, at, or near Knoxville to the Ohio River and maximum flood control in the Tennessee, Ohio, and Mississippi River basins and of otherwise carrying out the Tennessee Valley Authority Act of 1933, the Tennessee Valley Authority is authorized and directed, out of the funds herein and heretofore appropriated, to continue the construction of Norris Dam, Wheeler Dam, and Pickwick Dam, to begin a dam at or near Guntersville, Alabama, a dam at Chickamauga Creek on the Tennessee River, a dam at or near Aurora Landing, and at Whites Creek on the Tennessee River. . . .[58]

The Tennessee senator was in reality seeking to deprive the TVA of its financial flexibility as granted in the enacting statute. For did not the provision to the effect that "the Tennessee Valley Authority is authorized and directed" imply a rigid limitation on the Authority's use of its funds? It also indicated McKellar's distrust of the TVA board since he was unwilling to follow the language of the House bill which made a lump sum appropriation with only a verbal agreement to ensure the carrying out of the lower house's intent. This particular phraseology which McKellar sought to insert in the House bill did not meet with committee approval,[59] but the attempt to "strait-jacket" the agency's use of funds reveals one method by which certain "pork-minded" congressmen endeavored to bring the Authority's program firmly under their control.[60]

A second modification of the House bill was the itemized listing of those projects which were to be initiated by the TVA during the next fiscal year. Once again it was McKellar who insisted that the bill be made specific enough to bind the agency to a definite program. McKellar said,

> The purpose of this amendment is that, last year, [1934] when a similar appropriation was made, we were told by the head of the Tennessee Valley Authority, that those dams would be built. . . . We were told that those four dams were to be built. Only one has been started, and we think that the Congress ought to direct that the money be used for the purpose of building dams.[61]

Although the Tennessee senator was unable to secure an amendment as binding as he had hoped, he was successful in rewording the House bill so that the TVA was told specifically which dams it must construct with its appropriation. The McKellar proposal, as included in the bill by the Senate subcommittee and finally enacted into law, provided for

> the continued construction of Norris Dam, Wheeler Dam, Pickwick Landing Dam, and the beginning of construction on a dam at or near Chickamauga Creek, both on the Tennessee River, and a dam on the Hiwassee River, a tributary of the Tennessee River, at or near Fowlers Bend, and the construction of preliminary investigations as to the location and desirability of a dam at or near Aurora Landing, a dam at or near Whites Creek.[62]

A third change in the House bill concerned the total appropriation to the Authority. The Senate committee increased by $3,324,808 the House recommendation of $34,675,192. This added amount was cut in half when the bill went to conference. When finally passed, the second Deficiency Appropriations Bill of 1935 provided a sum of $36,000,000 for the Tennessee Valley Authority.[63]

In regard to the Authority's navigation assignment, the approval of the McKellar amendment in modified form as a part of the 1935 appropriations bill is noteworthy. Through its appropriating powers, Congress took the initiative in determining the time and sequence of the construction of the river control structures. By providing or withholding funds, Congress could and did tell the Authority which dams to construct. The Deficiency Appropriations Bill of 1935 definitely committed the Authority to an extension of the navigation channel beyond Chattanooga to the head of the river at Knoxville. The appropriations bill provided money for the building of Chickamauga Dam and for the preliminary investigation of a dam at Whites Creek (Watts Bar), both located in the upper portion of the river above Chattanooga. Only one other high dam, the Coulter Shoals (Fort Loudoun) project not mentioned in the 1935 money bill, would need to be built in order to provide a 9-foot channel the full length of the river. The depth of the channel was not determined by the Congressional appropriations committees; but this was not necessary, for Congress stipulated that a 9-foot channel was to be the minimum navigation depth when it amended the basic law. Congress passed the amendments to the enacting statute.

By the end of August, 1935, the high-dam scheme for providing 9-foot navigation on the Tennessee River was largely a settled matter. Two high dams, the Wilson and Hales Bar dams, were in existence before the creation of the TVA. The Wheeler Dam, built by the Authority, was nearing completion, and an auspicious beginning had been made on the Pickwick Landing Dam. A part of the necessary funds had been provided for the construction of the Guntersville and Chickamauga dams and for foundation studies at Aurora Landing and Whites Creek. In the following year, 1936, as a result of Senator McKellar's vigorous efforts, a small sum was provided for determining the precise location of the Coulter Shoals Dam.[64] Two tributary dams, which would aid navigation by storing water for release during the seasons of low water flow in the main river, were at various stages of construction. The Norris Dam on the Clinch River was practically complete, and the Hiwassee site on the Hiwassee River east of the Tennessee–North Carolina state line had already undergone preliminary investigation and foundation drilling preparatory to construction.[65]

By mid-1935, the TVA's constitutional battle also had turned in favor of the Authority. The United States Circuit Court of Appeals reversed the district court decision of Judge Grubb on July 17, 1935, but like the lower court it confined its opinion to the power generated at the Wilson Dam and the validity of the contract which the stockholders of the Alabama Power Company sought to annul. Judge Grubb's narrow definition of "surplus power" was broadened by the circuit court. It reasoned as follows: "Under the property clause of the Constitution, Congress might provide for disposition of the power [at Wilson Dam] as freely as in the case of other Government property, and the right of ownership and disposition extended to all of the power which the dam was capable of generating and not merely to the surplus which was accidentally created in excess of the Government's needs." [66] The TVA had won the second round in the courts, but both adversaries would meet again in the United States Supreme Court. Seven months later, in February, 1936, the Court sustained the decision of the appellate court and likewise presented a restricted opinion.[67] Since the courts limited their opinions to the power operations at the Wilson Dam, a loophole was left for a renewed attack on the TVA program by the utility companies. Also, immediately after the Supreme Court issued its ruling in the Ashwander case, the second attack was launched by the private power companies throughout the Southeast. This story can best be told in connection with the TVA's dam-building activities.

After two years, the Authority and Congress appeared to have clarified their thinking as to the means of developing the river for navigation and the limits to which they would go to secure a 9-foot channel for modern barge transportation. Many of the details still remained to be worked out, but the course of development was now firmly decided. The planning of the navigation channel was the work of several groups. Authority engineers, local pressure groups, Congress, and the courts all shared in the decision to make the Tennessee River a modern transportation artery. All the critics were not silenced nor were all the hurdles surmounted, and the TVA had not become institutionalized. What may be emphasized is that the Authority was now ready to develop the river with navigation as a primary goal and not as an incidental result of the building of a series of power dams.

3

DEVELOPING THE CHANNEL, 1936-1945

The plan for the development of the Tennessee River from Paducah to Knoxville for navigation purposes was fully clarified by the fall of 1935. Since it had already been decided that a 9-foot depth[1] should be secured by the building of a series of high dams, the major responsibility of the Authority became that of planning, designing, and building the structures necessary to extend the channel the length of the river. For the next decade the Tennessee Valley Authority was primarily a construction organization. In this role the TVA would enjoy its greatest acclaim.

The Authority's record as a builder antedated the 1935 reorientation of the agency. In the fall of 1933—after its first few months of seemingly slow development, a period when the organization was being readied and the recruitment of its staff was taking place—the TVA began to build the Norris and Wheeler dams with amazing speed. Before the constitutional litigation was begun late in 1934, preliminary plans and cost estimates also had been prepared for dams at Pickwick Landing, Aurora Landing on the main river, and for various sites on the Hiwassee River. Construction of the Pickwick Landing Dam was initiated one month after the Ashwander case was instituted. As the record clearly indicates, the TVA's construction forces already had achieved splendid results when the Authority was told to concentrate on building those dams that would provide a 9-foot navigation channel.

Much of the credit for its rapid rate of construction belongs to the Corps of Engineers, the Bureau of Reclamation, and the United States Geological Survey. In their 1930 report the engineers had furnished a skeleton plan to provide a 9-foot waterway by a system of high dams. This became the "Bible" for improvement of the Tennessee. Dam sites had been located which, except in one instance, became the present-day sites of the main-river dams built by the Tennessee Valley Authority.[2] Because of limited funds, these sites were given only preliminary foundation exploration. The TVA, after more extensive geological examination, occasionally found it necessary to build its dams a few miles upstream or downstream from these locations, but site locations varied little from earlier determinations. The Corps of Engineers' plan included other pertinent information such as tentative pool levels, power possibilities, and designs for navigation facilities at each of the recommended projects. In brief, a system of seven high dams in addition to the existing Wilson Dam, Hales Bar Dam, and the low-navigation dam, Dam No. 1, were considered adequate for establishing the 9-foot channel from Knoxville to Paducah. These basic studies, though incomplete for building purposes, were invaluable to the Authority in its development of the river.[3]

The Corps of Engineers, in addition to its general survey of the entire basin, had given particular attention to the Norris and Wheeler sites. It appears that even though Congress had committed itself to the development of the Tennessee Valley by a government corporation, the War Department took preparatory steps to build the Norris Dam only six weeks before the passage of the Tennessee Valley Authority statute.[4] It should be noted, however, that the act was vague in regard to the department or agency that should construct the Norris Dam.[5] This seems to be another indication of congressional misunderstanding or perhaps a failure to comprehend the Tennessee Valley Authority's role in developing the valley. It implies that Congress did not think of the corporation as a construction organization. Roosevelt, in accordance with the provisions of the statute, immediately turned over the building of the dam to Arthur E. Morgan, who was acting for the TVA.[6] Thus, because of special investigations by the Corps of Engineers at the Norris site, the Authority was able to proceed rapidly with construction of the project. The role of the engineers in the development of the Wheeler Lock has already been treated.

One other contribution to the Tennessee Valley Authority's construction program by the War Department engineers should be noted. Section 5-K of the enacting statute delegated the responsibility of operating the navigation facilities of the Authority's dams to the Corps of Engineers. Why the TVA was not given this assignment in view of the comprehensiveness of its task is open to question. A number of reasons can be suggested. First, the Corps of Engineers had traditionally performed lock operation duties on navigable streams.[7] Second, the newly created agency had no experience in such work. A third factor may have been the general attitude of Congress toward the function of the TVA—that is, it was viewed as being primarily a power corporation. Regardless of what prompted Congress to place the operation of the navigation locks in the hands of the Corps of Engineers, the engineers thereby secured an important part in the building of the navigation channel.

In the building of the Authority's first dam, the War Department's engineers were largely spectators. They had, of course, furnished the agency with a vast collection of maps, drawings, and data gained from their study of the river in the 1920's. They also had the Wheeler Lock under construction before the TVA was created. Not until June, 1934, however, did the corps begin to play a larger part in the construction program. On this date Carl A. Bock, chief assistant to Arthur E. Morgan, recommended that the engineers be given the task of designing the lock in the proposed Pickwick Dam. In making this recommendation to the board, he pointed out that the Corps of Engineers had the responsibility for navigation on the river, that it was responsible for lock operation, and that it was experienced in lock design.[8] The board approved Bock's recommendation. This initiated the policy of depending on the Corps of Engineers for the designing of the locks in the Tennessee Valley Authority-constructed dams, except for the lock in the Kentucky Dam, which the TVA designed because of the possibility of earth tremors in the lower river region.[9]

The control over the navigation locks given to the Corps of Engineers by the Tennessee Valley Authority Act of 1933, plus the constitutional importance of navigation in the Authority's program, forced the agency to lean heavily upon the corps in carrying out its navigation assignment.

Lock design constituted only a part of the Corps of Engineers' contribution to the development of the waterway. During the building years the corporation worked closely with the engineers on problems relating to channel improvement. The Authority sought the guidance of the engineers when it might have followed an independent course to a large degree. It should be pointed out, however, that much of the cooperation which took place in the construction period came almost a year after the Authority was organized. As suggested in the previous chapter, certain factors probably prompted the TVA to seek the advice of the Corps of Engineers on navigation problems when the Authority realized the necessity of giving more attention to its navigation objective. In the planning and building years, the Authority sought and gained the advice of the Corps of Engineers on such significant navigation problems as lock design, channel marking, dredging, lock size, and lock location in the dams.[10] Thus, the role of the War Department in building a navigable channel in the Tennessee, while largely of an advisory nature, has been significant.

Another governmental agency whose assistance to the Tennessee Valley Authority helped make possible the rapid accomplishment in the corporation's first two years was the Bureau of Reclamation. This organization, at the request of the Authority, prepared the detailed designs and contract drawings for the Norris and Wheeler projects.[11] The Corps of Engineers had already drawn tentative plans for the Norris Dam, but these were rejected in favor of a design that would be more economical to construct. During the first two years the bureau and the Authority worked hand in hand in building the Norris and Wheeler dams. Construction work usually began as soon as the blueprints were ready for use. The design work of the bureau enabled the corporation to put men to work immediately, and it is estimated that a year's time was saved in the building of Norris Dam by using the force account system of construction in cooperation with the use of plans prepared by the reclamation agency.[12]

As the Norris and Wheeler dams neared completion, the builders turned their attention to another main-river dam. The third major dam, the Pickwick Landing Dam, had been authorized in November, 1934, and active construction was begun in January, 1935. Its completion was planned for 1938. The Pickwick Landing Dam was an essential link in the navigation channel and would eliminate one of the less navigable sections of the river. Men, materials, and equipment were shifted from the Norris and Wheeler projects when they were no longer needed there. The economy of an ordered sequence of construction began to prove its value. Heavy machinery which was purchased for the earlier projects could be used at other dams, thus reducing building costs.[13] Workers attaining a high degree of efficiency and familiarity with one type of structure could be transferred to another dam of a similar nature. This, of course, enabled the Authority to build more economically and rapidly. Progress at the Pickwick site was rapid. The navigation lock, 600 by 110 feet, was designed by the Corps of Engineers and erected first so that traffic would not be blocked while the dam was being constructed. By the end of the fiscal year 1936, the lock was practically completed and excavation work and cofferdamming were well under way.

In the period from 1933 to 1936 construction work was affected little by the attack on the Authority's power distribution program. While the legal staff of the corporation fought the Authority's battles in the courts and the board of directors was coming to terms with Congress, the agency's engineers were swiftly throwing massive concrete barriers across the river. The hard-hatted legions, a combination of northern engineering skill and southern labor,[14] acquired land, cleared reservoirs, removed families, relocated highways and railroads, reburied the dead, dug gaping holes at foundation sites and filled them with concrete, built intricate powerhouses, and then distributed the energy created by the humming generators over an endless network of transmission lines. By June, 1936, the last concrete was poured at the Norris Dam and the Wheeler project was 98 percent completed. The construction of Pickwick Dam was ahead of schedule.[15]

While the TVA's forces were in the process of completing the Norris, Wheeler, and Pickwick projects, a beginning was made on two more main-river dams. The 1936 appropriations bill directed the Authority to initiate projects at the Guntersville and Chickamauga sites. Since preliminary investigations at these locations had been started several months before Congress assumed control over the time and sequence of dam construction, the TVA was in a position to begin building at Guntersville and Chickamauga shortly after the appropriation was made on August 12, 1935. The Guntersville Dam was authorized for construction by TVA on November 28, 1935, and the building of the Chickamauga project received TVA's approval on January 2, 1936. As the fiscal year 1936 ended, men and machinery were at work preparing the river bed for the foundations of the dams and the reservoir areas for eventual inundation.

A navigation channel, nine feet in depth, was beginning to take form. The Norris Dam with its large reservoir would store water for use during the dry months. A larger flow in the river would increase navigable depths. The Wheeler Dam would eliminate a difficult stretch of the river for a distance of 74 miles and provide a channel which would accommodate the heaviest equipment in use on the inland waterways. Thus, by 1936 the Tennessee could offer barge operators a disconnected 9-foot channel approximately 145 miles[16] in length as compared to a 70-mile length in 1933. In addition, an 8-foot depth was available for 184 miles and a 6-foot channel for approximately 60 miles.[17]

While the Authority was building the dams that extended the navigation channel, it was having to prepare an overall plan of development to pacify its congressional critics. The unified plan of 1936 was a blueprint of the way in which the agency expected to develop the resources of the river. Its building program offered little that was new. Actually, the dams it proposed in order to create a channel differed little from those of the Corps of Engineers' plan of 1930. Only the location of the lower-river dam (Kentucky Dam) was changed to any great extent. The old plan of nine high dams plus one low-navigation dam was proposed for the main river. The plan differed from the Corps of Engineers' proposals in that the Authority included three tributary dams as part of its navigation system. Two of these were the Norris Dam and the Hiwassee Dam, the former already constructed, and the latter in the preliminary stage of development. The third tributary dam proposed was the present-day Fontana Dam. At the time the unified plan was submitted, this last-named site belonged to the Aluminum Company of America, but negotiations were under way to secure the site. Additional dams for storage purposes on the Holston and French Broad rivers were proposed, but not for immediate construction.[18]

A suggested program of dam construction was made by the Authority. This feature concerned the time and sequence of building the various projects in the system. The economy of building the right dam at the proper time, in order to secure the greatest efficiency from its men, materials, and equipment, led the TVA to formulate a systematic plan of development. The agency expected to build ten dams by 1943. However, it was unable to do so, for, beginning in 1939, greater attention had to be given to power development for national defense. Although its entire program was speeded up, the necessity of building several additional dams not included in the unified plan of 1936 delayed the navigation portion of its plans. The following chart illustrates graphically the sequence of construction as proposed by the Authority.

The TVA also advanced a long-time, inclusive policy for the unified development of the Tennessee River system. The policy declarations concerning navigation are worthy of detailed treatment. The Authority recognized the importance of building a navigation channel that would become a part of the nation's inland waterway system. This consideration meant that the Tennessee River would be developed so that its physical features would compare favorably with the Ohio and Mississippi rivers. This type of development ensured that operating equipment on other streams could move on the Tennessee with no need of shifting cargo to lighter draft vessels. Another aspect of this farsighted policy of planning anticipated the significance of the Tennessee River in possible future development of adjacent waterways. Much thought was given to the idea of placing a dam on the Ohio River just below the point at which the Cumberland River enters that stream, ten miles upstream from Paducah. The project would have provided approximately 550 miles of continuous navigable water at a single level. This could be done by placing the lower Tennessee River dam (Kentucky Dam) at its present site and by constructing a canal between the Cumberland and Tennessee rivers. Such farsighted planning accounts in part for the location of the Kentucky Dam at a point farther downstream than it was originally located by the Corps of Engineers.[19]

Another future project which was closely related to the development of Tennessee River navigation was also incorporated in the Authority's planning. The ancient idea of connecting the Tennessee with the Tombigbee and Warrior rivers in Alabama was not overlooked. When plans were being made for the Pickwick and Guntersville dams, the eventual development of a canal between these reservoirs and the Alabama rivers was considered by the Authority. The history of the agitation for the building of the Tennessee–Tombigbee connection is not of major importance here, but it should be pointed out that many efforts have been made since 1933 to put this development under the jurisdiction of the TVA.[20] Thus far, these

SUGGESTED PROGRAM OF DAM CONSTRUCTION

The execution of this program would require appropriations for dam construction based on the schedule shown below, in addition to investments, which may prove to be necessary for generating electric power on projects other than those shown.

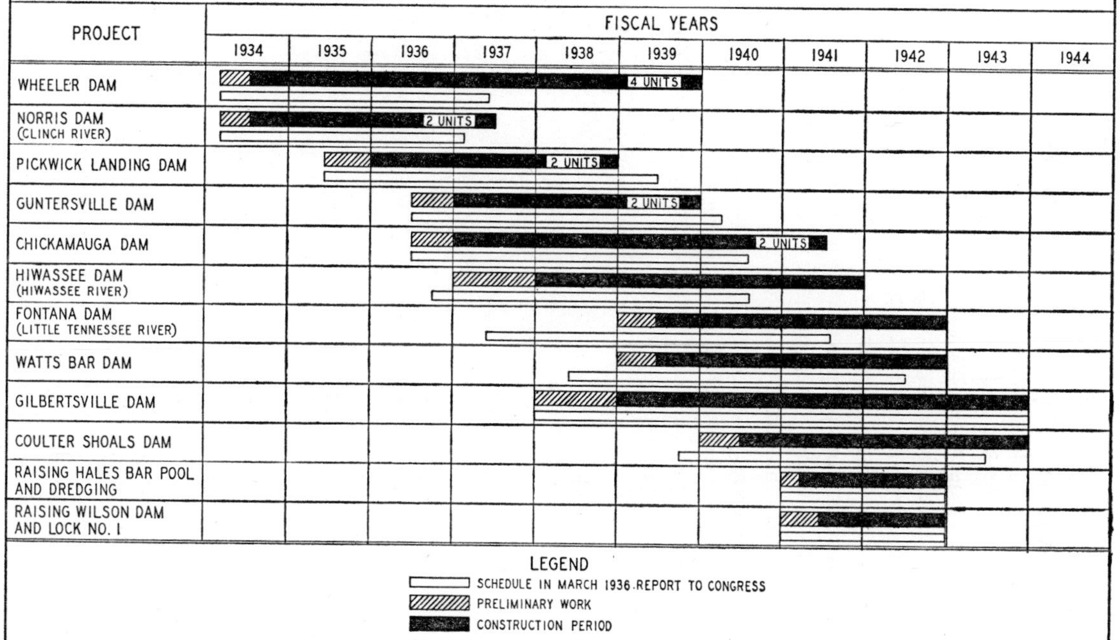

PROJECT
FISCAL YEARS
1934
1935
1936
1937
1938
1939
1940
1941
1942
1943
1944
WHEELER DAM
4 UNITS
NORRIS DAM (CLINCH RIVER)
2 UNITS
PICKWICK LANDING DAM
2 UNITS
GUNTERSVILLE DAM
2 UNITS
CHICKAMAUGA DAM
2 UNITS
HIWASSEE DAM (HIWASSEE RIVER)
FONTANA DAM (LITTLE TENNESSEE RIVER)
WATTS BAR DAM
GILBERTSVILLE DAM
COULTER SHOALS DAM
RAISING HALES BAR POOL AND DREDGING
RAISING WILSON DAM AND LOCK NO. 1
LEGEND
SCHEDULE IN MARCH 1936 REPORT TO CONGRESS
PRELIMINARY WORK
CONSTRUCTION PERIOD

GENERAL OFFICE ENGINEER - OCTOBER 12, 1936

GEDO 11BIR

efforts have not been successful. Opposition developed from those opposed to the extension of TVA's jurisdiction and from residents along the lower river who feared that a re-routing of the river might disrupt or damage their interests. In recent years the Corps of Engineers has restudied the feasibility of building a canal connection between the Tennessee and Tombigbee rivers.[21]

Two other policy declarations which were unique in regard to governmental development of navigable streams were made in the 1936 report. The first of these was not completely new. The TVA, as a part of its responsibility for promoting the economic development of the entire region, proposed that a system of freight terminals be developed in an integrated manner in order to coordinate the existing transportation arteries—truck and rail—with the future river channel. Its plans for a terminal system were incomplete at the time, but the foresight manifested by the agency indicated the possible values that could be obtained from a comprehensive approach to river navigation development.

The last of TVA's policy statements concerned its view regarding the levying of tolls on river users. The Authority favored an initial period of free use of the river to encourage water traffic. But it declared that "it seems reasonable to look forward, however, to a national policy that will require all river and harbor traffic to contribute to the cost of the facilities provided at public expense." [22] Just why the agency chose to take a stand on the issue is not clear. Apparently, the decision was the result of the TVA's unbiased attitude toward river transportation and a personal sense of fairmindedness on the part of the directors. The advocacy of user tolls certainly was not calculated to win friends in river transportation circles. Lobbying organizations that sponsor inland waterway improvements have consistently opposed the levying of user tolls on the nation's waterways. The TVA position on user tolls probably encouraged an unfriendly attitude toward the valley-authority method of river improvement.[23]

The estimated cost of the proposed program was revealed in the TVA's 1936 report. This aspect of the plan held special interest for Congress since the funds would have to come from appropriations. The cost of developing an adequate channel and providing a large amount of flood-control storage was estimated at $329,688,525. Included in the cost estimate was the amount necessary to complete the six dams under construction, to build four additional structures, and to raise the Wilson and Hales Bar dams in order to fit them into the integrated scheme of development. A sum of about $8,000,000 was included within the total estimate for activities preliminary to the actual construction of the projects. These activities consisted of a valley-mapping program, engineering studies, geological studies, and tentative planning for multipurpose construction.[24]

With the submission of the unified plan to Congress in March, 1936, the program for developing the Tennessee River for navigation, flood control, and incidental power generation was practically complete. It was a limited program in comparison with the present-day system of dams and steam plants owned and operated by the TVA. The plan called for the construction of seven dams on the main river: Gilbertsville (Kentucky), Pickwick Landing, Wheeler, Guntersville, Chickamauga, Watts Bar, and Coulter Shoals (Fort Loudoun), in addition to those already completed at Hales Bar and Muscle Shoals (Wilson Dam). Three dams were also proposed for the tributaries: Norris on the Clinch River, Fowler Bend (Hiwassee) on the Hiwassee River, and Fontana on the Little Tennessee River. The plan did not cover all the projects that would contribute to navigation and flood control. The Authority had only about nine months to produce its unified plan; and, consequently, it was hesitant to propose projects about which it had little information. Even where studies had been made, preliminary cost estimates were of a tentative nature.

Although the Tennessee Valley Authority did not consider immediate improvement of navigation on the tributaries of the Tennessee feasible, it did not overlook the possibility of future development of these streams. It suggested two methods by which these streams could be developed to provide water transportation. One called for low-navigation dams between the proposed high dams and the main river, while the other contemplated a system of transfer facilities at the high dam. Norris Dam was constructed with the view that if it became feasible to develop navigation on the Clinch River, a conveyer device could be installed to move commodities over the dam.[25] The failure to give attention to immediate development of navigation on the tributaries later brought severe criticism from TVA's opponents during the TEP case.[26]

With its plans formulated, its statutory duties clearly defined by Congress, and its construction crews hastily building five huge dams, the TVA appeared to be in position to relax and complete its proposed program. On May 29, 1936, eighteen power companies, whose operating territories were adjacent to one or another of TVA's generating facilities, made a second attempt to have the Authority's constitutional status defined by the courts.[27] When the Supreme Court limited its opinion in the Ashwander case to the legality of the generation and transmission of the power produced at the Wilson Dam, a loophole was left for the utilities to challenge the constitutionality of other TVA river-control structures and the generation of power at those installations. The companies charged that "the Federal government through TVA was unconstitutionally engaged in conducting an electric power business, and that consummation of the project would irreparably injure their business interests." [28] The utilities claimed that the government was entering the power business under the pretense of developing navigation, flood control, and national defense. In brief, the case hinged on the question of whether power production or navigation and flood control were the primary objectives of the TVA.

The question could be answered only by subjecting every facet of the TVA Act and program to a searching inquiry. In November, 1937, the United States District Court for the Eastern District of Tennessee began hearing the case. The power companies attempted to show that the Authority would have constructed a series of low dams had it been seriously interested in providing an adequate navigation system. The utilities argued that a low-dam program, as conditionally proposed by the Corps of Engineers in 1930, would have made the river navigable for far less money than TVA was spending for navigation in its high-dam project.[29] Flood control benefits in conjunction with a low-dam system, the power interests asserted, could have been provided for a relatively modest expenditure. They concluded that since

> TVA, with Congressional concurrence, [chose] to adopt the much more expensive alternative of high dams, [this decision] proved that the whole scheme was primarily a power project with no real relation to navigation or flood control needs; and that completed TVA projects had actually been operated primarily in the interests of generating power rather than of navigation and flood control.[30]

The TVA was faced with the problem of proving that its high-dam system would provide greater navigation and flood control benefits than might have been obtained by an alternative means. It also had to defend the operation of its water-control structures in order to prove that navigation and flood control had received first consideration where water usage was concerned. The TVA's multiple-purpose scheme for the unified development of the Tennessee River was placed on trial. The forthcoming decision would be extremely important, for it might not only determine the Authority's constitutional status, but it might also delay or defeat a major governmental experiment in water-resources control and use. The principle recognized by the National Conservation Commission in 1909 that "navigation is interdependent with other uses of the streams; [and] that each stream is essentially a unit from its source to the sea" was clearly endangered.[31] Furthermore, the concept that power should be the "paying partner" in river development was being questioned, for low dams could provide only an insignificant amount of energy and none whatever of salable value.

For almost two months the three-judge tribunal listened to a low-dam versus high-dam argument. The utilities urged that a navigation channel created by high dams was inferior to one provided by dams which formed broad reservoirs, that such a channel had less navigable capacity than that of run-of-river navigation which would be created by low dams and only about equal efficiency. The cost of a high-dam system which resulted in an inferior channel was impossible to justify from an economic basis, alleged the power interests, since estimates of future commerce on the river were far too high.[32]

Numerous other charges were leveled at the Authority's high-dam program. It was claimed by TVA's opponents that the wide reservoirs created by high dams would act as obstacles to navigation and that commerce on the Tennessee would be restricted, that navigation of the broad lakes would be hazardous for watercraft, since wind and wave action resulting from the greater fetch of a wide pool increased the danger of capsizing. Such an accusation had alarming implications. It implied that navigation on the Tennessee River would require larger and more expensive vessels, thus necessitating greater capital outlays for operating equipment and higher insurance rates on watercraft and their cargoes. Furthermore, if heavier draft vessels were required, integration of traffic from the Tennessee with that from the Ohio and Mississippi rivers might be seriously hampered. Such a development would have increased by a substantial amount the cost of shipping goods by water to points to and from the valley because freight would have to be transferred at the river's mouth where it joins the Ohio River. As charge after charge was leveled at TVA's multiple-purpose projects, the utility companies offered elaborate charts, graphs, and statistical information to support their contentions. Experts on navigation, flood control, and power generation testified to the accuracy of the power companies' assertions.[33]

Each argument presented by the utilities was answered by a long succession of engineers and experts on river navigation, drawn from private life, government agencies concerned with river development and transportation, and TVA's staff. The TVA contended that its high-dam system provided a superior waterway. Witnesses for the Authority declared that its slack-water navigation project had substantial advantages over a low-dam, run-of-the-river system. Benefits accruing to navigation from a slack-water development were said to include greater speed of tows, fewer interruptions of service, less costly freight terminals, and less danger from wind and wave action.[34] From an economic standpoint, one expert declared, future traffic on the river would doubtless justify the economic feasibility of the navigation project.[35] Probably TVA's most convincing argument concerning the cost of its high-dam project was its contention that the power created as a result of a navigation and flood-control project could be disposed of by the government to help defray the cost of those non-paying partners in the multiple-purpose scheme. To the utilities' charge that the water-control units had not been operated in the primary interests of navigation and flood control, the Authority produced operational bulletins which clearly indicated that the accusation was groundless.[36]

The three-judge tribunal, after hearing thousands of words of testimony and viewing numerous exhibits, in all instances where issues of fact were concerned, found in TVA's favor. The high-dam system, it ruled, provided a superior navigation channel to that which might have been obtained by a low-dam plan. In addition, the court found that TVA's high dams provided the most effective method of aiding flood control and navigation on the Mississippi River as well as the Tennessee. The design and construction of the projects were primarily for the improvement of navigation and flood control, said the court. The tribunal rejected the utilities' argument that the dams had been operated primarily for power generation. It found that the TVA board of directors required operating personnel at the projects to follow the TVA statute to the letter and that such instructions had been uniformly obeyed.[37]

Once these determinations had been made, the court then considered the constitutional issue. It concluded that the construction of the Authority's projects was within the government's powers to regulate commerce and provide for the nation's defense. If electrical energy was generated at the dams in carrying out the powers mentioned above, then such energy could be sold under the property clause of the Constitution, declared the judges. The opinion cleared the Authority of all charges of unconstitutionality. It remained to be seen whether the Supreme Court would do likewise.

The Supreme Court decision came approximately a year later, in 1939. The high court did not choose to examine the merits of the case as the district court had so thoroughly done. It rendered its opinion on the issue of whether the utilities had standing to sue. The Supreme Court held that the power companies had suffered no legal injury; therefore no basis existed for bringing suit against the TVA. The Court dismissed the case, and the last major legal assault on the Authority was ended.[38]

The lengthy litigation in which the Authority was involved affected its developmental program, but it is difficult to tell what effect it had on the navigation. That it had caused serious damages to the overall program of the agency is attested to by the joint committee which investigated the corporation in 1938:

> Mr. Lilienthal testified that attacks on the constitutionality of the Authority have succeeded in causing serious damage to the operations of the organization. In addition to direct costs of litigation, and large, though somewhat speculative, losses through delay in selling power, there have been further intangible losses in the form of confusion and disorganization among the Authority's personnel.
>
> At best, as Mr. Lilienthal points out, there are grave problems to be met in assembling a new organization, and in preparing to start a large construction program with a minimum of delay and waste. In certain parts of the Tennessee Valley Authority work, the schedules have been delayed by injunctions, suspending operations, and disrupting the organization; and similar delays were threatened at other points.
>
> To the responsible officials of the Authority, according to testimony, the necessity of proceeding with large commitments in the shadow of constant attacks upon the validity of their enabling act was a harassing and disturbing obstacle to efficient planning. By the duties of their office they were obliged to proceed on faith, knowing that any contract or commitment upon which they entered might be subjected at once to legal attack.
>
> The committee recognizes that there is justice in Mr. Lilienthal's complaint. It notes that the lack of a speedy and final determination of the

principal constitutional questions involved has been unduly costly to the Authority and to the public, and that it has undoubtedly caused disorganization and waste in the work of the Authority.[39]

While the Authority was battling the power companies in the courts, a civil war erupted among its board members. Two months after the trial court's ruling in the Eighteen Power Companies case, another searching inquiry into the agency's activities was begun. This time it was undertaken by Congress. The fight within the TVA board was not an overnight development. It appears that as early as August, 1933, a division began to take place between Chairman Arthur E. Morgan on the one hand and Directors David E. Lilienthal and Harcourt A. Morgan on the other.[40] By 1936, the conflicting attitudes of the board members began seriously to disturb the entire organization. During the next year the agency was reorganized, and its policy-forming directors were separated from the business of actively administering the Authority. A general manager was appointed to administer the TVA. This action soothed the tempers of the board members for a time and tended to reduce dissension at subordinate levels which had resulted from the practice of combining policy formulation and administrative function according to the area of interest of each director.[41]

The board feud in the Authority seems to have had little effect on the construction program. It is true that Arthur E. Morgan and Lilienthal had conflicting views with respect to the scope of the TVA's dam-building activities prior to 1936. The major disagreements in regard to the enlargement of the construction program were resolved by outside factors over which the directors had no control. The plans for developing the river and for providing a navigation channel were substantially complete before the dissension in the board reached serious proportions in 1936. After the reorganization of the corporation took place in 1937, the engineering aspect of the agency was no longer subjected to the disruptive forces working within the board. Arthur E. Morgan was relieved of his administrative duties as chief engineer, and thereafter a newly appointed engineering supervisor was made responsible to the general manager of the corporation.

The reorganization of the Authority in 1937 had only a sedative effect. By March, 1938, the feud was being aired publicly in the nation's press.[42] Needless to say, opponents of the Authority were jubilant, for a welcome scandal appeared to be right around the corner.

Events moved rapidly after this time. In mid-March, 1938, President Roosevelt intervened in the dispute, but he was unable to bring harmony among the directors. Chairman Morgan refused to cooperate with the President and insisted on a congressional investigation of his charges of dishonesty and corruption against his fellow directors. Morgan's defiant attitude brought about his removal by Roosevelt on March 23, 1938.[43]

Shortly after Morgan was dismissed by President Roosevelt, Congress provided for a sweeping investigation by a joint congressional committee of the policies, administration, and overall program of the Authority. Thus began the TVA's most searching examination. Between May 25, and December 21, 1938, hearings were held in Washington, Knoxville, and Chattanooga. The investigating committee made a five-day tour through the Tennessee Valley and inspected all of the TVA's projects. After its seven-month inquiry was completed, the committee found no earth-shaking scandals. A veteran political observer who had watched the Authority's development from its inception and who had personally known the directors said that "it all boiled down to very little, except as a drama of personalities." [44] The committee made its report to Congress in April, 1939. The committee majority group found little to criticize in the Authority's program. As for the charges of dishonesty brought by Arthur E. Morgan, the committee majority reported that such accusations were "without foundation, not supported by the evidence, and made without due consideration of the available facts." [45] Some dissatisfaction was found with the TVA's accounting system and its land-purchasing program, but its overall record was regarded as highly satisfactory. The committee expressed the hope that TVA's program could now be carried to completion and reported that "the Authority should be regarded as a settled and established institution in the Valley." [46]

The Republican minority on the committee did not share the majority's hope for the TVA's future success. It chose instead to disagree with practically every finding determined by the committee majority. It charged that the intent of Congress had been ignored by the majority because the investigation was limited in scope. Even so, minority members declared that the evidence clearly showed that the Authority was guilty of inefficiency, lack of economy, and that the board was hopelessly in discord. Such a situation demanded drastic measures, argued the Republican minority, which proposed a complete reorganization of the TVA. Their proposal completely rejected the wisdom of integrated river development and administration. The minority members recommended that the TVA be stripped of its navigation, flood control, fertilizer, and agricultural functions. These activities were to be turned over to the War Department and the Department of Agriculture. The minority sought to make the TVA a power corporation which sold electrical energy at the bus bar to private utility companies.[47] The scheme to wreck the government's experiment in unified development of water resources was rejected by Congress. The acceptance of the majority report by Congress represented another victory for the public power supporters over the advocates of private development.[48]

The investigation and its results were significant in the life of the Authority. In the first place, its conclusion marked the end of a five-year fight for legality and public support. Herman Finer noted that "the investigation marked a turning point in the career of the Authority: it was a dividing line between the years of trial and the years of assurance." [49] In the second place, the dissension in the TVA board was eliminated. Arthur E. Morgan, after having been removed from office by the President, challenged the action of the Chief Executive. The Supreme Court upheld the President's authority to dismiss the chairman. Former Senator James P. Pope of Idaho was selected to be a director of the TVA, and Harcourt A. Morgan was named as the new chairman. Congress did not tamper with the three-man governing board of the Authority. The investigation itself, by sustaining the views of Harcourt A. Morgan and David E. Lilienthal, had the effect of reducing the power of chairman of the board to that of chief spokesman of TVA. After the dismissal of Arthur E. Morgan, the directors were equals in board meetings at which policy was being formulated. Although some authorities on public administration have regarded the three-man directorate as an unworkable administrative device, it has been used successfully by the Authority since the board feud in 1938.[50] Much of the success, however, appears to have stemmed from the fact that the three directors have been substantially in agreement on major policy formulation. In recent years the board again has been subject to friction because of basic differences in the philosophy of the directors. General Herbert D. Vogel, after being named chairman of the TVA board by President Eisenhower, immediately found himself at odds with his fellow directors over the Authority's request for appropriations.[51]

A third valuable result of the congressional inquiry was the process of self-examination which took place during the long months of national publicity. Herman Finer concludes that

> It [the Congressional investigation] had a healthy effect on the whole organization. While it necessarily threw an enormous burden on the directors and officers of the TVA in the marshalling of information and opinion about their activities and procedures, clarification of the TVA's aims and methods resulted from the process of self-justification and cross-examination.
>
> The officials felt the disciplinary energy of Congress, and the effect was substantial, pervasive, and lasting.[52]

Perhaps the best lesson gained from this soul-searching was the realization that internal cooperation was absolutely necessary if the TVA was to survive attacks by its opponents. The multiple-purpose nature of the TVA's program provided a natural weakness which encouraged attacks by its adversaries. Divide and conquer appeared to be sound strategy for those interests opposed to the valley-authority device of river resource development. The fact that TVA's activities vary widely and also overlap with the work of other government agencies has consistently led its critics to suggest that the various functions of the Authority be returned to traditional resource development organs of government. Of course, to do so would destroy the whole scheme of unified development and the very heart of the TVA idea.

With the conclusion of the Congressional investigation and the dismissal of the Eighteen Power Companies case against the Authority, a feeling of relief pervaded the controversial valley. The TVA's arch competitor in the region, the Tennessee Electric Power Company, unwilling to fight further, agreed to sell its properties to the government corporation. Wendell L. Willkie, president of the holding company that controlled the Tennessee company, and David E. Lilienthal settled on a purchase price of $78,500,000. The TVA's share of the properties amounted to $45,000,000, which was financed through a bond issue sold to the U.S. Treasury. Other properties included in the total purchase price went to twenty-two municipalities and eleven cooperatives.[53] The Tennessee River and its drainage basin had now become the kingdom of TVA. The years when the battles between the Authority and its adversaries (private utility companies) were most bitter now ended. All would not be peaceful in the future, for further fights would develop in the congressional arena, where tactics designed to contain the TVA by limiting its construction funds or its service area would continue until the present day.[54] But for the time being, TVA could breathe easier and concentrate more fully on carrying out its plan for an integrated development of the river.

Whatever hopes the TVA may have had for a leisurely program of construction unhampered by external forces were destroyed when the German legions crossed the Polish border on September 1, 1939. World War I had led to the building of the first government-financed dam on the river—Wilson Dam—and now World War II would increase the demand for electrical energy so greatly that even the fondest dreams of Senators Norris and McKellar for the utmost development of hydroelectric power sites on the Tennessee River and its tributaries would be realized by 1945. The Authority, at the request of President Roosevelt and with the cooperation of a defense-minded Congress, embarked upon a highly accelerated construction program to develop the power resources of the river for the nation's defense. Power for the reduction of ores in the development of aluminum for aircraft manufacture was essential, since air power was now recognized as an indispensable element in modern warfare. For the next five years the TVA's construction crews were increased until a work force of slightly over 40,000 was engaged in constructing dams and steam plants for power, navigation, and flood control.[55]

While TVA's management had been fighting for its life in the years between the formulation of its unified plan in 1936 and the end of its court battles in 1939, the engineering and construction forces had been busy shaping the course of the river. In these years Wheeler, Pickwick Landing, and Guntersville dams on the main river were completed. By the spring of 1939, almost a year before the war emergency program was initiated, a channel depth of six feet was available from Paducah to Chattanooga. The lower 184 miles of the river had not at this time been improved, since present-day Kentucky Dam had not been completed. In the lower section, however, two feet of additional depth had been obtained through the release of water from up-river dams on the Tennessee and Norris Dam on the Clinch River. The Chickamauga Dam, which would extend the existing 6-foot channel one third of the distance to Knoxville, and the Hiwassee Dam on the Hiwassee River, which would provide greater quantities of water during the season of low water flow, were nearly completed at this time. Both of these projects were finished early in

1940. Thus, when a war emergency came, a 6-foot navigation channel spanning about two thirds of the distance of the river was available, and only the closure of Kentucky Dam and the construction of dams at Watts Bar and Coulter Shoals sites were needed to provide the authorized project depth of nine feet. The national emergency would hasten the completion of these vital links in the channel.[56]

In 1940 the TVA turned its attention to building for defense purposes in order to supply an ever-increasing demand for electrical power. The construction program outlined in its 1936 report was expanded to include the building of several tributary dams not in the integrated plan, the construction of a steam plant near the Watts Bar Dam, and the installation of additional generating units in those dams already completed. The construction program of three main-river dams was re-scheduled so that the completion dates of the projects were advanced by seven months. While the remaining main-river dams were being brought to completion, the then available 6-foot channel was put to use as a supply artery for civilian and military goods being moved between the Southeast and the upper Mississippi Valley, the Great Lakes industrial centers, and Gulf coastal ports via the Mississippi and Ohio rivers.[57]

As the demand for power was increased, the Authority was requested to enlarge its construction program even more. By 1942, when the first emergency program was substantially carried out, two more emergency programs had been instituted. Within seven months after the Japanese attack on Pearl Harbor, TVA had nine dams and a steam plant under simultaneous construction.[58] Records were broken and then broken again as TVA's well-trained and well-managed engineering and construction forces worked around the clock to harness the waters of the Tennessee and its tributaries for electrical power.[59]

The accelerated building program, primarily for power purposes, carried in its wake the quick completion of the three main-river dams necessary to provide the 9-foot channel on the Tennessee. In March, 1941, the navigation lock in the Watts Bar Dam was placed in temporary operation. On August 2, 1943, the closure of Fort Loudoun Dam took place, and with the filling of that reservoir the century-old dream of opening up the Tennessee for commercial navigation to Knoxville was realized.[60] Two months after the completion of the Fort Loudoun Dam, the last dam up-river necessary to extend the channel to Knoxville, the Memphis *Commercial Appeal* announced to its readers that the Tennessee had become the "world's most modern waterway." [61] Six months later, on February 16, 1944, the port of Knoxville was officially opened amidst a host of federal, state, and TVA officials. To enhance the significance of the occasion, the first commercial tow reached Knoxville the evening before the celebration. The part of the tow consigned to Knoxville consisted of 70,000 bushels of wheat from St. Louis.[62]

Despite the fact that the river was now open its entire commercial length of 650 miles, an all-year full project depth of nine feet to accommodate boats and barges of 9-foot draft had not been accomplished. Channel depths of six to eight feet still existed in several portions of the stream. To obtain the required depth would necessitate the closing of Kentucky Dam, the raising of the Hales Bar Dam, and a great deal of dredging in the upper part of the reservoirs and in the approaches to the navigation locks. Wartime restrictions had forced TVA to postpone this part of its navigation program. The late closure of the Kentucky Dam, however, was the result of the magnitude of that particular project rather than defense restrictions.[63]

The completion of the navigation channel had to await closure of the Kentucky Dam, which took place on August 30, 1944. Early in September the district engineer's office in Nashville announced that the Kentucky Dam lock would be open for navigation officially with eight feet of water by September 15, 1944.[64] The TVA's task of building water-control structures to provide slack-water navigation with a minimum depth of nine feet was virtually completed. Ironically, on September 2, three days after the closure of Kentucky Dam, the last of the main-river structures to be finished, former Senator George W. Norris, widely revered as the "Father of the TVA," died at his Nebraska home. One year prior to Norris' death, TVA Chairman Lilienthal told the House Subcommittee on Appropriations:

> The 1944 fiscal year budget winds up the major construction in the development of the Tennessee River. There is a good deal of satisfaction in making that statement because it has involved very large expenditures of funds which have been approved from year to year by this committee and Congress, and it was a great strain on this organization [TVA] to do that job in the ten year period in which it was done.[65]

By 1945 the task of harnessing the Tennessee had been accomplished. To be sure, the ideal channel as conceived by TVA's engineers still needed some finishing touches, but the basic work was a reality. The Tennessee River had become an important extension to the nation's 5,100-mile system of inland waterways. Knoxville, at the head of the river, now enjoyed a water connection with Pittsburgh, Chicago, Minneapolis, St. Louis, New Orleans, Houston, and Mobile. The century-old problem of providing a dependable, commercially usable channel from Knoxville to Paducah had been solved by TVA's high multiple-purpose dams which furnished 9-foot, slack-water navigation for a distance of 627 miles, only 22 miles shorter than the course of the old river.

What exactly had TVA wrought? What changes had the Authority's engineers and workers made in the Tennessee? Was Tennessee River navigation different from that of other rivers which had been improved for inland water transport? The answers to these questions reveal an astounding accomplishment by the Authority in engineering, water control, and the administration of a drainage basin area.

In the first place, the Tennessee Valley Authority had built a waterway which was—as a veteran riverboat operator described it in 1939 after having taken an experimental tow of grain from Paducah to Chattanooga—"the easiest and fastest to navigate anywhere in the country."[66] The TVA had transformed a river, which prior to 1933 had a year-round minimum depth of four feet upon 40 percent of its course, two feet upon 30 percent of its course, and one and one-half feet upon the remaining 30 percent of its length, into a safe and dependable transportation artery usable the year round by river craft loaded to 9-foot depths. This transformation resulted from the construction of seven main-river locks and dams by TVA, two high dams already in existence, and one low-navigation dam built by the Corps of Engineers. During the same period, five large tributary dams plus several others of lesser importance were constructed to provide water for the navigation channel. At the same time the structures would furnish storage for flood control and produce millions of kilowatts of electricity. That such an immense water control system was developed in a twelve-year period is a remarkable feat in itself. Not to be overlooked is the uniqueness of Tennessee River navigation from an administrative point of view and as a pioneering attempt in conservation of water resources. Clifton T. Barker, a TVA navigation expert, observed, "The Tennessee was the first of the nation's major rivers to be developed for navigation as only one phase of a comprehensive multi-purpose water control plan, and it is the only river whose development has been undertaken by a regional agency charged with encouraging the development of the whole economy of the tributary area." [67]

The TVA Information Office never fails to point up how the Authority has transformed the unruly Tennessee and made it flow slowly and evenly to the Ohio. The advantages of the TVA-created channel are not unreal or overemphasized. One would expect TVA to present its navigation accomplishment in a glowing manner, but it is not uncommon to find former and present-day critics of the Authority in general agreement that the channel on the Tennessee surpasses facilities elsewhere. An official of the largest common carrier domiciled on the Tennessee River reported that the high-dam system which provides slack-water navigation was far superior to waterways elsewhere.[68]

One of the major criticisms made of TVA's navigation channel during the building decade was that the wide lakes created by the high dams would endanger river craft because of wind and wave action. One of the staunchest supporters of this view was Captain Donald T. Wright, river pilot and editor of the *Waterways Journal*, a weekly devoted to furthering inland waterway development. Captain Wright, who made a trip from Paducah to Knoxville in the spring of 1954, was forced to admit that his 1937 testimony before a House committee was not well founded.[69] After almost fourteen years of river use, this criticism has been found to be largely unwarranted. In testimony given before a Senate committee in 1946, David E. Lilienthal stated, "As to this wave action bogey, there is nothing to it. . . . the concern about wave action is unfounded." [70]

While it is true that the slack-water lakes created by TVA's dams are no place for a rowboat, the records do not show an unusual number of sinkings. Probably much of the discontent manifested by conservative rivermen stemmed from their distaste for change. The attitude of a veteran river pilot seems to reflect this basic dislike of slack water for navigation. The following incident, as reported in the Louisville *Courier-Journal*, illustrates this attitude: "Papa Underwood, veteran pilot of 86 years, with no love for impounded water, snorted to his sons, pilots Paul and Harris Underwood—'covers up too many good steering landmarks, any fool can follow buoys. Pond pilots, that's what you are.' " [71]

One other criticism made of the Tennessee Valley Authority's channel has been that the Authority neglected or limited navigation on the upper Tennessee by constructing small locks.[72] Here, again,

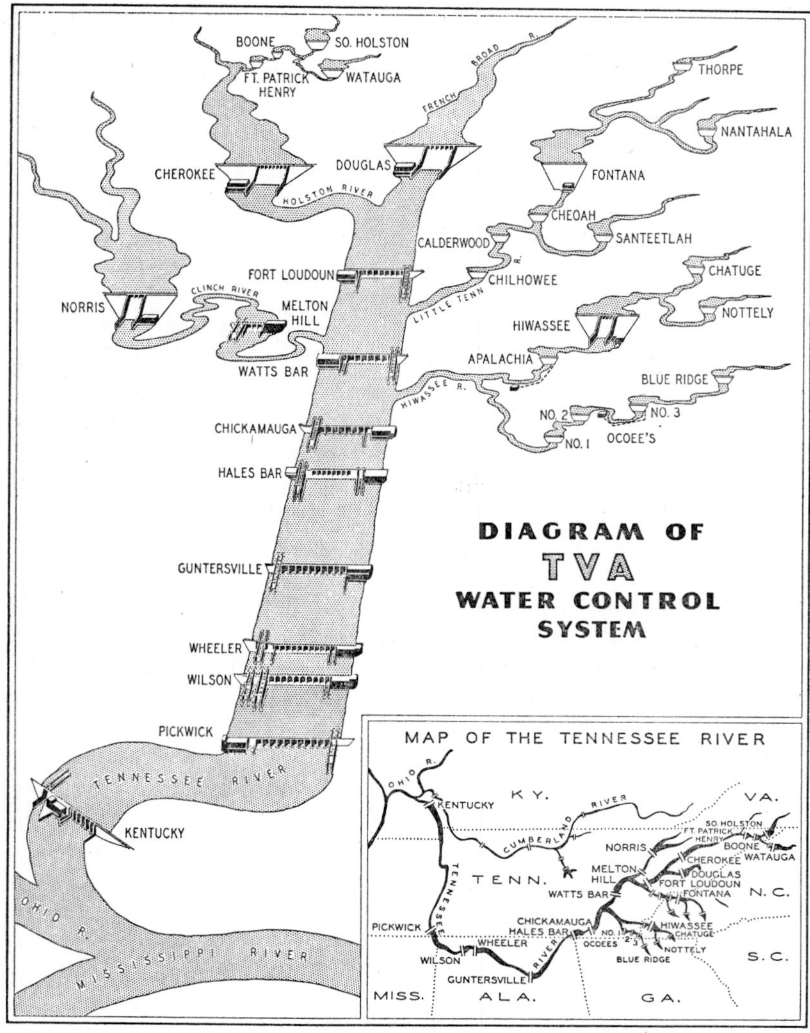

the criticism is somewhat unjust or at least misplaced. When lock sizes were determined for the upper river, the Authority consulted the Corps of Engineers to determine the size of lock necessary to handle the traffic in this portion of the river. The corps' recommendations of lock sizes 60 by 360 feet were followed by TVA. After fourteen years of use, these locks, except on unusual occasions, appear to be adequate to handle the present-day traffic on the river. One thing is clear: except for the outdated locks at Wilson Dam, which are being replaced at the present date, and the small lock at Hales Bar Dam, both built before TVA was created, little agitation has developed for building larger locks in those dams on the upper Tennessee. One might also note that the TVA considered future traffic demands on the smaller locks and left room for 600- by 110-foot locks in those dams above Muscle Shoals where the smaller locks exist.

The Tennessee Valley Authority has been a controversial institution since its inception. The fact that so little criticism has been directed toward its navigation system is in itself evidence of the quality of the transportation artery which has been created. Therefore, one must conclude that the engineering and construction efforts of the Authority to provide a 9-foot navigation channel on the Tennessee have been eminently successful. To the statutory mandate laid down by Congress in 1933 to develop the Tennessee River for navigation, TVA has responded generously and efficiently.

According to the Authority's logic, the building of a navigation channel was only a part of its responsibility. As Clifton T. Barker has said about engineers, their first reaction to anything new is "What good is it?" [73] Thus, TVA's next assignment was to promote its newly constructed waterway and thereby make the $148,915,775 investment [74] in its navigation system merit this expenditure.

4

PROMOTING WATER WAY TRAFFIC

By 1946 the Tennessee Valley Authority had substantially completed its task of transforming an unruly stream into a modern, navigable waterway. The river had been changed from a watercourse of shallow depths, uneven flows, and impassable shoals into a chain of slackwater lakes connected by nine high-lift locks and one low-navigation lock. Huge reservoirs located on the tributaries of the main river provided an ample water supply for navigation during all seasons of the year. The Authority boasted enthusiastically about "the most modern inland waterway in the world." [1] Director James P. Pope, successor to Arthur E. Morgan on the TVA board, declared on the eve of the channel's completion that the Tennessee River would soon "be ready to carry boats and barges ten times the size of Columbus's flagship." [2] From a monetary standpoint, TVA valued its navigation facilities at $158,000,000.[3] If the towboats did not come and the freight tonnage figures failed to increase, no one could blame the Authority, for the physical facilities of the stream were second to none in the nation's inland waterways.

Once the TVA had created a physically navigable waterway, its statutory obligation to navigation was complete. The act specifically delegated to the Corps of Engineers the task of lock operation, and, presumably, the corps was to perform such other functions related to navigation as determining the amount of commerce using the river and maintaining the navigation channel. Nevertheless, the federal agency "has assumed an unconventional measure of responsibility for seeing that the Tennessee River is used for commercial transportation." [4] Thus, the TVA was not only a navigation project but a navigation program as well.

TVA's decision to embark upon a policy of river-transportation promotion designed to assure the success of its navigation channel was motivated by several factors. Certain sections of the enacting law served as one stepping stone. The TVA Act required the Authority to apportion its developmental costs among its major objectives. This obligation forced the agency to place a fixed valuation on its navigation and flood-control systems in order to isolate the expense of its power operations which were expected to be self-supporting and self-liquidating.[5] Furthermore, Congress had been pursuing a policy since 1913 to the effect that river-development projects had to be worthy of improvement from the standpoint of future benefits to the public. The Tennessee River project, although the TVA statute did not explicitly say so, apparently was to be subjected to the same test. The Authority, then, could not very well ignore its navigation investment while other rivers improved at federal expense were being evaluated in terms of their public value. In short, transportation benefits and savings had to exceed the expenditures for developing, operating, and maintaining the navigation channel. Faced with the necessity of proving the economic feasibility of its navigation investment, the Tennessee Valley Authority determined that its waterway would not be idle.

The enacting statute also directed the TVA to further the economic development of the valley region.[6] The Authority recognized early the importance of transportation to this assignment. Navigation economics, transportation rates, and the region's transportation complex began to receive TVA's attention in 1934.[7] It learned that the estimates of transportation savings and future traffic on the river made by the Corps of Engineers in 1930 were too uncritical. As Elliott Roberts has written, "the [1930] analysis was inadequate to the TVA's needs. . . . A more realistic and defensible basis for the navigation expenditure had to be found." [8]

Research and analysis revealed other problems of river transportation. Terminal facilities along the river were unequal to the task of handling anticipated traffic, for too few were available and existent terminals were little more than cleared spaces along the bank of the river.[9] The Authority also learned that it could not expect an automatic shift of freight from the railroads to the waterway once a navigable transportation artery had been provided.[10] As it probed deeper into questions of transportation policy and transportation economics, the agency began to realize that its goal of developing traffic on the river would be profoundly influenced by the regulatory activities of the Interstate Commerce Commission (ICC), which fixed railroad rates and, after 1940, governed both the rates and the areas of service of major water carriers.

Expressed differently, the Authority found that artificial barriers to river commerce threatened the use of its waterway. Although familiar with this problem for several years, the corporation was rather belated in expressing itself on the subject. In its annual report for 1951 the TVA stated:

> . . . full use of the waterway is being hampered by some existing transportation and regulatory practices. Some of these can be solved only by legislative changes; others may yield to aggressive action by shippers, bargelines, and people of the Valley. In both areas, TVA can and does help.
>
> Among the barriers are unduly low rail rates on commodities best suited to water transportation. Rail freight rates, as shippers are well aware, have increased about 61 percent since World War II. Less widely known is the fact that rail rates on items best suited to water transportation have increased far less—coal rates 49 percent, grain rates 51 percent, and sulfur only 18 percent. . . . Where through rail rates cannot be held sufficiently low to prevent barge shipments, high rail rates to and from a river port can effectively block inland shippers from using the waterway even though barge rates are low. On the opposite side of the coin are instances of higher rail rates charged on perishables not suited to water transportation or on freight between inland points in order to make up costs which are not recovered from low rates on water-competitive traffic.[11]

Another factor which probably induced the TVA to embark upon a policy of promoting water transportation was its study of the interterritorial freight problem.[12] The Authority's obligation to further the development of the natural resources of the Tennessee River area was interpreted to mean that it should promote an economy balanced between industry and agriculture. From its study of the structure of national freight rates, it found that "manufacturing in the outlying territories [the South, the Southwest, and the West] was hampered, discouraged, and retarded"[13] by rate barriers which prevented those regions from marketing manufactured and processed goods in the nation's industrial heartland, located north of the Ohio and Potomac rivers and east of the Mississippi River. David E. Lilienthal expressed the problem in this manner:

> It became apparent in the first months of the TVA that an integrated development of the resources of the Tennessee Valley region required consideration of the freight transportation rate structure. A study was initiated. The facts showed that the free flow of commerce between the South and other sections of the country was being hindered by what appeared to be a discriminatory freight differential between the South and the North and East, a differential unfair to southern business and harmful to the whole country.[14]

Recognition of the problem was far easier than obtaining a solution. Elimination of freight-rate barriers to southern and western finished goods would necessitate a complete overhaul of the national freight-rate structure. Because the problem was national in scope, the regional agency could do little about it except to educate southerners regarding the limitations which the system placed upon their attempts to industrialize and report to the President and Congress on the desirability of changing public policy. Action of this type was taken, as is indicated by the Authority's having studied and publicized the effects of the freight-rate differentials on southern industry.[15] But these efforts have been slow in bearing fruit. In the meantime, the TVA discovered a new means of attacking the problem.

The Authority apparently determined that its navigation channel could be used as a weapon in the battle against the freight-rate barrier. In its annual report for 1936, TVA asked, "To what extent can water rates be made to offset carrying charges which now tend to drain the Valley of its raw materials and to penalize the establishment of local industries?" It answered, "Lowered transportation rates might well hasten the economic rehabilitation of the region."[16] The value of water transportation as a means of eliminating discriminatory freight practices against the South was voiced from Austin, Texas to Atlanta, Georgia. Lilienthal expressed this to a Rotary Club meeting in Atlanta:

> But it is the outbound traffic down the Tennessee River—the things you produce in surplus quantities for exchange with the North and East—that will especially interest and encourage your manufacturers. That is because . . . your Atlanta industries, in common with industries all over

the South, are handicapped in their trade with other regions by a combination of long distance, which we can take philosophically, and discriminatory railroad rates, which are not so easy to take and which we denounce as an injustice to this and similarly treated regions. Entirely apart from the effort to achieve rate reform . . . the Tennessee waterway cuts a deep channel through the trade barrier of discriminatory interterritorial rates.[17]

Thus, from statutory obligation, from its efforts to stimulate the economy of the valley, and from its realization of the use that the navigation channel might serve in offsetting the freight-rate barriers to the industrialization of the valley and its environs, there resulted a policy of promoting water transportation which has no parallel with the activities of other federal agencies concerned with river development. Because of those factors, the TVA initiated a navigation program designed to define and remove the impediments to the use of its waterway.

The program consists of four types of activities: engineering planning, designing, constructing, and maintaining the navigation facilities; operation of the reservoirs so as to maintain specified depths of nine feet in the channel plus two feet of overdepth as a safety factor; economic studies of traffic; and the provision of clientele services of a limited nature to shippers and others interested in water transportation.[18] The objectives of its program are to assure the valley's residents of a dependable waterway which will stimulate the region's economic development and to make the navigation channel yield benefits in the form of transportation savings to justify the public's investment in the navigation facilities. The program has cost the Authority approximately $200,000 annually since 1948 and lesser amounts prior to this date.[19]

The engineering phase of the navigation program is similar to the activities of other federal agencies concerned with the development of water resources. The Authority shares this responsibility with the Corps of Engineers. The TVA maintains the navigation channels in the feeder streams while the Corps of Engineers performs this task in the main river. This activity consists largely of dredging the rivers to remove foreign matter which may obstruct navigation. Repair and new construction having to do with the river-control structures is a TVA duty. Operation of the dams to provide a water supply for navigation, although a complex procedure and an essential part of the navigation program, may be regarded as a routine practice which is common to all multipurpose projects. The engineering aspects of the TVA's navigation program embody a series of activities which can hardly be defined as unconventional federal functions.

But when one removes the engineering portion of the program from consideration, the TVA's navigation operations become unique. For instance, the Authority has conducted numerous studies of the factors influencing river traffic, prepared elaborate analyses of shipments which could be freighted by water at a substantial saving over other means of transport, and published colorful brochures on the benefits which accrue to the shipper from using the navigation channel. Activities such as these greatly exceed those of the Corps of Engineers and the ICC, which confine their functions largely to the task of gathering statistics about inland waterway commerce.

The TVA's efforts to promote river commerce do not end with research and the dissemination of the results of its findings. It engages in a number of other practices—many of them quite extensive—aimed at the same objective. In providing clientele services to river shippers and others interested in water transportation, the Authority has constructed four public-use river terminals plus one for its own use; it has provided navigation charts of its reservoirs for a nominal sum; and it has furnished data concerning channel depths, waterway operating equipment, river-bank industrial sites, and other information related to river navigation. The Authority has on occasion intervened in rate cases before the ICC for both shippers and barge-line companies.[20] The scope of TVA's navigation program is indeed broad.

One of the first impediments to the expansion of river commerce recognized by the Authority was that of the inadequacy of terminal facilities along the river. In its report to Congress in 1936 the agency asserted: "It is the purpose of the Authority at a later date to present for the consideration of the Congress and of the several states a report concerning the location, construction, operation, and control of terminals on the Tennessee river system."[21] By June, 1937, the study was well under way. As it evolved, the TVA was introduced to other problems vital to the success of the channel as a commercial artery. The Authority reported in 1938 that "these surveys involve an analysis of waterway traffic of the future . . . and consideration of the possible development of private, contract, and common carrier barge lines."[22] The terminal study was completed in 1939 by the

TVA's commerce department, a group of transportation economists, freight-rate experts, and navigation engineers.

The department reported that traffic potential warranted the building of a system of public-use terminal facilities along the river. It reasoned that existing terminals were unsuitable for modern barge transportation and that "adequate and efficient public terminals are as essential to the success of inland navigation as are improved channels." [23] It estimated that future freight movements through the terminals would be some 2 million tons once the waterway was completed. It regarded the cost, approximately 3 million dollars, as nominal compared to the outlay for river-control structures on the main stream. The group felt that the construction of the terminals should be a gradual undertaking geared to the requirements of the public and the government. As for the ownership, construction, financing, and operation, the commerce department recommended that prime consideration be given to exclusive federal action through the TVA or some associated agency.[24]

Despite the concrete recommendation of the commerce department, the board of directors was hesitant to embark upon a policy of federal development. Elliott Roberts attributes TVA's hesitancy to the fact that terminal construction "lay outside the scope of TVA's clear legislative authorization for channel construction . . . [and] it involved touchy questions of local politics." [25] Both reasons appear to be valid, for TVA had once before experienced the wrath of the river cities when it was determining the sequence of its dam construction program, and the recent constitutional tests in the courts undoubtedly left the agency with no desire to create grounds for a new attack by its opponents. The course was clear; some other means would have to be found to secure adequate terminal facilities.

The TVA turned its attention to this task in the summer of 1940. The solution to the problem appeared to be through state action. The Authority encouraged the formation of the Tennessee Valley Waterways Conference, an organization composed of representatives from municipalities along the river, to lobby for state legislative appropriations for terminal construction.[26] The waterways committee of the Chattanooga Chamber of Commerce took the initiative in organizing the conference. On June 28, 1940, delegates from several river ports assembled at Chattanooga under the guidance of the Authority and the Chattanooga waterways committee. Director James

P. Pope served as keynote speaker, and the Authority provided river transportation experts, statistical materials, and plans for river terminal facilities. Pope told the delegates, "It is time to perfect an organization and to work out a program for terminal development so that terminals will be ready when they are needed. . . . I think the time has come for us to act together." [27] Organization followed the speeches and Earl P. Carter, chairman of the waterways committee of the Chattanooga Chamber of Commerce, was selected to head the pressure group. Action was now in order.

The problems facing the organization were threefold. It had to secure state funds and work out plans for an agency to construct, maintain, and operate the terminals once they had been completed. Finally, it had to formulate a plan which would be acceptable to the legislatures of Alabama and Tennessee. Several financial schemes were considered, but eventually it was decided that direct appropriations from the state legislatures offered the greatest hope of success. It was proposed that a Tennessee Valley terminal authority be set up as a joint agency of the two states to construct, maintain, and operate the terminals. Cooperation between the two states was to be obtained through an interstate compact. These proposals were considered and accepted by the conference at Decatur, Alabama, on December 20, 1940.[28]

In working out the plans, the TVA rendered significant support. The Authority's legal experts and its river transportation division prepared drafts of the interstate compact and the appropriations bills necessary to implement the program adopted by the conference. It studied the question of the legality of joint participation by Alabama and Tennessee in the project. The agency found that nothing in the constitution of the state of Tennessee prohibited such a course of action but that the Alabama constitution might require an amendment to permit that state to join in the undertaking.[29] This requirement was a major obstacle in the path of the planners, for the Alabama legislature was not in session and would not meet again until January, 1943, thus possibly delaying the project for two years unless a special session were called to expedite the matter. The TVA advised the conference at Decatur that a special session probably could be arranged if the citizens of North Alabama gave vigorous support to the proposals.[30] The Authority also furnished technical data concerning the engineering aspect of the terminals. It advised the conference on prospective costs, location of the facilities, methods of operation, and other pertinent matters.[31] The TVA had done its share. It was now up to private interests, largely local chambers of commerce, to marshal support for passage of the bills and other necessary action.

In the fall of 1940 plans were made to send delegations to Nashville and Montgomery to secure administration support for the terminal project.[32] Since the Alabama legislature was not in session, efforts were concentrated on getting Governor Frank Dixon to call a special session of the legislature. Attempts to secure a special session were unsuccessful. Alabama boosters of the river terminals then sought to procure whatever funds remained from the construction of the Mobile facilities, but none were available.[33] While Alabama advocates of the terminal program were meeting defeat at Montgomery, the Tennessee backers of the project were busy trying to put their state in the river-terminal business.

When the Tennessee legislature convened in January, 1941, the members of the Tennessee Valley Waterways Conference were ready for action. Both the Tennessee Valley Authority and the Waterways Conference had contacted Governor Prentice Cooper prior to the meeting of the legislature and had won his support for the program.[34] Efforts were now directed toward getting the Assembly to approve the project.[35] Bills to implement the terminal system were introduced and passed the first and second readings, but the legislature adjourned before the third and final reading was completed. Failure of the bill apparently stemmed from two factors: strong opposition from railroad interests [36] and the "customary closing-days rush of the Legislature." [37] In spite of this setback, the waterways committee of Chattanooga felt that the terminal measure would be passed at the next session of the legislature.[38]

State action on the development of terminals died at that time. As mentioned earlier, terminal promoters in Alabama were never able to secure a special session of the legislature, nor were they successful in obtaining state funds for terminals at Tennessee River ports. The Tennessee General Assembly never again gave consideration to the proposal, for when it met again the Authority already had a terminal development program under way. No other valley states made any concerted effort to secure state participation in the project.[39]

With the possibility of state aid highly uncertain and at best two years away, the TVA began to consider other means of getting the terminals built. Within a month after the state aid bill failed, the

Authority's commerce department began exploring the possibility of securing federal funds for the project as a national defense necessity.[40] Once again the Tennessee Valley Waterways Conference worked closely with the TVA. Throughout the year 1941 plans were developed looking toward the building of the facilities. When war came in December, 1941, the terminal problem became more acute than ever before because of the scarcity of labor and materials and the priorities required for any construction project. Furthermore, full-scale commercial navigation on the Tennessee was sure to be needed in view of the strain which would be put on the rail lines in the region. Thus, the stage had been set for a renewal of efforts to secure adequate terminal facilities.

In February, 1942, the Waterways Conference, unwilling to wait longer for state aid since the next legislative session was still one year away, requested that TVA build the terminals. The Authority responded with alacrity. It had already prepared a budget request for terminals in its 1942 appropriation, and it now urged the river cities to convince the Office of Defense Transportation of the need for the facilities.[41] In May, 1942, Congress appropriated a sum adequate to construct four public-use terminals, and the War Production Board and the Office of Defense Transportation released the construction materials as a defense undertaking. The terminals were to be located at Decatur, Guntersville, Knoxville, and Chattanooga. The facilities were less elaborate than the TVA had originally planned because wartime considerations forced the substitution of wood for steel construction.[42]

Building of the terminals was initiated immediately after Congress supplied the funds and the Office of Defense Transportation approved the project. Progress at Chattanooga, Decatur, and Guntersville was rapid, but at Knoxville complications of TVA's own making soon brought a halt to construction activity. Apparently the Authority in part determined upon the terminal sites according to the interest in water transportation which had been shown by the shippers at various river ports. The Alabama cities and Chattanooga were strong advocates of water transportation, and business interests in those cities had made many applications for joint rail and barge rates. At Knoxville, on the other hand, very little interest had been shown in barge-line service, and the TVA decided to focus greater attention on water commerce in that city. To accomplish this task, the Authority decided to postpone the building of the Knoxville terminal. On the basis of this action the War Production Board revoked the defense priorities for the facility. The postponement had the desired effect of stirring up interest in barge-line service in the area, and the Knoxville Chamber of Commerce organized an immediate campaign to enlist the support of local business leaders in encouraging barge services and joint barge and rail rates for the port. After the Knoxville interests had satisfied the Authority, they sought the aid of Senator McKellar to ensure the construction of the terminal. Together, the TVA and the Tennessee senator were able to convince the War Production Board of the defense value of the terminal and construction was resumed.[43]

While the Knoxville situation was evolving, the Authority continued its building of the terminals at Decatur, Guntersville, and Chattanooga. In the fall of 1943 these three facilities were completed, and in February, 1944, the terminal at Knoxville was officially dedicated.[44] A few months later a coal terminal at Harriman, Tennessee, was completed for the TVA's own use. The terminals were of simple design, consisting largely of wood and brick construction. Each unit was equipped with stiff-leg derricks for transferring bulk and package freight between land and water carriers, transit sheds for the storage of package freight on a temporary basis, highway and railroad connections, and the necessary docking and wharf facilities to accommodate the water carriers.[45]

Upon the completion of the terminals, the operation and management were assumed by the Authority, which did not intend to engage in permanent operation of the facilities. It anticipated that private, public, or quasi-public agencies, under appropriate agreements with TVA, would ultimately manage the terminals. The war emergency, the necessity of proving the economic feasibility of the terminals to private capital, and the desire to assure continuous and satisfactory service of the facilities were factors which led the Authority to manage the terminals upon their completion.[46]

The TVA's policy of terminal operation was governed by its desire to improve the overall transportation system of the valley region, to make the facilities self-sustaining, and to encourage the development of a coordinated terminal system. Therefore, during the eight-year period of Authority administration, the docks were uniformly operated. Rates for terminal services were kept low but generally in line with those at terminals elsewhere on the nation's inland waterways. High standards of service were maintained without discrimination among individual users and the same policies were in effect at all of the public-use terminals.

The docks were never as successful as the TVA had anticipated in terms of the tonnage which moved through the facilities. With the exception of the Guntersville unit, none of the other terminals has handled the amount of tonnage which the TVA estimated would be shipped through them. The port of Decatur is an illustrative case. In 1941 the Authority estimated that this unit, after a fifteen-year growth, would be receiving and shipping approximately 70,000 tons of freight annually.[47] In 1956, after twelve years of operation, this terminal during its most successful year handled only 35,000 tons of freight, about half of the original TVA estimate. The Chattanooga and Knoxville terminals also have failed to secure the estimated tonnage.[48]

The failure of the facilities to be fully utilized may be accounted for by several reasons. Probably the major cause for their poor showing is the fact that less than barge-load shipments of assorted freight have never developed on the river. The public-use terminal is designed to service the small shipper who has less than a barge load to ship. Provision of this kind of service is impractical for the barge-line companies since it entails frequent stops which are usually unprofitable if less than a barge load is received from a landing. Furthermore, shipper habits of routing goods must be overcome where a new form of transportation begins to compete with an older form. Competition between the two forms usually leads to rate reductions on freight, which in turn reduces the main advantage of water transport—its cheaper freight rate. Although traffic growth on the river has been substantial during the past several years, much of the increase is handled by private companies which furnish their own loading and unloading facilities. Consequently, a large segment of the Tennessee River traffic does not use public facilities. The war emergency probably hampered traffic development through the terminals, because the bulk of the goods transported on the river was not for public consumption and was used at plant locations along the river's edge. Another factor which prevented full use of the terminals was the absence of an organization to assemble freight in barge-load orders. Not until 1957 was such an organization set up to provide a forwarding service to smaller shippers.[49]

In 1952, in line with its plans to turn over the control of the terminals to private interests, the Authority leased the facilities to private operators. The TVA required the new operators to fix reasonable rates for terminal services in order to encourage use of the units, and provision was made to allow the lessors to purchase the docks if they desired. Under private control, the terminals have been used more extensively. In 1951, the last year of TVA operation, the docks handled 114,517 tons of freight while in 1956, after four years of private management, the total tonnage passing through the facilities was slightly over 200,000 tons. Probably the increase can be accounted for by the more comprehensive barge-line services, an increasing diversity in the type of freight, and the shipment of larger amounts of consumer products. The Authority's program of river-transportation promotion has also helped in making the shipping public more aware of the navigation channel's freight benefits. In 1957 the lessors of the Chattanooga terminal exercised their option to purchase that terminal, and its operation is now fully under the control of private capital.[50] At the time this study was terminated, the Knoxville and Guntersville facilities had been sold by the Authority.

The terminal problem and its solution represent only one aspect of the Tennessee Valley Authority's comprehensive program for the promotion of river traffic. It plunged with equal zeal into the study and identification of other problems which have adversely affected the use of the navigation channel. Elliott Roberts has said that many of the barriers to greater utilization of the waterway have been "less tangible than that of terminals—more complex, and ultimately more influential on the use of the Tennessee River as an avenue of commerce." [51]

The effect of these obstacles on Tennessee River traffic has been and continues to be substantial. In June, 1945, the president of the Tennessee Valley Waterways Conference reported that "the Tennessee [River] transports not more than ½ the immediately prospective long-haul high-value tonnage and not more than ⅓ the ton-mileage; and not more than ⅓ of the near-term savings are being realized." [52] The reason for this limitation on the use of the water artery stemmed from the failure of the federal government properly to coordinate the various components of the nations transportation complex. A TVA official summed up the problem as follows: "The present conflict in national policy . . . is expressed on the one hand in appropriations to develop waterways and on the other hand in numberless moves backed by the authority of the federal government to prevent the public from getting full benefit of the waterway."[53] The ICC and Congress, after having spent huge sums to provide the physical facilities for river transportation, have been guilty of throwing up barriers to the interchange of traffic between river and land carriers which effectively retard the development of water movements.

Several devices act as obstacles to an easy flow of commerce between river and land. Section 4 of the ICC Act allows railroads to lower their rates to meet water competition and to retain high rates where competition is not a factor. Such actions by the railroads with the approval of the commission prevent the full utilization of the waterway. The Guffey Coal Act, which fixed the price of delivered coal, discriminated against a major waterborne commodity since no differential was allowed for using a less costly mode of transportation. This act was repealed in 1943 at the insistence of waterway interests. Another obstacle to river traffic growth is the difficulty in securing the establishment of joint rates between the railroads and barge-line companies.[54] The railroads have stubbornly refused to enter into such agreements with Tennessee River water carriers.[55] Failure of the rail carriers to enter into joint rail-barge rate agreements has reduced the savings to shippers and thereby discouraged water movements. Another restriction involved railroad-assessed "switching charges" on waterborne freight which moved to and from the Knoxville public-use terminal.[56]

Finally, the failure of the railroads to grant transit privileges on water movements has acted as a deterrent to river traffic. The transit privilege allows freight stopped in transit for storage, processing, or transshipment to move to its destination on a lower through rate. The use of this device has substantially affected the grain trade on the Tennessee River. Some of the barriers to river commerce are still effective, but through the action of the Authority, shippers, and barge-line companies, several such barriers have been eliminated. The efforts which have been made to free water transport from these restrictions constitute a major part of the TVA's promotional program.

One official of the Authority has declared that "such impediments must be modified or eliminated entirely if the shipping public is to realize fully the inherent advantage of water transportation."[57] This militant attitude has prompted the corporation to act in a number of ways to rid river commerce of these artificial barriers. Initially, the problem or hindrance is defined through research. When findings indicate that transportation laws or regulatory practices are responsible for the barrier in question, remedies are then sought. Since the TVA does not write national transportation legislation nor engage in the administration of these laws, its actions are confined to education of the shipping public regarding the need for changes in basic transportation policies and to interventions before regulatory bodies in cases involving restrictions on water commerce. Thus, by one means or another, the Authority has been able to secure the abandonment of some of the discriminatory practices discussed in the preceding paragraph. The TVA has not been without supporters in its fight for unhampered inland waterway commerce. Frequently, however, the Authority has developed much of its support by marshaling evidence and disseminating information concerning an unfair practice or a drawback to utilization of the river for navigation.

The TVA's concern with the problem of artificial barriers to river commerce appears to have taken shape after 1936. The report on the unified development of the river published in that year more or less assumed that the chief obstacle to utilization of the river would be shipping habits. Converting shippers to the use of this new mode of transportation would require some time. The Authority apparently assumed that the ICC would effectively initiate an integrated system of water and land carrier rates in accordance with the Transportation Act of 1920, which charged the ICC with the responsibility of protecting water carriers against destructive competition. Several factors seem to have persuaded the corporation that more than a change in shipper habits would be necessary in order to secure full use of the navigation channel.

The cancellation of the joint water-rail rate on waterborne freight to and from Knoxville in 1936 was probably one factor. In 1939 the TVA was introduced to the use which could be made of the "fourth section" relief clause of the ICC Act when the railroads sought lower rail rates on oil shipments moving to the Tennessee Valley in order to prevent the loss of this business to the water carriers.[58] This attempt by the railroad companies to divert traffic from the river was followed by an effort to secure passage of a bill by the Tennessee legislature to impose a tax of one half cent per gallon on petroleum products barged into the state. The railroad-inspired measure never passed, for vigorous opposition to the bill developed. The TVA did not take an official stand on the issue, but its friends, especially its Chattanooga supporters, strongly protested the proposal.[59] Finally, the TVA's concern with the interterritorial freight-rate problem as an obstacle to the full economic development of its region undoubtedly provided the Authority with a vast knowledge of the competitive nature of rail and water transportation and the tactics used by the railroads to prevent water carriers from obtaining rail freight.

Once the Authority realized how completely future navigation on the river could be affected by the inconsistencies between national transportation policies and its aim of securing the full utilization of its channel, the agency set to work to influence transportation policy and to correct what it regarded as administrative abuses of the country's basic transportation laws.[60] Actions were initiated in several ways. The TVA encouraged the water carriers operating on the Tennessee River to seek joint rate agreements with truck transportation firms. In 1941 several water freight firms successfully established combined motor truck and barge freight rates between localities in northern Alabama and Georgia with points in the upper Mississippi River Valley. This attempt to overcome railroad resistance to providing a joint rail-barge rate, though sustained until 1947, was found to be unprofitable since it did not attract a sufficient volume of freight to the motor-water route.[61]

As World War II neared its end, the corporation stepped up its fight against the impediments to Tennessee River commerce. In 1945, officials of the TVA acting in conjunction with the Tennessee Valley Waterways Conference began to give consideration to what John P. Ferris, then director of TVA's commerce department, called "straightening out the inconsistency." [62] A few weeks later, the waterways committee of the Chattanooga Chamber of Commerce heard Ferris outline the principal barriers to the full development of the river, and it unanimously agreed to work toward relieving those conditions.[63] Statements of the problem were sent to members of the Tennessee Valley Waterways Conference, and the Authority urged the American Waterways Operators, Inc., an association of water carrier firms, to join the fight.[64] Joint efforts by the Authority and the Waterways Conference to further the development of river transport by the removal of artificial barriers to its growth continued through mid-1946, but little was accomplished.[65] Except for the business interests of Chattanooga, shippers along the river never manifested a great deal of concern over the impediments to river traffic growth. Therefore, such success as has been attained is largely a result of the single-handed efforts of the TVA. Elliot Roberts accounts for the limited response which the TVA has received from the valley public as follows:

> The TVA can, and does, make studies and put forward evidence, but these do not constitute a fully adequate vehicle for action. In such matters, furthermore, a large hidden resource on which the construction phase of the navigation program has relied heavily, the public acceptance of real tangible things, is not available. Here, where the issues are abstract and in some degree ideological, the TVA has been forced to move much more slowly than in its building program.[66]

The failure to overcome public apathy regarding the inconsistencies in national transportation policies has led the TVA to pursue a "go-it-alone" course in its fight to remove barriers to Tennessee River commerce. Here the agency must operate within rather narrow limits, for it can only follow the lead of other interested parties. It does, however, quite frequently initiate the action by pinpointing the problem and suggesting a solution to a particular difficulty. Two cases involving restrictions on water traffic illustrate the TVA's role in this capacity: the Knoxville Switching case and the Barge Grain case.

The Knoxville Switching case grew out of a railroad company action which increased switching charges on traffic that moved to or from the Knoxville public-use terminal. Only a small amount of the total Tennessee River traffic was affected, but the principle of fair and nondiscriminatory treatment of river traffic was involved and was clearly inconsistent with the provisions of the Transportation Act of 1940. The TVA researched the problem and interested several Knoxville shippers in the matter. The parties concerned lodged a protest before the ICC, and the Authority then intervened in the case in behalf of the Knoxville shippers. The ICC ruled in favor of the railroads, and the river interests appealed to a federal court. The court reversed the ICC ruling and ordered the ICC to reopen the case. The regulatory agency reopened the case, but before a hearing was completed a compromise agreement was reached and the matter was dropped. It might be said that the river interests had lost the battle but won the war.[67]

The second case, the Barge Grain case, was not so readily settled. Litigation was begun in 1951 when three barge lines entered a complaint before the ICC that ex-barge grain [68] moving from thirty-two ports located on the Mississippi, Illinois, Ohio, Missouri, and Tennessee rivers was not accorded the same rate treatment as ex-rail grain.[69] The water carriers sought an ex-barge proportional rate which would have reduced rail rates on grain when this commodity utilized both barge and rail transportation in moving to its destination. The practical result in the Tennessee Valley and the Southeast would be materially to reduce freight charges paid on grain that used the newly developed Tennessee River. The object of the barge companies—to develop more traffic—clearly paralleled the central purpose of TVA's navigation promotional program. In 1951 the Authority intervened in the case on behalf of the water carriers.[70]

The Authority's role as a litigant was no different from that of other interested parties. Its governmental status did not give it greater influence. It could only petition the ICC to redress what the Authority, along with other interveners, interpreted to be a discriminatory policy which was made illegal by Congress in the Transportation Act of 1940 which instructed the ICC to preserve the inherent advantages of all forms of transportation. The corporation was limited in its action as a petitioner, but this did not mean that it would not resort to other measures. The agency did not sit idly by and engage in a policy of watchful waiting; it channeled its energies into a campaign to educate numerous groups and the general public as to the issues involved and the impact of a favorable ruling on the economic development of the valley.

In November, 1951, the TVA's Navigation and Transportation Branch prepared a "competent, semi-technical analysis of the case and its bearing on the region's economy." [71] This publication, vividly illustrated and simply written, made a clear case for ex-barge proportional rates. Its broad appeal encompassed industrial, commercial, consumer, and agricultural interests in twenty-five states and parts of two others. The case for reduced rail rates on ex-barge grain was translated into terms which expressed a glowing future for the Southeast. The Authority stated its position in the following manner:

> In the long run the result of such reduced rates should be reflected in the price which consumers pay for shipped-in grain and grain products. Reduced prices are normally followed by expanded markets and increased consumption.
>
> An expanded volume of grain transported via barge-rail routes through the Tennessee River ports would help those cities become gateways, rate-break points, and centers of concentration in the grain trade. That result would in turn tend to attract brokers, commission merchants, banking

and credit facilities, storage and warehousing companies, and the whole interrelated complex of highly skilled and extremely productive occupations that exist in an important grain market. If the enterprises centering on grain should profit, other types of businesses would naturally gravitate to the Tennessee River ports and these communities would become centers of communication, manufacturing, and commerce.[72]

According to Elliott Roberts, the brochure was widely disseminated.[73]

Research, publication, and distribution did not end the TVA's efforts to marshal support for the barge lines. After interested persons had had time to digest the printed material in the report, members of the Authority's staff contacted the heads of farm organizations, milling and feed manufacturers and distributors, state utilities commissioners, and key persons in other commercial and semipublic groups. The TVA's actions bore fruit, for twenty-three organizations had filed petitions with the ICC in support of the Authority and the barge companies by June, 1952.[74]

In spite of the array of supporters for rate revision, the ICC, after extensive hearings, dismissed the complaint on July 18, 1955, and the complainants turned to the courts. Prior to court action, the ICC reopened the case in light of a Supreme Court decision which had ordered the commission to establish proportional rates on ex-barge sulphur at ports where ex-rail sulphur was handled on a division of a joint rate. After further hearings, the ICC in March, 1958, reaffirmed its 1955 findings on the grounds that no rail proportional rates were published from Tennessee River ports to the South, which meant that the railroads could freely vary charges for ex-barge and ex-rail reshipments as long as they did so by means of unpublished divisions of a through rate rather than published proportional rates.[75]

The effect of this ruling on grain movements to destinations beyond the port cities along the Tennessee River is illustrated by the following example. A Chattanooga grain dealer wishes to ship grain from Kansas City to Chattanooga and subsequently reship it to Orangeburg, South Carolina. He can purchase grain in Kansas City and arrange for shipment to Chattanooga by barge or rail. In either case, the grain is shipped on a bill of lading showing Chattanooga as the destination, and the delivery is completed when the barge or car is placed for unloading at the dealer's elevator or mill. The difficulty arises when he wishes to reship at a later date to Orangeburg over the Southern Railway. If the grain came in by rail, he can surrender his inbound bill of lading and ship either the grain or grain products into which it has been manufactured from Chattanooga to Orangeburg for sixteen cents per hundredweight. If the grain was brought in by barge, however, he has to pay a rail rate of fifty-four cents for the movement from Chattanooga to Orangeburg. Therefore, in the absence of a joint proportional rate agreement between rail and water carriers, the savings inherent in lower-cost, inbound barge transportation are lost.[76]

The latest ICC ruling was immediately challenged by the barge companies and other petitioners. Once again, before the case came up for trial, the ICC modified its stand of 1958 when two of the barge companies, the American and Federal barge lines, sought reconsideration of its order of March, 1958, which related to ports on all rivers other than the Tennessee. A rehearing was scheduled for October, 1958. At this juncture the Arrow Transportation Company filed a second complaint with the court to force the ICC to end its delaying tactics and thereby achieve a determination of the issues in a federal court. The district court enjoined the ICC from further action and then reversed its order to allow the ICC to make a final and definitive ruling in the case. In March, 1959, the ICC issued an order and an accompanying report which eliminated preferential and prejudicial rates against ex-barge grain movements but disallowed the Arrow Transportation Company's status as a connecting carrier. This section excluded Arrow from participating in a rate agreement with the railroads and thereby continued a discriminatory rate system under a different guise.

The Arrow company then lodged a third supplemental complaint with the district court on the ICC's March, 1959 decision. The court reviewed all the outstanding issues in the case and decided that the ICC was guilty of maladministering the Transportation Act of 1940, which clearly imposed upon the ICC the duty of preserving the inherent advantages of each mode of transportation. Having found accordingly, the court, on July 20, 1959, ordered the ICC to act as promptly as possible to institute "lawful, reasonable, and non-discriminatory ex-barge rail rates on grain and grain products"[77] from Tennessee River ports to destinations in the South. In 1964 the problem still awaits ICC action.[78]

The settlement of the Barge Grain case, if favorable to the barge lines, is of major significance to Tennessee River navigation. In the first place, the actions of the Authority to assist the barge lines and shippers in the litigation should do much to enlist the support of river shippers in the TVA's fight to remove artificial barriers to the use of its waterway. Secondly, grain movements on the river which have steadily increased despite the lack of rate integration between land and water carriers should grow increasingly larger. A third possible result of the decision may be that water-transported commodities other than grain can be expected to enjoy a reduced rail rate when outbound from Tennessee ports. If these results should materialize, traffic on the river may well exceed those optimistic estimates calculated by the Corps of Engineers in 1930. Before full utilization of the waterway can be accomplished, however, the carrier services along the river will have to be substantially expanded. Here again the Authority, in conjunction with shippers and barge-line companies, has acted to provide the river user with more comprehensive services.

In still another way TVA has sought to promote traffic on the Tennessee River. It has attempted to secure more adequate barge-line services for river shippers. Prior to 1940 it was thought that the improved waterway and the anticipated traffic would be sufficient magnets to motivate the barge-line companies to extend their services to the Tennessee River. The services of these additional carriers plus that of already established barge lines[79] appeared adequate to handle the expected increase in river traffic. Once again the TVA was forced to revise its assumptions as a result of national transportation policies.

The passage of the Transportation Act of 1940 brought certain water carriers under the jurisdiction of the Interstate Commerce Commision. Part III of the act divided water carriers into three categories according to the type of service the carrier rendered.[80] Private carriers were exempted from regulation. Common carriers "were required to obtain certificates of public convenience and necessity," and "contract carriers subject to the act had to secure permits" to operate over certain rivers.[81] Under the provisions of Section 309a of the act, a carrier, in order to continue its service over a given route, had to convince the ICC that such a service had been performed prior to January 1, 1940. Permission also had to be obtained from the ICC to perform services over newly improved portions of a waterway.

It was unforeseen and unfortunate for the TVA and other Tennessee River boosters that ICC regulation of water carriers came when it did, for the "grandfather" provisions of the 1940 act had the effect of limiting the number of common and contract carriers which could operate on the river. Under the "grandfather" clause, carriers had to be in bona fide operation over a given route in January, 1940, in order to qualify for operating rights thereafter. In case of the Tennessee channel, which was still in the construction stage, this meant that many of the larger carriers were unable to secure rights. Moreover, it meant that future permits to operate over the completed channel would have to be granted on the basis that public convenience and necessity required additional services as evidenced by shipper demand. Of great importance also was the fact that the Tennessee channel was completed during World War II when few applications were made to conduct new operations. The limited number of applications at this time is accounted for by the lack of equipment during wartime and by the growth in freight traffic on established routes as a result of the war emergency.[82]

On the surface, the granting of operating rights over a newly improved waterway by the ICC might appear to be a routine matter. This, however, is not the case, for before operating rights are granted to an applicant a hearing must be held where opposition to such an extension of service can be heard.[83] In almost every case, this leads to a vigorous protest on the part of the railroad companies and those water carriers which already have such rights. Thus, the threat of having to share the freight quickly brings opposition from affected carriers which often prevents the granting of rights to applicant barge lines. That such proceedings have often in the past acted as a deterrent to more extensive barge-line services on the Tennessee River is evidenced by the large number of denials made by the ICC of applications for the expansion of operating rights on the river.[84]

It is obvious that the ICC has felt that common carrier barge-line services over the river have been adequate. The Tennessee Valley Authority has not thought so, for it has striven since 1938 to procure the services of both private barge-line companies and the Federal Barge Lines, formerly a government-owned and -operated facility. The story of the corporation's attempts to secure operating rights on the Tennessee River for the government barge line will be developed subsequently. The building of the public-use terminals during the war was in part a TVA effort to attract carriers to the river. Since 1938 the Authority has allocated a portion of the funds from its navigation operations budget for the gathering of data which could be used in encouraging carriers to extend their services to the waterway.

The compilation and dissemination of such information has been rather extensive in nature. An illustration of the diversity of TVA's activities in this respect is afforded by its budget request for the fiscal year 1941:

> While the unified river system is being constructed, it is of great importance that problems and potentialities of navigation be under constant scrutiny, so that policies may be developed and facilities provided which will insure the maximum utilization of the 9-foot channel. The amount requested for 1941 [$73,000] includes provisions for studies of the proper location of sailing lines, channel markers, and safety in the reservoirs still under construction . . . and continuation of the preparation of navigation charts which will permit craft to navigate the river in safety while taking advantage of the shortest possible distances.
>
> The assembly of data on the types of commodities available for river shipment, their probable origin and destination, and rates for water and other modes of transport will also be continued. This and other information will be assembled and made available to prospective navigators and shippers. The types of equipment best suited for operations on the Tennessee River will be determined. . . . The results of these investigations will also be made available to prospective operators.
>
> Studies were made in 1939 of the possibilities for the development of private, contract, and common carriers, and co-operation will be extended to them [the carriers] in 1940 and 1941 in establishing their services.[85]

Obviously, the Authority was leaving nothing to chance. When the Transportation Act of 1940 vested control of contract and common carriers in the ICC, it practically ensured a clash between the two agencies, for frequently the policies of one did not agree with those of the other. There is no clear-cut evidence that the two organizations have purposely sought to block each other's program, but a former high official in the TVA revealed that the Authority has been a thorn in the side of the ICC over the years and that the ICC has in turn been unfriendly toward the Authority on many occasions. Whether or not this unwholesome relationship has been a major factor in retarding carrier service on the river is open to question. The evidence available does not seem to indicate that such is the case.[86]

Another phase of the TVA's struggle to secure adequate barge-line services for the river deserves comment. In July, 1941, the corporation began to give consideration to the possibility of persuading the federally owned Inland Waterways Corporation to extend its operations to the Tennessee River. Accordingly, a conference between the TVA and the Inland Waterways Corporation was held in Knoxville. It appears that the officials of the Inland Waterways Corporation were rather hesitant about seeking such rights, but the TVA apparently decided to go ahead with its plans for procuring the services of the federally owned transport facility.[87] Efforts in this direction were not successful. The failure to secure the services of the government-owned facility was a result of the war emergency situation. The need for the Federal Barge Lines on the Mississippi River system outweighed the requirements of the Tennessee. This setback, while it may have forced the TVA to shelve its plans for a time, did not destroy the agency's hopes for future success.

Since the war, two additional legislative attempts have been made to amend the Denison Act in order to allow the Federal Barge Lines to operate over the Tennessee. In 1947 Representatives Albert Gore and Estes Kefauver of Tennessee endeavored to push through such amendments. Efforts have also been made to secure a wider interpretation of the provisions of the 1928 act so that they could be construed to mean that the Tennessee River was not excluded from the service area of the government barge line. Both of these attempts ended in failure. The opposition of private water-carrier interests and of the rail carriers has been credited with blocking the efforts. The most recent attempt to extend the service area of the Federal Barge Lines to the Tennessee River came in 1951. In that year Representative Robert E. Jones, Jr. of Alabama introduced a bill which would have effected this change in the Denison Act. Once again the effort ended in failure. Agitation ceased when the Federal Barge Lines were sold to private interests in July, 1953.[88]

The attempt by the TVA and its supporters to extend the operating rights of the Federal Barge Lines to the Tennessee River represented an effort to solve a problem of enduring nature on the Tennessee and other rivers—that is, the absence of frequent and regular common carrier barge-line service for less-than-barge-load shipments.[89] This problem continues to exist. It stems from the inability of the barge lines to operate at a profit if less-than-barge-load lots are freighted. The operation is impractical because of the frequent stops that have to be made and the time-consuming nature of such stops. Both of the requirements result in added fuel and labor costs, and they materially reduce the time required to move freight, which is of great importance to the shipper.

From the foregoing discussion, it should be clear that TVA was a novice when it began to consider the use that would be made of the waterway. Its apparently naïve attitude toward the competitive nature of transportation was soon revised when it realized that the navigation channel offered a means of circumventing the freight-rate barriers that retarded valley economic development. Furthermore, few people expected navigation to be more than a constitutional peg. This lack of experience with water transport on the part of TVA's early policy-makers was clearly a fault of the Roosevelt administration, which was responsible for naming the first TVA board members. The fact that none of the directors had previous experience in dealing with the problems of inland waterway carriers appears to be substantial evidence that the navigation aspect of TVA's assignment was rather lightly regarded by its creator. This situation, fortunately for navigation in the TVA program, lasted only a short time. For, as the Authority acquired a greater understanding of the valley and the importance of transportation to its overall program, the advantages of a modern inland water transportation artery began to exercise a positive influence on the TVA's thinking about its navigation channel. From this thought, the navigation program emerged. Its success is evident in the ever-increasing amount of freight tonnages hauled on the river, the decreasing number of restrictions on waterway use, and the larger number of water carriers which now operate on the Tennessee River.

5

GROWTH OF RIVER COMMERCE

The initiation of the TVA's river-improvement program marked the beginning of a new phase in water transportation on the Tennessee River. Basic changes that resulted include greater volume of traffic, greater diversification of commodities transported, and vastly increased lengths of haul. These three modifications in the traffic picture of the Tennessee are characteristic of changes which have occurred elsewhere on the nation's waterways. The new trends in river traffic have been emerging since 1920, but the Tennessee River did not share in the rapid expansion of inland commerce until the TVA provided a modernized navigation channel for this watercourse. Although the major interest here is Tennessee River commerce, it is necessary at the beginning to consider the experience of inland waterway commerce in other parts of the country and the forces which have brought about the revival of water transportation.

Several factors have contributed to the revival of water transport in the United States. First has been the role of the federal government in encouraging and promoting water conveyance by improving the inland rivers for deep-draft vessels and by providing lockage facilities adequate to accommodate modern waterway equipment; by constructing multipurpose projects which have ensured a year-round regulated supply of water for these streams; by attempting to stimulate the development of privately owned water transportation facilities through government ownership and operation of the Federal Barge Lines; and by legislating to prevent "unjust discrimination, undue preferences or disadvantages, or unfair or destructive competitive practices" among the various transportation forms.[1]

A second element in the expansion of waterborne commerce has been technological improvement of floating equipment. Progress in this respect has been a joint contribution of government and private enterprise. The function of the federal government has been to study various problems associated with carrier performance on the waterways in an attempt to translate the results into more efficient methods of navigation and improved towboats and barges. Private enterprise has contributed by invention and adaptation of modern technology. Space does not permit a full discussion of all the improvements that have been effected, but mention of a few of the more important ones will illustrate what has been done.[2]

Generally, advancement has been made in perfecting electronic navigation devices which enable the modern mariner to navigate in bad weather, over unfamiliar channels, and at night when darkness prevents visual contact with shore points. Such equipment as radar, ship-to-ship and ship-to-shore radio, depth finders, and other devices have greatly aided river transport by reducing the delays brought about by fog, reprovisioning, and operational adjustment of locks, and by permitting twenty-four-hour movement. Of major importance to river transport has been the adaptation of the diesel engine as a power unit for towboats. A recent report of the American Waterways Operators, Inc. declared:

> The Diesel engine is perhaps the factor which has most influenced the modern trend in towboat design. This engine, a more compact unit requiring less space than a steam engine of equal power, can be operated by fewer personnel and generally at lower cost. Consequently Dieselized towboats can be built to smaller over-all dimensions than a steamboat of identical power and do not require a large crew. This has effected a saving in the capital outlay for floating equipment.[3]

The advantages of the dieselization of towboats to water transportation are more extensive than the mere reduction of operational expenses. This advance has made power transmission from engines to propulsion devices far less complex and more efficient. Smaller towboats with powerful engines can do more work than steam-propelled craft of larger dimensions. Furthermore, a shorter towboat "facilitates the handling of tows of barges through locks [thus] enabling the avoidance of double lockages required with respect to tows moved by larger towboats." [4] The importance of this change is that the ratio of load to power—the ratio of tonnage carried to the power unit necessary to move that tonnage—has been maximized. Engineering experts have said "the optimum of transportation economy is one which maximizes the ratio of load to power." [5] From an operational standpoint this has meant an increased tonnage transported at greater speeds through the water.

Many other improvements have also served to increase load sizes and towboat speeds. Barges of greater capactiy have been developed. The use of nozzles around propellers to provide greater thrust has augmented both load and speed. Better means of steering, of connecting barges, and of barge design to prevent diving, as well as many other innovations, have contributed to more rapid and more economical water transportation. The effect of these developments has been to make water transport more competitive with other transportation media and thereby to attract more freight.

Third, and equally important as a determinant in influencing the expansion of river commerce, has been the increase in the number of terminals and their modernization. In the words of experts, "Terminal facilities are the gateways to our waterways, and the increase in number of these gateways and the reduction of the money, time, and effort required to pass through them have been vital in bringing more freight to the water's edge." [6] While the total number of terminals constructed or modernized throughout the Mississippi River system since 1933 would probably amount to hundreds, a better picture of this growth can be obtained by noting what happened on a particular stream. In 1927 the Tennessee River had sixty-nine terminals or landings. None of these was considered suitable for modern barge transportation, and most of them were hardly more than open spaces along the river's banks.[7] The terminal situation has changed since 1927. As a result of increased traffic on the river, the TVA, state government, municipal ports, and private firms have constructed many additional freight exchange facilities. As of December, 1955, the Authority listed 107 major freight landings on the river which had modernized loading and unloading machinery.[8] On the national scene comparable progress has been made; according to the American Waterways Operators, "Terminal facilities on inland waterways are keeping pace with the construction of new floating equipment."[9]

A fourth factor in the growth of water commerce has been the rapid expansion of the nation's economy since 1940. The entire transportation complex has benefited from the vast increase in the country's productivity. Freight traffic moved by all forms of transport in the United States totaled 608 billion ton-miles in 1940. After fifteen years of unprecedented industrial expansion and sustained high levels of agricultural production, the total national freight traffic increased 1,274 billion ton-miles. The later sum was divided among the several forms of transport as follows: railways, 49.3 percent; motor trucks, 17.7 percent; Great Lakes carriers, 9.4 percent; inland waterways, 7.7 percent; and pipelines, 15.9 percent. In 1940, waterway traffic amounted to only 3.6 percent of the total ton-miles of traffic. Since 1940, the percentage of ton-mile traffic carried by the railways and Great Lakes carriers has declined 12.4 and 6.4 percent of the national total, respectively.[10] Despite this decreasing trend in the amount of traffic carried by the railroads, net railway operating income was almost 60 percent larger in 1955 than it was in 1940.[11]

The effect of these developments on waterborne commerce has been prodigious. Tons transported by inland waterway barge lines on the Mississippi River system increased from 26 million in 1920 to about 64 million in 1929, or nearly 142 percent. From 1930 to 1940, river traffic rose to approximately 89 million tons, an increase of 40 percent. During the decade from 1940 to 1950, an increase of 55 percent was made in tonnage, which by the latter year amounted to 138 million tons. Since 1950, the trend has continued upward. In 1957 the Mississippi River system accounted for 227 million tons, an increase in seven years of almost 65 percent. Measured in ton-miles this figure amounted to 60.7 billion such miles. For comparison purposes, only 5.5 billion ton-miles were recorded in 1931. The increase in this twenty-six year period was nearly 1,000 percent.[12]

Along with the increase in traffic volume has come a change in the character of freight. The major portion of the traffic on the inland waterways consists of bulk commodities in raw or semimanufactured form. Generally this traffic has constituted some 90 percent of the total waterborne commerce. While bulk freight has accounted for the greatest proportion of the aggregate waterway tonnage, significant changes have occurred in the value and in the percentage of such freight. Charles S. Morgan has presented an interesting analysis of the trends in the character of freight moved by domestic water carriers from 1926 to 1940:

> Coal . . . constituted approximately a fourth of the total tonnage. . . . petroleum oils rose from about a fifth to about a third of the total; iron ore traffic fluctuated greatly in volume, but, in years of depression, constituted from about 11 to 16 per cent of the total tonnage; the tonnage of stone associated with iron ore tonnage, generally represented 4 to 5 per cent of the total; logs, lumber and pulpwood fell from about 10 to about 7 per cent of the total; sand and gravel traffic fell from about 11 per cent to about 8 per cent of the total. Cement and sulphur, never more than half of 1 per cent of the total, held their own; grain and sugar, slightly more important, generally declined in relation to all traffic. The 12 commodities named constituted from 83.5 to 95 per cent of the total traffic, 1926 to 1940. . . .[13]

By 1957 several notable changes had taken place in the character of traffic. Coal tonnage declined to about one fifth of the total tonnage, while petroleum and petroleum products constituted 38.8 percent of the total traffic in 1957. Iron ore tonnage decreased from one fifth of the total in 1944 to only 11 percent in 1957. The percentage of logs and lumber decreased by almost one half (from 7.2 percent to 3.4 percent). Sand, gravel, and stone traffic increased about 2 percent. Grain tonnage declined very slightly between 1944 and 1957. A notable change in traffic was the beginning movement of large amounts of chemicals over the waterways. In 1944, the amount was negligible, but by 1957, chemical products totaled 1.8 percent of the gross tonnage. Also of note was the increase of 4.4 percent in miscellaneous commodities moved by water. This last item includes many products classified as non-bulk freight, which normally moves at higher rates.[14]

The question now arises, what has been the impact of this changed character of freight on water carriers and shippers? Generally, the modification has produced advantages to both groups in the terms of dollars earned by the carriers and savings achieved by shippers. This result has stemmed from the fact that water lines are transporting higher grade freight which produces greater revenue; and shippers, despite having to pay a higher rate for shipping more valuable commodities, are still able to effect a saving by utilizing water transport rather than rail or truck facilities.

Another important result of the increasing amount of freight

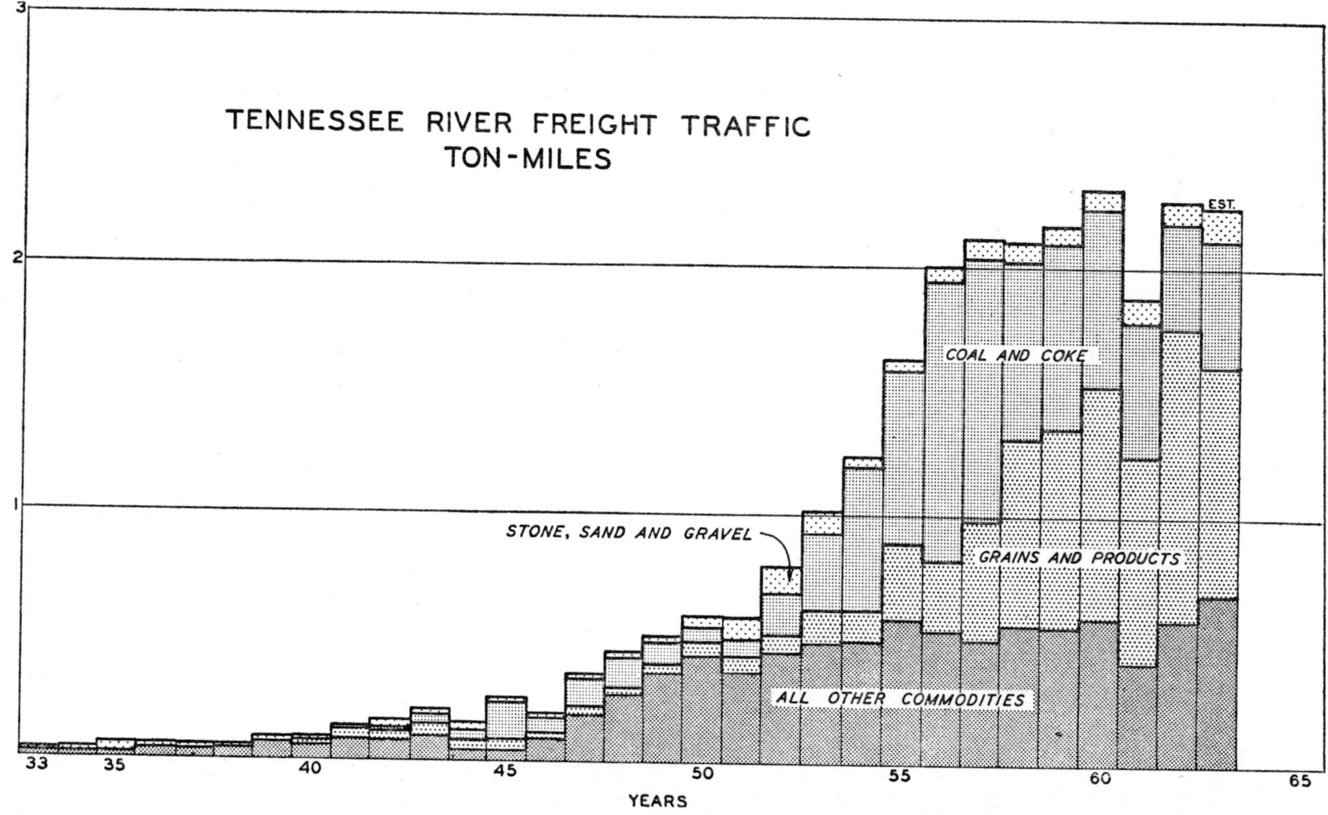

TENNESSEE RIVER FREIGHT TRAFFIC
TON-MILES
BILLIONS OF TON-MILES
3
2
1
COAL AND COKE
STONE, SAND AND GRAVEL
GRAINS AND PRODUCTS
ALL OTHER COMMODITIES
EST.
33
35
40
45
50
55
60
65
YEARS

carried by waterways has been the parallel expansion of carrier capacity. Charles S. Morgan reported that in the period from 1939 to 1941 the total-vessel capacity of regulated inland water carriers operating on the inland waterways was 1,391,234 tons. This represented 44.5 percent of the total-vessel capacity of both regulated and nonregulated carriers in operation.[15] Fourteen years later, at the end of 1955, regulated carriers alone had a cargo capacity of 2,573,856 tons.[16] Viewed from the standpoint of particular carriers' financial investments in transportation equipment, a similar expansion is evident. In 1944 the American Barge Lines reported an investment of $4,496,305 in transportation property and equipment.[17] As of December, 1955, their investment in such facilities stood at $14,433,331.[18]

Foremost as a determinant in the expansion of waterborne commerce has been the continued effort on the part of federal and state governments[19] to provide a system of navigable waterways adequate for modern barge transportation. Progress in this respect has been rapid. In 1929, 220 miles of the Mississippi River system had been modernized to nine feet in depth, and about 1,400 miles had been improved to at least six feet in depth.[20] By 1939, the Mississippi River system had 4,037 miles of 9-foot channel.[21] During the following twenty-year period another 2,000-mile extension was improved to make a total of about 6,000 miles of 9-foot channel throughout the system.[22]

The expansion of the nation's system of inland waterways has had a significant effect on the distance over which products are transported. It is axiomatic that an improved watercourse results in longer hauls. The Allegheny River, which rises in northern Pennsylvania and empties into the Ohio River at Pittsburgh, flows a distance of 325 miles. The lower portion of this stream, a distance of 72 miles, has been improved for 9-foot navigation. The rest of the river is unimproved. Over the improved part, the average length of haul in 1956 was 14 miles, whereas it was only one mile over the unimproved section. Traffic on improved sections of the Missouri River—to cite another example—enjoys a greater length of haul than that which moves over those portions which have shallower depths.[23]

Much progress has been made since Congress initiated a broadened policy of inland river improvement and promotion of waterway services and facilities. Government encouragement has stimulated private enterprise to expand its operations and to modernize its fleets.

Altogether, these efforts have contributed to a revival of inland river commerce. The effects of this revivification have been greater traffic volume, a change in the character of freight carried, longer hauls for waterborne goods, and the expansion and improvement of water-carrier services and facilities.

The Tennessee River is a part of the nation's 10,000-mile system of 9-foot waterways. In 1943, as a result of the Tennessee Valley Authority's river improvement program, a 6.5-foot depth prevailed throughout the river. In 1952 the channel was completed. Today a 630-mile, 9-foot waterway with a minimum channel width of three hundred feet, except for the locks, is a link in the national system of inland waterways.[24] Therefore, the physical development of a navigation channel on the Tennessee represents on a smaller scale what has been taking place nationally. One recognizes, of course, that certain unique elements are contained in the Tennessee Valley Authority developmental program. Specific features of the TVA's navigation scheme may still be regarded as unparalleled; but its channel improvement program of constructing high multipurpose dams to provide slack-water navigation, although controversial, was never unprecedented and is an accepted method of river development on other streams where engineering logic dictates such a course of action.[25]

188512

The growth of commerce on the Tennessee was once regarded with skepticism by opponents of the Authority and even by valley residents. A TVA official recently said,

> During the early days of TVA, navigation was referred to by some as one of the two constitutional pegs on which the whole TVA program was hung. The implication frequently was that navigation did not amount to very much and probably would never be more than a mere peg. When Pickwick Dam was under construction someone observed that it would be cheaper for TVA, instead of building a navigation lock in the dam, just to buy every boat that came up the river and wanted to get through.[26]

A Knoxville *Journal* reporter once questioned five persons at random: "Do you think that construction of heavy duty highways for rapid truck transportation would be more desirable than the expenditure of the same funds for river transportation?"[27] Interestingly enough, three of the five felt that money spent on highway development would be more beneficial, one appeared undecided, and the fifth strongly favored river development. Those who supported motor transportation viewed river transport as obsolete, and one of these persons said, "Money spent on rivers nowadays is money wasted in most cases, I believe." [28]

Even Stuart Chase, who publicly vowed that the Tennessee Valley Authority was the New Deal's best asset, took a dim view of the navigation purpose. Chase declared, "As a matter of fact—and I trust the Supreme Court is safely asleep as I whisper it—navigation is probably the least important aspect of the cycle, from the point of view of the well-being of the people of the Valley." [29] Despite the fact that Shell Oil was shipping 500,000 gallons of gasoline per year up the Mississippi, Ohio, and Cumberland rivers to Nashville between 1931 and 1933, at a transportation saving of over one cent per gallon,[30] critics on both sides of Nashville's Twenty-First Avenue, the site of the city's two leading educational institutions, declared that navigation on the Tennessee River was not economically feasible.[31]

There were others, of course, who thought that "navigation on the Tennessee River between Knoxville and Paducah will prove to be the foundation of success of the Roosevelt Tennessee Valley development. . . ." [32] Chattanooga spokesmen were especially vigorous in asserting that the river's improvement for 9-foot navigation was essential to the valley's economic development.[33] The Corps of Engineers had predicted a rosy future for navigation if the river were improved. The TVA, which accepted the view of the engineers, appears to have regarded its navigation assignment primarily as a congressional mandate to be carried out, and for a time it disregarded the question of economic feasibility.[34]

Despite the gloomy predictions made by persons unenthusiastic about future commercial prospects of the river, the rate of growth of water transportation on the Tennessee in recent years has exceeded that of other waterways. Between 1946 and 1957 tonnage rose from 2,399,250 tons to 12,742,769 tons, representing an increase of 430 percent. During the period 1948 to 1957, traffic tonnage on the Mississippi River system, not including the Tennessee River, increased only about 70 percent.[35] The Authority claims that the Tennessee River tonnage increase nearly doubled that of its nearest rival, the Missouri.[36] The forces responsible for these changes are similar to those which accounted for the national revival of water transportation. But this is not all of the story; it does not explain why the rate of increase of Tennessee River traffic has exceeded the national average, which is some seven times less than that of the Tennessee. Tennessee River tonnage figures are given in the table on page 97.

Several factors have contributed to the more rapid growth of traffic on the Tennessee, but they can be grouped into three basic classifications. First, the Tennessee Valley Authority has carried on an effective program of river transportation promotion; second, the valley has enjoyed several years of economic prosperity which began just at the time when the river was first opened to economical navigation along its entire length; and third, the tonnage increase on the river represents a substantial amount of TVA coal which is used by the Authority's steam-generating plants. A fourth factor, of less importance, is that the Tennessee River is favorably located in regard to climatic conditions. Seasonal navigation plays no significant role in its use, whereas on rivers in the northern United States navigation ends when the rivers freeze or is curtailed by summer droughts. E. P. Ericson, a former member of the TVA's Navigation and Transportation Branch, has stated that three principal factors account for the significant growth in Tennessee River traffic during the last twenty years. These are "the technical revolution in water transportation, the improvement of the river and its facilities, and the extraordinary industrial growth of the Valley. . . ."[37]

Some of the causes need little explanation, but two deserve further consideration at this point. Let us first consider coal movements on the river. In 1957 coal, lignite, and coke made up slightly over 50 percent of the total river traffic, or 6,725,645 tons out of the total tonnage of 12,742,769 tons.[38] In that year the TVA was shipped 7,750,000 tons of coal by barge and rail-barge facilities. Rail-delivered coal amounted to 8,973,000 tons.[39] These figures reveal that practically all the coal moving on the river was destined for TVA consumption. It is clear that if one excluded these coal shipments from the aggregate river tonnage, the traffic picture on the Tennessee would be vastly altered. If this exclusion were made, the total tonnage would then be 6,015,588 tons, or an increase of approximately 130 percent instead of 430 percent for the period 1946 to 1957. Even so, this would still be considerably higher than the growth rate of the Mississippi River system generally.

The inclusion of TVA coal tonnage in Tennessee River traffic has led to much criticism of the Authority's reports on the progress of river transportation.[40] Many people feel that freight which is destined for use by the Authority should not be counted in the total tonnage. This view is unrealistic, for it seems logical to assume that if the federal government had not developed the power resources of the valley, private interests would have done so. If private enterprises had provided the generating capacity for TVA's domain, it is certain that they, also, would have had to supplement their hydroelectrical power-dam facilities with steam-power plants in order to meet the increasing demands for electrical energy. Since no criticism is leveled at the Corps of Engineers for including coal traffic which moves to privately owned steam generation plants on other rivers, it hardly seems fair to exclude such traffic from the total tonnage figures for the Tennessee River.

A second important factor in helping to establish traffic records on the Tennessee River as compared with tonnage increases on other streams was the completion of the Tennessee River channel on the eve of an era of unprecedented business prosperity. Traffic on the river remained relatively stable from 1924 to 1933, when river tonnage dropped below one million tons for the first time in ten years. With the coming of the Tennessee Valley Authority, whose building program stimulated river commercial activity, tonnage figures began to move slowly upward again.[41] On the eve of World War II, as channel depths of 6.5 feet were made available to Chattanooga, substantial amounts of grain and petroleum began to move on the river. These commodities, plus a heavy tonnage of sand, gravel, and related products used in TVA's expanded construction program and in the building of defense establishments in the region, caused tonnage figures to soar to an all-time high of slightly more than three million tons in 1941.[42] Wartime conditions limited this growth, however, for a shortage of barge equipment, brought about by an inadequate supply of steel available to manufacturers, forced many barge lines to curtail their operations. This condition, along with nation-wide strikes in the coal and steel industries, played a significant role in retarding traffic gains until 1949.[43] The rapid expansion in Tennessee River commerce had developed in the years since 1949.

It is apparent that river traffic development did not make great strides until the postwar economic spiral began. This retardation of water commerce is accounted for by the war, by the fact that a 9-foot channel was still unavailable until 1945, and by other forces referred to earlier, including the lack of joint rail-barge rates on freight which moved beyond the Tennessee River ports. By 1950 several of these adverse influences had been removed, and a rapid expansion of traffic began to take place. Since river commerce had not undergone any drastic expansion prior to 1949, it was only natural that once these limiting factors were removed a rapid advance in tonnage figures would take place. Meanwhile, Mississippi River system watercourses which were completed before the TVA channel was improved had already attained a substantial amount of matured traffic. Therefore, it appears that recent traffic developments on the Tennessee, which certainly have been outstanding, represent a youthful growth that will level off as the commerce reaches its maturity. It is still too early in the life of the channel to determine whether or not that level has been attained.

Commodity movements on the Tennessee River showed some diversity before TVA improvements. The 1926 traffic consisted of sand and gravel, pig iron or ore, forest products, farm goods, and a small amount of miscellaneous freight.[44] When traffic increased, as a result of the Authority's improvement program, greater variety was soon manifested in freight shipments. David E. Lilienthal noted this change in traffic composition in 1937 when he stated that "the number and variety of commodities moving on the river—and this is especially significant—have increased."[45] This trend continued as the channel was extended, and in 1944 Lilienthal, then chairman of the agency, reported as follows:

> . . . there has been a change in the character of the freight carried. This is disproving the old notion that inland water transportation is suited only to low-grade products. Iron and steel products, automobiles and military vehicles, petroleum products, grain originating at Middle West ports, and coal are some of the goods which have been shipped in increasing quantities in the past few years.[46]

Since 1944, the traffic has consistently increased its variety as different commodities have supplemented existing commerce. A 1956 analysis showed that "of the different commodity groups moved on the river, 16 moved in greater volume than ever before . . . and [3] moved for the first time on the Tennessee."[47]

River commerce in 1957 reflects this growing diversification of commodity shipments. Forty-eight different products were listed as having moved on the river in that year. These commodities made up ten classifications, including inedible animal and animal products, vegetable food products and beverages, inedible vegetable products exclusive of wood and fibers, wood and paper goods, nonmetallic minerals, metal and manufactures exclusive of machinery and vehicles, machinery and vehicles, chemicals and related products, waste materials, and government freight. Approximately 90 percent of this freight consisted of coal, sand and gravel, petroleum products, and grain, in this order of importance. The remaining traffic was made up of such goods as soybeans, crushed limestone, iron and steel products, various metallic ores, industrial chemicals, vehicles, pulpwood, and phosphate fertilizer material. Waste materials disposed of in the reservoirs constituted a sizable movement, and government freight, consisting of materials for improvement of the waterway, was about 2 percent of the total freight traffic.[48]

The changing composition of Tennessee River traffic is a significant development. It means that more shippers are using the river and that a wider margin of transportation savings is being realized by these firms and individuals. A changing traffic composition reflects a utilization of the stream by shippers other than those who are resident along its banks. Diversification of river commerce also implies that traffic is no longer local in character but has expanded into interterritorial and perhaps even international trade, since valley business and agricultural establishments do not produce many of the goods which are transported on the river. In fact, the Tennessee Valley receives by river almost four times as much freight from other regions as it ships to those areas.[49] Also important as a factor in the evolution of freight traffic has been the greater earning opportunity presented to carriers which provide the equipment for transporting these commodities.[50]

The new traffic has meant greater business for barge lines, including those domiciled outside of the valley. In 1949 the TVA reported:

> Prior to 1933 by far the major portion of Tennessee River traffic consisted of short haul movements which locally owned companies hauled in their own equipment. There was very little business to attract for-hire carriers. Since 1933 the traffic in higher value commodities moving longer distances has increased nearly ten-fold from 126,000 tons to 1,174,000 tons annually. Virtually all of this new traffic is hauled by for-hire carriers, of which there are about a dozen now actively operating on the Tennessee. Most of these companies have their headquarters outside the Valley.

Just what this has meant in revenues to barge lines is difficult to estimate. But here is an indication: prior to development of the new waterway no petroleum products moved by barge to Tennessee River ports. In 1948 over 480,000 tons of this traffic moved an average distance of 476 miles on the Tennessee and about 530 additional miles on other waterways. This was new traffic for which presumably new equipment has had to be built. Assuming the very best operating conditions, with equipment operating 24 hours a day, 7 days a week, 95 per cent of the year,

> this traffic was a full-time job for about 6 towboats and 22 barges. . . .
> At present [1949] prices 6 towboats and 22 petroleum barges would cost between $3½ and $4 million. A conservative estimate of annual barge line revenue from the traffic would be about $1¼ million.[51]

This increase in barge line business can be demonstrated in another way. In 1944 the Arrow Transportation Company, which has consistently carried a large share of the Tennessee River traffic, reported a revenue of $122,695 from its freighting operations.[52] Its 1955 freight revenues totaled $1,450,465.[53]

This new traffic has led barge companies to expand their facilities to service the additional freight volume. Here again, the Arrow Transportation Company provides a good example. In 1939 this company was operating two steam towboats and about five barges, two of which were of wood construction. In 1959, after merging with two small companies and adding new vessels to its existing fleet, the firm had a carrier fleet of nine towboats and about ninety-five barges. Its physical expansion has paralleled its financial growth.[54]

Along with the internal expansion of locally owned barge line companies, there has developed an ever-increasing amount of barge service furnished by water transportation firms located outside the valley. In 1938, before depression conditions severely curtailed freight movements on the river, thirty-nine establishments were operating vessels on the stream. Vessel capacity totaled 42,550 tons. Two of the carriers were classified as "common carriers," one was engaged in ferrying railroad cars, twenty-one handled private freight, and fifteen did contract towing. About one third of the towboats and one half of the barges, with a capacity of 10,390 tons, were employed in sand and gravel operations. Almost all of these operators, except for several of those in the sand and gravel business, confined their operations to the section of the river below Florence, Alabama. Only two of the firms transported freight beyond the mouth of the Tennessee River. One operated between St. Louis and Florence, and the other between Sheffield, Alabama and Metropolis, Illinois. Obviously, commerce was restricted to local hauls between Tennessee River ports.[55]

Four years after the TVA's river improvement program was initiated, notable changes began to occur in the amount of carrier facilities available to shippers of water freight. The number of operating firms had declined to thirty-one, but the towboats in operation on the river remained the same. More significant was the increasing number of new firms with headquarters outside the valley which had begun to use the river. Apparently, larger quantities of freight were now being moved to and from the valley region. Transportation service to points beyond the river's mouth was made more convenient. Equally significant was the fact that, despite the severe economic setback which occurred in the period under consideration, facilities did not suffer a major decline in number.[56] It also should be remembered that channel conditions were practically unchanged since only three high dams in the navigable stretch of the river had been completed by 1937—Wilson, Wheeler, and Hales Bar dams—and freight tonnage at the end of the year was only slightly over one half of that of 1933.[57] Obviously, the TVA construction activities were the prime cause in the prevention of a considerable loss of carrier services on the river.

As the channel was lengthened and deepened by the Authority's high dams and as business activity continued its upward trend after the hesitant years from 1937 to 1939, when Tennessee River tonnage figures declined, water carriers began to make more extensive use of the stream. Substantial movements of petroleum products, grain, pig iron, and automobiles, which began between 1938 and 1941, along with the increased tonnage of other commodities, attracted additional firms to participate in the new traffic. It should be recalled also that by this date the Authority had embarked upon its promotional program of informing barge companies and shippers of the waterway's advantages.[58]

The inducements were adequate, for the number of barge-line operators increased from thirty-one in 1933 to forty-two by 1941. Towboats in operation remained about the same in number, but the barge fleet was greatly expanded.[59] In 1928 operating companies had 183 barges in service. By 1941 the number had grown to well over 300. Especially significant was the number of firms that had extended their operations to the Tennessee River. At least fifteen lines could be classified as interregional carriers while several others were seeking permits from the ICC to use the river. Most of these carriers were private or contract carriers. Only two common-carrier companies were in operation: the Eagle Packet Company of St. Louis and Greenline Steamers, Inc., of Cincinnati.[60] This was a temporary situation, for the ICC had just begun its regulation of water carriers and was in the process of examining "grandfather" rights in order to establish the operating routes for waterway transport companies.

But even those firms which had applied for common-carrier status did not contemplate furnishing comprehensive common-carrier freight service on the river.[61]

The four-fold increase in Tennessee River freight tonnage since World War II has encouraged many new barge companies to extend their operations to the river. Most of these operators perform contract towing of exempt commodities, a service which is unregulated by the ICC; therefore, profits alone determine the extensiveness of their routes. Many more private business firms which operate their own vessels have made use of the channel to transport their raw materials and processed goods. The era has also witnessed a slight increase in the number of common carriers, which must secure permission from the ICC to operate over designated routes and to carry specific commodities. In 1950, the year in which tonnage figures began to move sharply upward, approximately forty carrier firms were in operation on the river. By 1956, as commerce grew to 12 million tons, an increase of about 10 million tons, 104 commercial operators sent their towboats and barges over the "Great Lakes of the South." In mid-1959, at least ten additional water-freight firms were dispatching their vessels to destinations on the Tennessee River.[62] Although an increasingly larger number of carrier operators are making use of the river, the problem of serving the small shipper remains.

One of the most striking changes in the evolution of traffic development on the Tennessee River has been the increased length of haul of many commodities. In 1932 goods were transported about an average of 22 miles. Ten years later, with a 6-foot channel to Chattanooga, the average haul had grown to 140 miles, and by 1952 it was 205 miles, if sand and gravel shipments are excluded. Only three other inland rivers with tonnages greater than the Tennessee—the Mississippi, Ohio, and Illinois rivers—surpassed this average in 1957.[63]

One meaning of this new characteristic of Tennessee River commerce is that local traffic has expanded into interregional navigation. An analysis of the 1954 traffic showed that "three regions—the upper Mississippi, the lower Mississippi and Gulf Coast, and the Ohio River—interchanged river traffic with the Southeastern states served by the Tennessee River." [64] Principal commodities shipped into the valley included coal, petroleum, grain, soybeans, iron and steel products, and automobiles. Major commodity movements shipped from the valley consisted of coal, pulpwood, sand and gravel, pig iron, fertilizer, and chrome and ferrochrome products. The valley received more than it shipped. Inbound freight totaled slightly less than two and one-half million tons while outbound traffic was less than a million tons. Of a total traffic of 8,415,769 tons, approximately 37 percent was local freight, whereas 63 percent was classified as interregional traffic. Most of the inbound freight came from the Ohio River section.[65]

Since the completion of the channel, a relatively fixed pattern of commodity exchange has developed. Five basic commodity groups —coal and coke, grain, petroleum products, industrial chemicals, and iron and steel goods—make up the major portion of the interregional traffic. Under normal conditions the trade balance has favored the shipping areas outside the valley; however, during the war the Tennessee River shipped more goods than it received. This deviation from the normal occurred because large amounts of sand and gravel were being barged to Ohio River points for use in defense construction.[66]

The patterns of exchange between the Tennessee region and other economic sections of the nation have developed primarily because of the difference in natural resources of each area. Simply put, the valley is deficient in certain basic resources and must secure these products from other regions, and the same is true of those sections which ship to the valley. Petroleum goods, one of the first interregional commodities to move on the river in quantity, are barged to the valley from the Southwest, the Midwest, and points on the Ohio River. The TVA reported in 1949 that the city of Knoxville was receiving 40 percent of its total gasoline supply by the water route. This movement did not exist in 1945. Despite increasingly greater competition from pipeline companies, barge shipments of petroleum products to the head of the river at Knoxville amounted to 334,028 tons in 1958. This compares with the 1949 shipment of 265,000 tons.

In the exchange with the Southwest, the Tennessee region suffered an extremely adverse trade balance. In 1957 the Southwest shipped approximately 300,000 tons of petroleum supplies to the valley and was sent small amounts of finished steel goods, industrial chemicals, and newsprint paper. The difficulty in this relationship is the circuity of the water route. The river route is almost twice as long as rail and truck connections. It is more economical to ship the higher valued goods produced in the valley by land route than to use the water connection.[67] Since few markets have developed in the Southwest for low-grade bulk commodities produced in the valley area, it is not likely that the trade balance will be appreciably altered. For several reasons, circuity does not play such an important role in the movement of incoming oil products. First, petroleum products lend themselves well to bulk shipment; second, transfer from river to land is not a difficult operation; and third, the economical storage of large quantities of petroleum is easily arranged by the construction of tank-farm terminals along the river.[68] Consequently, petroleum shipments can be moved economically to the region despite the fact that the water distance is almost twice that of land connections.[69]

The other major commodity groups which make up the interregional freight move over less circuitous routes than do petroleum goods. Grain, a commodity which is not produced in great quantities in the southeastern states, is imported from the upper Mississippi and Ohio valleys. The ports of Chattanooga and Guntersville are the largest receivers of grain products. A small portion of this produce is also barged to Knoxville. In exchange for midwestern grain products, the Tennessee Valley ships principally coal and industrial chemicals. Once again the two-way trade is heavily in favor of the upper Mississippi River section.[70]

The Ohio River area provides the Tennessee region with its greatest market and also acts as the chief supply region for the valley. Coal is the prime import from Ohio River ports, and, strangely enough, it is also the chief export of the Tennessee Valley to the Ohio area. In 1957, Tennessee River terminals received 1,880,942 tons of coal from mines along the Ohio River. Conversely, 293,808 tons of coal were sent from the valley to the Louisville area on the Ohio River.[71] Other imports from the Ohio region that year included grains, petroleum products, automobiles, iron and steel goods, and chemicals (largely coal tar products). In return, the Tennessee Valley shipped, in addition to coal, lumber and pulpwood, iron and steel scrap, industrial chemicals, and a small number of finished steel products. As with other regions, the trade relationship between the Ohio and Tennessee valleys greatly favors the former.

The above analysis of major routes and the commodities transported over those routes applies only to the principal products which enter into the interregional commerce. In 1958 this type of trade constituted a little more than 50 percent of the total river tonnage. It is apparent, therefore, that the rest of the commerce was local in nature and moved within the valley area. The direction of trade within the region parallels that of the interregional trade in that tonnages moving upstream are substantially larger than those moving in the opposite direction. The 1958 traffic figures show an upbound traffic of 4,513,835 tons and a downbound movement of 1,292,041 tons. Over 90 percent of the internal upstream commerce was overwhelmingly sand and gravel. The remaining up and down internal traffic was mostly agricultural goods, pulpwood, and clays.[72]

The ports of Chattanooga, Guntersville, and Knoxville are the three leading exchange points on the river for both interregional and local freight. Together, they handled 3,226,952 tons of freight in 1958. The major river port, Chattanooga, shipped or received approximately 50 percent of this total.[73] Most of the freight traffic is delivered to private docks or terminals along the river. The five public-use terminals constructed by the TVA during the war, including the coal terminal at Harriman, Tennessee, handled only about 3 percent of the total river traffic in 1956.[74] The public dock at Guntersville handled the largest tonnage among the TVA-built terminals. Heavy movements of automobiles and grain through this port account for its greater activity. The coal terminal at Harriman showed extensive use for the first time since it was built in 1944. In 1956 there was a transfer of 258,833 tons of coal from rail and truck facilities to barges on the river at Harriman.[75]

Although commercial use of the Tennessee River has undergone a remarkable expansion since the war and reached the TVA's estimated "mature" traffic of 7 million tons in 1953 instead of in 1960, a large segment of the general public has not participated in this enlarged use of the river. As noted earlier, it is the bulk shippers using their own facilities who have accounted for 90 percent of the total ton-miles of traffic. This is not what the Authority anticipated in its 1941 report on prospective commerce. That survey predicted that coal, petroleum, and grain movements would amount to about 50 percent of the prospective commerce after the channel had been improved. In 1958 these commodities composed over 60 percent of all the traffic. It was estimated that sand and gravel traffic, the second largest movement on the river in 1958 (about 20 percent of the total tonnage), would make up 40 percent of the traffic in 1945 when the channel was opened for the entire length of the river. The remaining 10 percent of the traffic, the TVA estimated, would consist of such diverse items as beer, brick, textile goods, lumber, iron and steel products, and a host of other manufactured products.[76]

Actually, the 1945 traffic in coal, sand and gravel, and petroleum products was relatively close to the Authority's 1941 estimates. The grain trade equaled only about half the amount anticipated. The downbound flow of diversified commodities did not take place. The predicted movement of 927 tons of downbound stoves, ranges, and heaters, if they moved at all, went by rail or truck. The 3,050 tons of beer, whiskey, and other alcoholic beverages which were expected to be barged up the river in 1945 did not show up in the statistics for that year. In 1958 small shipments of merchandise freight were still absent. The figures for 1958 did reveal a downbound shipment of 618 tons of metal manufactures and parts. This amount was negligible as compared with TVA's estimate for 1945.

It is clear that the wide variety of commodities that TVA estimated would be transported by barge has not been routed by way of the river. It is also evident that the small shipper who would supply the commodities for this type of traffic has not been able to use the river. The case was succinctly stated by a journalist in 1949:

> Most of the traffic which has moved on the Tennessee to date has been in bargeload or even towload quantities amounting to 1,000 tons or more in each shipment, TVA studies reveal.
>
> Small shippers, the average businessmen in the valley, have not yet used barge transportation. In fact they have been unable to use it because no barge line is yet offering service for less-than-barge-load quantities.
>
> . . . . . .
>
> In other words, barge service has to be made about as convenient and usable as the service offered by other kinds of transportation.[77]

The obstacles which prevent the utilization of water transportation by firms and individuals constitute the major unsolved traffic problem, not only on the Tennessee River but on other inland waterways as well.[78] The solution to this problem is one that neither the Tennessee Valley Authority, the Interstate Commerce Commission, nor the water carriers have been able to discover. But attempts to overcome the deterrent have received the attention of all three parties. Before this kind of movement can take place, three changes must be made: more extensive public-use docking facilities will have to be provided; regular and frequent common carrier barge-line service must be offered so that uncertainty of delivery can be eliminated; and the ICC must promulgate a set of joint barge-rail and joint barge-truck rates.

Some headway has been made in overcoming these obstacles. The construction of the wartime public-use terminals by the TVA represented one effort to aid the small shipper. In 1953 the agency supported the efforts of the Commercial Barge Lines, Inc. to secure operating rights from the ICC to transport less-than-barge-load quantities by organizing a trailer-barge operation over the river. This service would have included a store-door pickup and delivery service of freight by trailer trucks and the subsequent carriage of the trailers on the docks or in the holds of the barges. The barge-line company argued that this would eliminate the problem of expensive transfer of freight at terminal points. The pickup and delivery service would have been performed by any motor carrier, and the company's own vehicles might be used in the operation.[79]

The ICC refused to approve the application of the barge line for the right to perform this service. Its action appears to have been justified. The barge company had conditioned the inauguration of the trailer-barge service upon the granting of extensive operating rights over the entire Mississippi River system for barge-load services only.[80] The protesting carriers, seeking to prevent this additional barge-load service competition, maintained that the applicant carrier was interested primarily in transporting general commodities in barge loads, but that, realizing the difficulty of establishing a need for additional barge-load service, the applicant proposed the establishment of the trailer-barge service as a device to gain support for his application from small-lot shippers. The ICC supported the protesting carriers and ruled that barging rights of such scope would not be issued merely to sustain a proposed trailer-barge service.[81]

Another recent aid to the small shipper has been the establishment of a freight-forwarding company. The I and S Forwarding Company of Atlanta made its first shipment on the river in 1957. This company assembles less-than-barge-load orders into barge-load shipments. Its operations thus far have been limited to the assembling of iron and steel products for movement from Ohio River points to southern destinations. The commodities leave the river at Chattanooga and Guntersville for rail shipment to locations in Georgia, Alabama, Tennessee, Mississippi, and Florida. An expansion of these operations to include other products may prove to be of great help in making water transportation more convenient to the less-than-barge-load shipper.[82]

The terminal problem is also receiving additional attention. In 1957 the voters of Alabama, through a constitutional amendment, approved a ten million dollar bond issue to finance a system of docks for the state's inland streams. According to one official of the Alabama State Docks Department, popular demand for such a program resulted in legislative action.[83] Two forces apparently brought matters to a head in 1957. One was the growing prosperity of the North Alabama cities located on the Tennessee River where increasing barge traffic had stimulated new agricultural and manufacturing industries. Another factor was the improvement of other Alabama rivers for water transportation. Since World War II, dam construction by the federal government and the Alabama Power Company has provided 9-foot depths for navigation on several of those streams in Alabama which flow southward into the Gulf of Mexico.[84] Therefore, citizens in those areas bordering on the state's navigable streams—a substantial proportion of Alabama's population—voted to put the state in the waterway terminal business in the hope that such a program would bring greater economic development in their regions.

Since the first bond issue of three million dollars was marketed in 1957, the Alabama State Docks Department has made rapid progress. Terminal facilities have been built at Decatur, Huntsville, and Florence, Alabama, on the Tennessee River, and a dock is in the process of construction at Columbia on the Chattahoochee River. The latter facility will not be utilized until the multiple-purpose dam is completed at Columbia, Alabama. In May, 1960, a second bond issue of three and one-half million dollars was sold to continue the program. This money has not been earmarked for use in any particular area thus far. The docks department is at present conducting feasibility studies to determine where the additional terminals should be located.[85]

The Tennessee River docks at Decatur, Huntsville, and Florence have been completed and are being used, though not extensively. The terminals are supposed to be self-liquidating projects, but there seems to be some doubt in the mind of the director of the program that this can be accomplished.[86] According to the TVA's experience in operating its terminals, which in practically every case was a financial disappointment, the goal of the state agency at this time appears to be unattainable. On the other hand, the terminal is such an important component of a water transportation system that its value is difficult to measure from a strictly dollar-and-cents standpoint. Like the first transcontinental railroads, public capital had to venture where private capital would not. Thus, the expense of the program may have to be justified in terms of public benefits rather than on a profit-and-loss basis.

Some of the river cities have invested in the construction of municipal docking facilities. Such terminals, which are available to the general public on a fee basis, exist at Paducah, Sheffield, and Chattanooga. The state of Tennessee has shown little interest in providing shipping facilities for its citizens. Since the terminal bill of 1941 failed of passage in the Tennessee legislature, the subject of state action in this direction has been revived only once. In the 1957 gubernatorial campaign, state Senator Clifford A. Allen promised to support a program of state dock construction along the river. Allen was defeated in the Democratic primary and the idea seems to have been forgotten.[87]

Other obstacles to the full use of the Tennessee River are more formidable since they have national instead of local implications. The problems of joint rail-barge and joint truck-barge rates and comprehensive common-carrier service are matters which are under the jurisdiction of the ICC and are administered to conform to a nationally-oriented policy. The Tennessee Valley Authority is limited in taking action on these problems to representation before regulatory bodies such as the ICC and the courts and to investigating and reporting what it considers unfair practices. The Authority's endeavors in these matters have been explored in an earlier chapter. It is only necessary to add that the TVA is aware of these deterrents to the use of the river and has tried to eliminate them whenever the opportunity arises.

Despite the barriers to full development of navigation on the river, the traffic on the Tennessee has undergone a rapid expansion since the TVA came to the valley in 1933. The development of river commerce has been accomplished by TVA, state governments, port cities, and private enterprise. The river, although it has already reached and exceeded estimated mature tonnage, is still awaiting maximum utilization for certain kinds of traffic. This will come when technological progress permits a reduction in the cost of terminal operations, when artificial barriers to river usage are eliminated by the ICC, and when the barge lines are able to perfect methods of operation which will allow water transportation rates to remain low while providing more comprehensive service on a systematic basis. In time, perhaps, the solutions to such problems will be found, but at present they still exist and prevent the maximum utilization of the navigation channel.

6

TENNESSEE RIVER NAVIGATION: A FACTOR IN SOUTHERN ECONOMIC GROWTH

The conversion of the Tennessee River from an undependable stream into a reliable commercial artery has contributed measurably to industrial expansion and agricultural diversification in the Tennessee Valley and large areas of its hinterland. Canalization of the river was accomplished by the construction of nine high dams and locks between Knoxville and Paducah.[1] What was once a wild river in the winter and spring and a rivulet in the summer and fall is now a series of slack-water lakes which provide 9-foot navigation for a distance of 650 miles. The improvement of the river linked the South with practically all parts of the Mississippi Valley. Petroleum and sulphur products from the Gulf Coast, coal from the Ohio Valley, steel and other metal products from Pittsburgh and the Great Lakes region, and grain from the Middle West now move leisurely into the ports of Chattanooga and Knoxville, both only a relatively short distance from Atlanta in the heart of the South. Gordon R. Clapp, former chairman of the TVA, said, "This new commerce is discovering again the affinity between the Southeast and the great Middle West." [2] The impact of this water-transportation route on southern economic growth has been of a quantity which submits to a reasonable, if not definitive, measurement.

The growth of industry along the Tennessee River is a fascinating story.[3] Riverside plant location has been extensive and much of it has been of recent origin. Since the TVA began its improvement of the river in 1933, private investors and government have expended huge sums for plant development. Most of the expansion has occurred since 1951. Between 1951 and 1963 more than one billion dollars have been invested by private interests alone. Government's expenditures more than doubled that of private entrepreneurs. Since 1940, the TVA has spent more than a billion dollars on steam-plant construction. Other public facilities such as the Arnold Aero Development Corporation at Tullahoma, Tennessee, the Redstone Arsenal at Huntsville, Alabama, and the atomic energy center at Oak Ridge, Tennessee, account for another sum of well over one billion dollars. A 1964 estimate placed total water-front investment, both private and government, at 3.8 billion dollars.[4]

What has brought about this extensive appropriation of water-front sites, and what role has the existence of a navigable waterway played in this expansion of industrial activity? No fixed answer is adequate to explain why an industry chooses a plant site. Several conditions usually govern the selection of a factory location. Prime considerations are proximity of raw materials, markets, labor, and water supply, and transportation, as well as waste disposal possibilities, climate, and political attitudes. These factors would influence locational decisions regardless of whether or not an industrialist determined upon a waterside position. Therefore, other determinants must be involved in the selection process whenever a riverside setting is chosen. What are these added factors, and is the availability of river transportation a significant influence? Finally, which of these factors have been at work to produce the vast industrialization which has developed along the Tennessee River?

A TVA analysis is helpful in our search for answers. An extensive field survey made in 1953 to determine the character of existing business and industrial development on the river resulted in the following conclusions. One hundred and seven firms had located along the Tennessee River and its tributaries between 1933 and 1953. Fifty-six of these establishments were manufacturing plants. The survey showed that thirty-six of the fifty-six plants made some use of the river, either for navigation, for cooling or processing water, or for water supply and transportation. The report concluded:

> . . . manufacturing establishments located on the waterfront since the construction of the navigable channel make more extensive use of the

river than those established before that time. Out of 27 in the former category, 21 make some use of the river. Twelve out of the 27 now use the river for navigation; two using the river only for water supply and two others making no use of the river at present are potential navigation users. Of the 29 plants established before the construction of the navigable channel, on the other hand, only 15 out of the 29 use the river; only 5 of the 29 use the river for navigation at the present time and only three others are potential navigation users. Eleven in this group make no use of the river and expect to make no use of it in the future.[5]

While it is recognized that the absence of an improved waterway prevented utilization of the river for navigation by those firms built before canalization of the stream, the argument also may be advanced that barge transportation was a significant locational factor since those businesses established after the river was improved used water transportation. In fact, 44 percent of the firms built after the stream was improved utilized the water artery for transportation whereas only 17 percent of the older plants made use of the watercourse. More recent evidence supports the above conclusion. J. Porter Taylor, TVA's director of navigation, testified in an ICC hearing in 1962 that of the 150 waterfront industrial plants and terminals along the river, approximately 60 percent used barge transportation.[6]

Although only 60 percent of the 150 firms employed the river for transportation purposes, one might argue that the influence of navigation on industrial site location was relatively unimportant. This is not necessarily true, for the existence of a navigable waterway, whether actually used or not, may yet serve as a magnet for attracting industry to a waterfront site. Taylor holds that industries seek a waterfront location "to use the threat of water transportation as a lever to obtain favorable [rail] freight rates." [7] Thus an industry does not have to have riparian rights to secure preferential rail-freight rates. As long as a firm has reasonably large shipments to transport and is near enough to a navigable stream to effect a transportation saving by using water transport, concessions can be forced from the rail carriers.[8]

Manufacturing industries have located along the banks of the Tennessee River for a variety of reasons. Twenty of the fifty-six firms which have been established there, but which make no use of the waterway for transportation or water supply, were situated along the waterfront for one or more of the following reasons: availability of sufficient land with suitable topography, availability of buildings, easy accessibility to rail and highway transportation, the possibility of obtaining preferential freight rates, and the scenic values of a site bordering on the river.[9] Although low-cost electrical power has played a key role in attracting industry to the valley and certainly has encouraged several of the waterfront industries to settle along the river, this factor can be discounted as a major determinant in waterside industrial development since cheap power could be obtained anywhere within the TVA's electric service area.

There are three prime reasons for the location of industry along the Tennessee River. First is the desire for an adequate water supply and a place to dispose of waste materials; second is the possibility of using the threat of water transportation as a lever to obtain favorable rail-freight rates; and third is the expectation of using barge transportation as a means of bringing in raw materials and shipping out finished products. Several other factors influenced the decisions of many firms to place their plants on waterfront sites. Many of the industries which are located along the river would not have settled in the valley under any circumstances if water transportation had not been made possible by the TVA or some other agency. Whether or not the others would have sought a location in the region if water transportation and water supply had not been available is uncertain.

Another unknown factor is the effect of navigation on plant location at substantial distances from the river's edge. Frequently rail carriers grant preferential freight rates in the form of "blanket" rates to an area which theoretically could secure lower transportation costs if waterways were utilized.[10] D. Phillip Locklin reported that this device is frequently used by the railroad companies to discourage water hauls.[11] In other words, the threat of using barge transportation exerts an influence which extends miles beyond the banks of rivers and may have affected the location in the valley of numerous plants which have no expectation or desire of ever using the river for transportation. Since the rail carriers have successfully used this "blanketing" system of rate fixing in the Authority's domain, it appears that the impact of navigation on industrial development may be more substantial than is actually measurable.

Because of the transportation advantages offered by a riparian location, and for other reasons, the banks of the Tennessee River and its immediate hinterland have become an area of rapid industrial growth. Both private sources and governmental organizations have spent huge sums for facilities which make use of the navigation channel. Navigation's availability has been a determinant in the choice of the locations for these installations. In several instances it has been a major though certainly not the sole factor; often it was only of secondary importance. Of the various government plants along the river, only the TVA steam plants were located so that water transport could be utilized. A TVA official noted that "getting the coal [for the steam plants] hinged on adequate transportation facilities that would open up these fields [Alabama, Kentucky, Illinois, Tennessee, and Virginia] to water transportation on the Tennessee River at reasonable rates. Such rates are highly important, since transportation costs represent from 15 to 50 per cent of the delivered price of coal." [12] Nine of the twelve steam plants are located at points which can be served directly by barge lines. When the Authority set up its coal-buying program, it purposely arranged to buy barge-delivered coal for economic reasons and to encourage the use of its waterway.[13] The huge tonnages of coal barged on the river annually, which push freight statistics upward and TVA coal costs downward, attest to the wisdom of this consideration.

Other federal installations situated beside or near the waterway were located there for various reasons. Navigation played little if any part in their placement. The availability of adequate electrical power and of government-owned land and buildings and the need for a large and dependable water supply were the key factors which determined their location. Of course, political considerations also may have been the overriding factor in the selection of such sites. While navigation probably was not an important influence in their location, all of these enterprises use the river for transportation to some extent.[14]

Industrial growth along the river has occurred largely in the stretch from Paducah to Chattanooga. Among the manufacturing enterprises found along the waterway are chemical, synthetic fibers, primary metals, pulp and paper, meat packing, prepared feeds, and cement factories.[15] Three areas adjacent to the river have gained the major share of industrial growth. The first important industrial complex is that at Calvert City, Kentucky, about sixteen miles upstream from the mouth of the river. Its growth as an industrial center has been phenomenal. In 1948, there were 319 persons dwelling in that city. In that year chemical and electrometallurgical plants were located there in order to take advantage of low-cost power, water transportation, and an adequate supply of water. During the course of the next eleven years "more than 20 separate plants and processing units manufacturing chemicals, chemical products, and ferroalloys . . . employ[ing] more than 2,000 workers and represent[ing] a total investment of $115,000,000" were developed.[16] As a result of this rapid industrialization more jobs were created and the city's leaders were anticipating a population of 10,000 in 1960,[17] a dream which was not realized.

For the next 184 miles upstream from Calvert City, between the Kentucky and Pickwick dams, industrial development has been spotty. Although several river terminals have been built in this section for transferring timber, coal, and stone to the barges, only eight large manufacturing firms have been built. At New Johnsonville, Tennessee, the E. I. Du Pont de Nemours Company has constructed a $30,000,000 titanium dioxide plant and the Air Products Company, Inc. has developed a $2,000,000 factory to supply oxygen and nitrogen to the Du Pont concern. Just downstream from the Pickwick Dam, the Tennessee River Pulp and Paper Company has constructed a $40,000,000 paper manufacturing facility. All of these firms were expected to utilize the river for transportation purposes.[18]

The second important industrial area is the Muscle Shoals region. This section includes that part of the river from the Wilson Dam at Florence upstream to Guntersville, a distance of approximately 107 miles. In this belt industrial growth has been extensive. Manufacturing activity began in the Wilson Dam vicinity during World War I. During the 1920's the pace was slowed, but with the initiation of the TVA's construction program in the 1930's industrialization gained momentum. The expansion of manufacturing operations has centered in the river cities of Florence, Sheffield, Tuscumbia, Decatur, Huntsville,[19] and Guntersville, all located in northern Alabama.

Three factors have furthered the growth of industry in this region: the availability of low-cost power, the abundance of water for industrial purposes, and the existence of water transportation. An additional stimulus to industrial development in this sector, and in the Calvert City, Kentucky region as well, has been the effect of already established manufacturing firms encouraging the development of "satellite" plants. Linkage between plants tends to develop "where the products of one plant provide the raw materials for another."[20] The relationship between the Reynolds Metals Company and the Ford Motor Company plants located near the Wilson Dam illustrates this point. In 1941, the Reynolds Metals Company established an aluminum factory at a cost of 2 million dollars. Since 1941, plant expansion has reached an investment of 234 million dollars. In 1956, the Ford Motor Company located a die-casting plant adjacent to the Reynolds firm in order to obtain molten aluminum for casting directly into engine and other automobile parts.[21] This tendency of older factories to spawn newer ones has been an important factor in the industrial development of the river.[22]

Industrial types common to the North Alabama region are power-oriented and water-transportation-oriented establishments. Moreover, specialization according to municipal centers has occurred as one or the other of these determinants assumed the leading role in fostering the growth of a particular industrial operation. The tri-cities[23] sector is one of chemical and primary metals manufacture, while Decatur's industrialization has inclined toward grain processing, machinery manufacture, vessel construction, and steel goods production. In the Huntsville section, government-sponsored missile production and privately owned chemical firms predominate; and at Guntersville, grain processing plants and formerly automobile distribution facilities formed the basis for that city's economy. These are the basic industrial types found in this region of the river, but by no means do they include all of the industrial operations found there. Numerous other factories, usually of a smaller nature, dot the riverfront from Florence to Guntersville. Oil and coal terminals, public-use terminals, and smaller plants, frequently linked to the larger industrial units, exist abundantly.[24] The electrometallurgical and chemical industries were attracted by low-cost power and a dependable water supply, while the rapidly expanding grain processing plants, the vessel construction, and all of the terminal facilities developed as a result of the improvement of the river for economical navigation.

The Chattanooga district constitutes the third major industrialized portion of the waterway. This city was a manufacturing center long before the river was improved, but since the Tennessee River was developed for 9-foot navigation, industrial growth in that section has greatly increased and become more diversified. Chattanooga, like Guntersville, has become a feed grains and flour milling center. Over 9 million dollars have been invested in grain elevators and milling facilities. Other large firms include Combustion Engineering, Inc., which produces soil pipe and atomic reactor vessels, the General Portland Cement Company, and a 30-million-dollar nylon factory. Several other firms devoted to the production of chemicals and iron products have located in the Chattanooga area since the river was improved. In most instances water transportation was a consideration in the location of the plants, and in the case of the grain processing companies it was the principal factor.[25]

Above Chattanooga, the last upstream section of the river, and on to Knoxville at the head of navigation, the waterway is less industrialized. In fact, except at certain locations, very few major industrial installations have been built. Even at Knoxville the rate of industrial growth has been slow compared to that which has occurred elsewhere. Three notable firms have been built in this region. At Calhoun, Tennessee, some eighteen miles from the mouth of the Hiwassee River, an English-controlled corporation has built the South's largest newsprint mill. The Bowaters Southern Paper Corporation's plant, established in 1952 at a cost of 60 million dollars, now represents an investment of over 126 million dollars. The availability of water transportation was a prime factor for its location along the stream. The firm has been utilizing barges to obtain pulpwood and fuel oil and in shipping out newsprint, some of which has been sent as far away as Corpus Christi, Texas.[26] Across the river from the Bowaters plant, the Olin Mathieson Chemical Corporation has constructed an 18-million-dollar chemical concern to supply the Bowaters Company and for general sale. It also makes use of river transportation. At Rockwood, Tennessee, a second large industrial concern has been built. The Tennessee Products and Chemical Corporation has invested 12 million dollars in a ferroalloy plant and rehabilitated the old Rockwood iron furnaces. Products of this firm, pig iron and ferroalloys, are shipped by barge.[27]

Several factors are responsible for the fact that Knoxville and the upper portion of the river have not enjoyed the same rate of industrial growth as the Chattanooga area and the cities in North Alabama. Industrial sites in Knoxville are small and the tendency of newly developed industry in the valley has been to locate on large acreages which allow for future expansion and the possible location of "satellite" plants nearby.[28] Another consideration has been the preemption of waterfront plots by industries which make no use of water transportation. This factor frequently forces many other firms into "backyard" locations which materially increase water supply and barge transportation costs to a point which may effectively discourage an industrial placement.[29]

An unmeasurable element which probably accounts for some of

Knoxville's industrial lag may be the lack of promotional zeal in behalf of industrialization. At both Calvert City and in the cities of northern Alabama, local interests have played significant roles in persuading business firms to locate there.[30] Donald Davidson described Knoxville's interest in its waterfront accordingly: "Knoxville had a plan for improving its waterfront. Someday it might be turned into a kind of park . . . though, in its casual disarray, it was an interesting spot on a sunny morning, one knew that the real business of Knoxville was on the heights where the modern city towered, not in the semislum where the steamboats and the keelboats once tied up." [31]

Despite the obstacles to the development of river-transportation-oriented industries in the Knoxville area, some firms have located in that city. Since 1946, Knoxville has become an important distribution center for petroleum products. The TVA reported that three fourths of all the oil supplies which are barged to Knoxville are transshipped to inland points by rail or truck.[32] In conjunction with this activity, a number of oil terminals have been constructed on the city's waterfront. Further, the livestock feed manufacturing industry has enjoyed some growth in the area as a result of barge transportation. An interesting movement, before the Castro regime took over in Cuba, was the shipment of molasses from Cuba to New Orleans and then by barge up the Mississippi, Ohio, and Tennessee rivers.[33] Mexico and the Dominican Republic now supply the molasses for this operation. The molasses, upon its arrival in Knoxville, was utilized by the feed manufacturers. Knoxville's public-use terminal, a TVA-built facility, serves as a connecting point between land and water carriers for such products as asphalt and iron and steel goods. Thus, some industrial gains have been registered in the upper section of the Tennessee, but major growth has occurred in the middle and extreme lower regions of the stream.

The disproportionate development of industry in the eastern part of the valley appears to have resulted from psychological, geographic, and economic factors. The urge to industrialize has probably been less strong in the eastern part of the valley than elsewhere since the two largest cities along the river had already experienced considerable manufacturing development before the navigation channel was completed. Circuity of the river is another factor which may have retarded industrial growth in this section because the cost of water transport approaches that of other forms of transportation in the portion of the valley which stretches from Chattanooga northward to Knoxville. In other words, the distance by land routes from the Ohio River region and the upper Mississippi Valley, the areas which send the bulk of the freight to the Tennessee Valley, is much shorter to Knoxville and its environs than to points such as Chattanooga and the cities of North Alabama. This condition has substantially affected traffic growth along the upper portion of the waterway and undoubtedly industrialization as well, for 70 percent of the total river tonnage is hauled over the middle and lower portions of the stream. Interestingly enough, three fourths of the industrial growth has occurred in those sections where traffic has been the heaviest.[34] While it is conceded that many variables affect the choice of industrial location, the close relationship between river-traffic increase and plant location warrants the conclusion that the improvement of the Tennessee River for 9-foot navigation has significantly stimulated business and industrial expansion along the river and far beyond.

The improvement of the Tennessee River has undoubtedly encouraged industrialization in those areas which exchange goods with the Tennessee Valley. A recent appraisal of Tennessee River traffic indicated that "3 out of every 4 tons of traffic that move on the Tennessee River either originate or are destined to points outside the valley. The trade area affected by the waterway's traffic encompasses some 30 states." [35] This new commerical exchange has resulted in the construction of many additional river terminals, grain elevators, and other businesses related to water transportation, as well as the expansion of barge-building activities throughout the inland waterway system. William J. Hull, chairman of the legislative committee of the Ohio Valley Improvement Association, a river-improvement pressure group, described the importance of inland waterways to the industrial development of the South as follows:

> To a remarkable degree, the American waterway system is a southern system. Industries in the Southern States have long been handicapped by higher rail freight rates than those their competitors in the North have to pay. This has been one of the factors contributing to the retarded economic growth and lower income levels in some of these states. Partially offsetting this, water transportation has been the foundation of much of the industrial growth in the South since the end of World War II.
>
> In 1955, 58.3 per cent of all freight hauled on the American inland waterway system moved on southern waters.[36]

The impact of Tennessee River navigation on valley industrial development or on the economic growth of those trade areas affected by the waterway is not yet susceptible of precise measurement. Two wide areas of study need further exploration. First, a comprehensive survey of the industrial expansion which has occurred in those regions that exchange goods with the Tennessee Valley and its hinterland is mandatory. Second, more specific data is needed regarding the factors which entered into the locational decisions reached by the numerous firms that have been established in the Tennessee Valley and the Southeast. In such a study, particular attention would need to be given to the role, if any, that navigation played in site selection and the direct or indirect use made of the navigation channel by these industries. Determination of the waterway's influence is further limited by the relative "newness" of the channel. Traffic growth on the river and industrial expansion are regarded as being far from mature. A TVA official has said that by 1975, tonnages will probably double the present twelve million ton figure.[37] Since industrial increase has tended to parallel traffic enlargement, it is too early to make a definite appraisal at this time. Judging by recent industrial expansion along the river, it appears that the existence of the navigation system will continue to significantly influence industrialization in the valley and its hinterland.

The improvement of the Tennessee River for barge transportation also has substantially influenced agricultural practices in several southern states. Gauging this outcome is exceedingly difficult, for many factors have been at work producing the changes which have occurred in southern agriculture. Nevertheless, in the case of certain agricultural operations it is possible to assign to water transportation the dominant role in producing much of the change which has come. To begin with, the relative importance of agriculture as an income producer in the South and in the Tennessee Valley has lessened considerably since 1929. In 1929 persons engaged in agriculture received 23 percent of the total regional income for the Tennessee Valley. By 1950 agriculturally produced income amounted to only 12 percent of the total. During the same era, industrial income climbed from 15 percent to approximately 20 percent of the total regional income for the 201 counties which make up the TVA power service area.[38] Navigation was instrumental in producing this change. Thus, it would appear that farm income has been adversely affected by the improvement of the river and other factors. On the other hand, a more realistic interpretation seems to be that declining agricultural income represents a shift in the southern economy to a more balanced system of agricultural-industrial production. This has been a desirable change which has been promoted and welcomed by southern leaders.[39]

Since 1933 the TVA has carried on a vigorous program designed to improve agricultural income in its watershed area.[40] The Authority has concentrated on fertilizer experimentation to produce cheaper but more valuable soil nutrients. In this activity its results have had nation-wide influence. Its program for the valley has been more extensive. The Authority has sought to readjust agricultural land use by encouraging the planting of soil-building crops, the reduction of acreage devoted to row crops, and reduction of acreage in bare lands. It also has attempted, through education and research, to supplement farm income by developing wider farm markets, encouraging the adoption of new farm production techniques such as "adequate fertilization of crops, new crop varieties, improved crop and livestock management, adoption of farm machinery, [and] better planning of farm operations." [41]

The program, as a TVA official views it, has succeeded. Leland G. Allbaugh recently wrote:

> Fertilizer use has expanded . . . . Corn acreage in the Valley has decreased 20 per cent since 1930, cotton acreage 18 per cent. Small grain acreage is up 17 per cent, hay acreage 57 per cent. Sixteen per cent more land is in pasture. Cattle and calves on the farm are up 38 per cent. The value of farm products, adjusted for price increases, is 17 per cent above what it was twenty years ago; and, while in 1939 the ratio of gross income from crops to that of livestock was roughly 60:40, in 1950 it was about 50:50.[42]

It is apparent that TVA's efforts to effect agricultural changes in the valley have been rewarded. Unquestionably the agricultural development program is due the major credit for effecting such change. Nevertheless, the existence of a navigable waterway and the use which has been made of the channel for the shipping of farm commodities, especially grain products, have been to a large degree the vital factors which have made the modifications possible. In particular, water-transported grain, barged from the upper Mississippi Valley to the TVA region and subsequently shipped by rail and truck to all parts of the South, has so cheapened the price of feed grains to southern farmers that livestock production has been made competitive with that industry in other parts of the nation. This reduction of grain prices has resulted in new industries and agricultural practices which formerly were alien to farmers in the South. The Authority has been aware of the role which navigation could play in remaking valley agriculture, and it has encouraged the use of the waterway whenever possible.

In the early years of the TVA, it was thought that the improvement of the waterway for low-cost barge transportation would materially aid the farmer by providing him with a cheaper means of getting his crops to the more populous markets in the Ohio and Mississippi valleys.[43] An early experiment in this direction was the construction by TVA of a refrigerated barge for shipping frozen strawberries to St. Louis. The effort was never really successful, even though one shipment of berries did reach the Missouri city.[44] In later years, hope remained that outgoing shipments would profitably use the channel to take advantage of lower-cost water-freight rates, but the outbound movement of agricultural commodities via the waterway always has been negligible. Consequently, the value of river transportation, except as it may have acted as a deterrent to excessive rail rates on outbound agricultural goods, has not been great for the farmer who markets his products outside or within the valley.

A severe critic of the TVA has said that "navigation on the Tennessee has served to open up the valley to imports and has not greatly assisted it in exporting its products."[45] This conclusion is justified, but the critic, Waldorf V. Howard, failed to determine why this situation exists. He chose rather to point to this adverse trade situation as an example of TVA's lack of concern with its navigation objective. Actually, artificial and technological barriers have retarded the shipment of farm products both to and from the region. Strong railroad and truck competition and the difficulty of transporting small shipments economically by barge have made it unprofitable for small-scale agricultural operators to take advantage of the new waterway for outgoing commodities. Moreover, as the costly refrigerated barge experiment showed, the perishable nature of many farm products precludes their movement by water transport.

It is because of this adverse trading relationship which the Tennessee Valley and other parts of the Southeast have with the upper Mississippi Valley that the river has had its greatest impact on southeastern agriculture. The South, long known for its one-crop economy built around cotton production, is a grain-deficit region. Ford K.

Edwards, transportation consultant and economist, found that in 1955 the South disposed of 83 percent of its feed grains on the farm and sold 17 percent to commercial outlets, whereas the nation as a whole disposed of 64 percent of its production on the farm as "feed and seed" and sold 36 percent.[46] One third of the production of food grains in the South, such as wheat and rye, also was channeled into the manufacture of animal feed. Approximately 67 percent of the South's food grain crop entered commercial channels. The nation, exclusive of the South, sold 90 percent of its food grains to other areas of the country and to foreign markets. Edwards concluded that "if one eliminates the farm disposition of the grains as 'feed and seed' and also household uses, leaving only the category of grains sold, the South's proportion of the United States farm sales of grain was a little over 4 per cent." [47]

From the foregoing analysis of southern grain production and consumption, several observations can be drawn. The amount of grain produced in the South is small when compared with that raised in other areas. The bulk of southern grain is disposed of on the farm for livestock production. Finally, the South is dependent on the grain producers of the Midwest for both its animal feed grains and its cereals.

In recent years the South has become a greater grain deficit region than ever before. As Allbaugh pointed out, in the TVA region livestock production now furnishes one half of gross farm income whereas in 1939 it provided only about one third of the total.[48] During the same period southern grain production has remained stable in relation to national grain production. Edwards found that "in both the 1937–41 period and the latest three-year period [1951, 1953, 1955], the production of feed grains in the South has remained at between 3 and 4 percent of the national production." [49] The Edwards study also revealed that between 1939 and 1956 grain-consuming industries in the South outgrew those for the rest of the nation.[50] In some areas, such as poultry production and the production and marketing of meat animals, the growth was described as phenomenal.

The importance of the expansion of these grain-related industries cannot be minimized. Gordon Sawyer, executive secretary of the Georgia Poultry Federation, who testified in the ICC hearings on the barge-grain rate case, told the commission,

> The economy of the State of Georgia is to a large measure affected by farm income. At present, however, Georgia farms earn only about 60 per

cent of the average income of farms in the United States as a whole. In recent years Georgia has become the largest broiler producing state in the United States and poultry and poultry products have become second only to cotton as a source of farm income in Georgia.[51]

The research of Robert W. Williams substantiated Sawyer's testimony. Williams found that "in . . . 1940, poultry production brought $750,000 to Hall County [Georgia] farmers while cotton brought only $745,000 which included subsidy and conservation payments of $205,000." [52]

Georgia is not an exception in this rapid expansion of the southern poultry and livestock industry. A recent report argued that the "expanding poultry and livestock industries of the Southeast created the need for more feed than this region produced. This was particularly true of the three-state area of Mississippi, Alabama, and Georgia —the fastest growing broiler region in the United States." [53] It is apparent that the Southeast is putting greater and greater emphasis upon the production of grain-consuming animal units. As a result of this modification of its economy, the region has become more dependent than ever before upon the importation of grains from the grain-belt of the upper Mississippi Valley. Since the most dynamic increase in grain consumption has occurred in that section of the South where producers of poultry and livestock can take advantage of the lower-cost, barge-hauled grain, it becomes conclusive that the importation of grains by water from the upper Mississippi Valley to such ports as Decatur, Guntersville, and Chattanooga must have been the vital factor in promoting this new development in southern agriculture.[54]

Midwestern grain began to move up the Tennessee River in 1939. The opening of the 9-foot navigation channel to Chattanooga in that year tapped the "golden grain belt of the Midwest by way of the Mississippi and its northern tributaries, and. . . [siphoned] grain into the feed-hungry Southeast." [55] From 1939 to 1959, grain shipments on the Tennessee River increased from 6,000 tons to 1,396,672 tons.[56] By 1961 grain tonnage on the waterway amounted to about 2,300,000 tons.[57] A Guntersville grain distributor reported that during one week in 1959 that port handled more corn than the Chicago Board of Trade for the corresponding period.[58] This increasingly heavy movement of grain and grain products—corn, wheat, oats, soybeans, and flour—has led to the creation of new processing industries, large scale poultry and livestock production, new grain distribution centers, and to a more diversified and larger income for many southern farmers.

The transformation of Guntersville over the last two decades from a small land-locked village to a bustling grain port capable of handling an estimated one third of a million bushels of grain [59] in a normal eight-hour day illustrates the role that Tennessee River navigation has played in producing such dynamic changes. Recently, it was reported that Guntersville "is now a feed and grain distribution and manufacturing center for the whole Southeast." [60] In Marshall County, Alabama, of which Guntersville is the county seat, "pin-money" poultry production has given way to large scale output. "The chicken is king in Marshall County, Alabama. He's such a regal ruler in fact, that an entire train was named for him. It was called —as you might well guess—'The Chicken Train'." [61] Since the river has been improved, sixteen mills or grain elevators have been established along its banks, representing an investment of 30 million dollars.[62] Most of these are located at Guntersville and Chattanooga. The railroad industry, an arch rival of the barge lines, attributed to water transportation the prime role in producing this new industry.[63]

The growth of the milling, poultry, and livestock industries has obviously not been limited to the Tennessee River cities. Milling operations utilizing barge-hauled grains have sprung up at Gainesville, Flowery Branch, and Cartersville, in Georgia. A poultry marketing specialist observed that "water transportation on feed grains and low labor costs seem to be secrets to success in the Southern broiler area. Of these two the lower freight rate on feed is the more important. There's no question that the Tennessee River development has put, and kept, Alabama and Georgia in the broiler business." [64]

An area of 39,000 square miles including portions of Alabama, Georgia, Mississippi, Tennessee, and the Carolinas has been affected by, and to a large degree is dependent upon, the grain which is transported up the Tennessee River. In a current contest for the grain trade of the Tennessee River between the Southern Railway and the barge companies which serve the Tennessee River, a TVA spokesman told the ICC that if the grain trade on the river were ended by railroad competition, "the port cities on the Tennessee River; the milling industry at such ports; the barge lines; the poultry business in Georgia, Alabama, and the Carolinas; the opportunities for industrial expansion in the region; and the railroads themselves" [65] would be adversely affected. Such a prediction is certainly not without merit if the ICC later permitted the railway companies to increase their rates.

For the southern farmer, the availability of cheaper grains has created opportunity for increased farm income. The story of poultry operations of a Georgia farmer engaged in the broiler business on a part-time basis supports this conclusion. He observed, "I figure I get about $1,000 cash from my 10,000 capacity [chicken] house a year. I grow six acres of cotton on shares, but by the time the bills are paid I don't see much cash from my cotton. I raised nine calves and 15 hogs last year and some corn to feed the hogs, but if it wasn't for broilers I don't know how I would make out." [36] Another Georgia farmer commented, "If we could not get that corn that far south [Guntersville] by water, we'd have a much higher basic cost of production. Competition keeps rail and truck rates in line." [67] A third poultry producer of Northeast Georgia not only raised his income from $407 in 1937 to $2,350 in 1940 but, by utilizing chicken manure fertilizer, increased his cotton yield from three to seven bales on a ten-acre holding.[68]

The creation of an expanding southern broiler industry as a result of cheaper transportation rates on grain products has affected the poultry industry from Texas to Maine. A recent visitor to the Tennessee Valley from the Delaware, Maryland, and Virginia broiler-producing region said, "The South is putting natural advantages to good use. Delmarva and other areas of the North will need to develop all of their natural advantages and abilities to meet their Southern friends on even terms." [69] Southern competition has been so painful to northern producers that poultrymen along the Northeast coast of the country have been "studying ways and means of employing the newly opened St. Lawrence Seaway to tap the upper Midwest grain belt." [70]

River-barged grain has also stimulated the dairying industry in the Southeast. As the TVA pointed out in the barge-grain case, "The Southeast is beginning to develop a farm economy based on poultry, dairy, and beef production. In the period 1940–1950 milk production in Tennessee jumped 50 per cent compared with an increase in the United States of 13 per cent." [71] Ford K. Edwards described the rapidity of this growth and showed its continuing nature. He wrote,

> From 1939 to 1955 the marketing of cattle, calves, and hogs increased sharply for the United States as a whole. . . . The marketing of cattle and calves in the South more than doubled, i.e., from 1,278 million pounds

> to 3,104 million pounds. This was an increase of 143 per cent. Marketing in the remainder of the United States (excluding the South) rose 83 per cent. . . . The marketing of hogs increased 63 per cent in the South from 1935 to 1955 while increasing 42 per cent in the rest of the nation.[72]

Further evidence of the dependency of the southern livestock and dairying industry on river-hauled grain is seen in the intervention of the Chattanooga Area Milk Producer's Association in the barge-grain case on behalf of the barge lines which sought to end railway discrimination on grain moving from Tennessee River ports to inland points. William C. List, speaking for that association, declared that "over the last twenty years [1934 to 1954] there has been a revolution in the agriculture of the region, and dairying and beef production are now the principal sources of income to the farmer." [73] These industries have become such important consumers of locally manufactured animal feeds that one milling company at Guntersville had to modify its production schedule in order to supply the quantity of feed needed for hog and dairying enterprises.[74]

The improvement of the Tennessee River for economical barge transportation has played an important role in the ever-changing nature of the southern economy. The South is one of the nation's fastest growing regions. The strides it has made in industrial and agricultural development since the 1940's is manifested not only in the statistics which yearly reveal a greater diversification of economic endeavors but also in an ever-growing annual output of goods and services. In the Tennessee Valley these growth trends have more than kept pace with other areas of the Southeast and the nation as well. Cheap power and nonunion labor do not account fully for this spiraling prosperity of the valley region. The availability of water transportation has had much to do with this economic growth. The huge investments by both government and private enterprise in manufacturing establishments and other industrial facilities along the waterway in many instances would not have been made if barge transportation had been unavailable. Moreover, the expanding grain trade which has stimulated agricultural opportunity and spawned new farm-related industries could not have taken place without the presence of cheap water transport. Navigation, which in 1933 was never expected to be more than a "constitutional peg" for the New Deal's power generation experiment, has become a vital part of the Tennessee Valley Authority's program to revitalize an entire river basin.

NOTES

Chapter 1

1 *Statutes at Large,* XXVI, 446.
2 *A History of Navigation on the Tennessee River System,* House Doc. 254, 75th Congress, 1st Session (1937), 6; hereinafter cited as *A History of Navigation.*
3 Donald Davidson, *The Tennessee* (New York, 1946–48), I, 208–211.
4 *A History of Navigation,* 51, 53.
5 Stanley J. Folmsbee, *Sectionalism and Internal Improvements in Tennessee* (Knoxville, 1939), 12–13; hereinafter cited as Folmsbee, *Sectionalism.* William E. Martin, *Internal Improvements in Alabama* ("Johns Hopkins University Studies in Historical and Political Science," XX, No. 4 [Baltimore, 1902]), 36; hereinafter cited as Martin, *Internal Improvements.*
6 Davidson, *The Tennessee,* I, 231.
7 Folmsbee, *Sectionalism,* 25–26, 125.
8 Philip Hamer, *Tennessee: A History* (New York, 1933), I, 389–95; Folmsbee, *Sectionalism,* 26.
9 Folmsbee, *Sectionalism,* 28.
10 *Ibid.,* 30.
11 *Ibid.,* 20, 32–33.
12 Huntsville (Ala.) *Southern Advocate,* March 21, 1821, quoted in Alldredge, *A History of Navigation,* 56.
13 *A History of Navigation,* 57; Folmsbee, *Sectionalism,* 16; Albert C. Holt, "Economic and Social Beginnings of Tennessee," *Tennessee Historical Magazine,* VII (January, 1922), 297–98; Davidson, *The Tennessee,* I, 239.
14 Thomas J. Campbell, *The Upper Tennessee* (Chattanooga, 1932), 9–45.
15 Folmsbee, *Sectionalism,* 71.

16 *A History of Navigation,* 59.
17 Davidson, *The Tennessee,* I, 243–44.
18 Folmsbee, *Sectionalism,* 70–83.
19 *Ibid.,* 20, 70–84, 216–20.
20 *Ibid.,* 217–20.
21 *Ibid.*
22 Although Middle Tennessee had been allocated $100,000 worth of the original river bond issue, it did not participate in this direct appropriation. East and West Tennessee argued that the middle region had already obtained more than a fair share of state aid for turnpikes.
23 Hamer, *Tennessee: A History,* I, 397; Folmsbee, *Sectionalism,* 221–222.
24 *A History of Navigation,* 129.
25 The region of the Tennessee River known as the Muscle Shoals was in reality a series of shoals with intervening pools of deep water. The entire stretch extended fifty-three miles. Beginning at river-mile 287.7 and moving downstream, one encountered first the Elk River Shoals, second the Big Muscle Shoals, third the Little Muscle Shoals, and finally the Colbert Shoals at mile 234.6.
26 Davidson, *The Tennessee,* I, 284.
27 Martin, *Internal Improvements,* 34–41.
28 *Ibid.,* 44; *A History of Navigation,* 126–27; Davidson, *The Tennessee,* I, 287–89.
29 Davidson, *The Tennessee,* I, 289; *Report on the Examination and Survey of the Tennessee River,* House Executive Doc. 271, 40th Congress, 2nd Session (1868), 30.
30 *A History of Navigation,* 126–27.
31 *Ibid.;* Martin, *Internal Improvements,* 34–42.
32 *Report on the Examination and Survey of the Tennessee River,* 30.
33 Martin, *Internal Improvements,* 35, 41.
34 Hamer, *Tennessee: A History,* I, 390; Folmsbee, *Sectionalism,* 200–22.
35 Folmsbee, *Sectionalism;* Hamer, *Tennessee: A History,* 395.
36 Folmsbee, *Sectionalism,* 222; Martin, *Internal Improvements,* 35–44.
37 *A History of Navigation,* 133.
38 A sum of $50,000 to improve approximately 200 miles of the Tennessee River in view of the numerous obstacles to navigation must be regarded as ridiculous.
39 River distances between these points are as follows: Knoxville to Chattanooga, 188 miles; Chattanooga to Riverton, Alabama, 237.4 miles; Riverton to Paducah, Kentucky, at the river's mouth, 226 miles.
40 *Tennessee River and Tributaries: North Carolina, Tennessee, Alabama, and Kentucky,* House Doc. 328, 71st Congress, 2nd Session (1930), Part I, 230; hereinafter cited as *Tennessee River and Tributaries. Statutes at Large,* XVI, 538, 542; XXVIII, 338, 354; XXXVII, 201, 215, XL, 918, 927–28. War Department, *Annual Report of the Chief of Engineers* (1933), Part I, 749.
41 *Statutes at Large,* XXXVII, 201, 215; Department of War, *Annual Report of the Chief of Engineers* (1933), Part I, 749; *A History of Navigation,* 135–46.
42 *Tennessee River and Tributaries,* 32.
43 *Annual Report of the Chief of Engineers* (1933), Part I, 207–10.
44 Davidson, *The Tennessee,* I, 250; *A History of Navigation,* 135–40.
45 Martin, *Internal Improvements,* 46.
46 *Statutes at Large,* XXXIV, 1073, 1093.

47 *A History of Navigation,* 136; *Tennessee River and Tributaries,* 32.

48 *A History of Navigation,* 137–39; *Statutes at Large,* XXVI, 426, 445–46.

49 This dam was officially titled Dam Number One. Its designation resulted from engineer plans to build three moderately high dams to provide slack-water navigation over the entire shoals region.

50 *Statutes at Large,* XXVI, 426, 444–46; *A History of Navigation,* 140.

51 *Tennessee River and Tributaries,* 32.

52 The Corps of Engineers reported in 1930 that total expenditures on the Tennessee, exclusive of $37,000,000 charged to power at Wilson Dam, amounted to $23,400,000. They estimated that it would require an additional $15,000,000 to complete projects currently underway. *Tennessee River and Tributaries,* 1–2.

53 A 9-foot channel was authorized for the Ohio River in 1907 and completed in 1929. By 1920, a 9-foot depth was available on the Mississippi River from New Orleans to Cairo, Illinois. Stuart Daggett, *Principles of Inland Transportation* (Rev. 3rd. ed.; New York, 1941), 47.

54 *Tennessee River and Tributaries,* 231.

55 *Ibid.,* 2.

56 Herbert D. Vogel, "Role of the Civil Engineer in Multipurpose River Development," *Civil Engineering,* XXVI (July, 1956), 436.

Chapter 2

1 Preston J. Hubbard, *Origins of the TVA: The Muscle Shoals Controversy, 1920–1932* (Nashville, 1961); Herman Pritchett, "The Development of the Tennessee Valley Authority Act," *Tennessee Law Review,* XV (February, 1938), 128–41; Norman Wengert, "Antecedents of TVA: The Legislative History of Muscle Shoals," *Agricultural History,* XXVI (October, 1952), 141–47.

2 *Message from the President Requesting Legislation to Create a Tennessee Valley Authority,* House Doc. 15, 73rd Congress, 1st Session (1933), 1.

3 The original directors were Arthur E. Morgan, a self-educated hydraulic engineer; Harcourt A. Morgan, an entomologist; and David E. Lilienthal, an attorney.

4 Cove Creek Dam was named in honor of Senator George W. Norris.

5 Dam No. 3 was later designated the Joseph T. Wheeler Dam.

6 *Tennessee River and Tributaries,* 7.

7 Chattanooga *News,* September 28, 1933.

8 House Subcommittee of the Committee on Appropriations, Hearings, *Additional Appropriations for Emergency Purposes,* 73rd Congress, 2nd Session (1934), 137–202; House Committee on Military Affairs, Hearings, *To Amend the Tennessee Valley Authority Act,* 74th Congress, 1st Session (1935), 97.

9 President, Executive Order No. 6162, June 8, 1933. Copy located in minute files of TVA Board of Directors, Knoxville, Tennessee; Chattanooga *News,* October 28, 1933; "No Present Need for Completion of Dam No. 3 on the Tennessee," *Engineering News-Record,* III (November 2, 1933), 537; David E. Lilienthal, *The Journals of David E. Lilienthal: The TVA Years, 1939–1945* (New York, 1964), I, 42.

10 *Tennessee River and Tributaries,* 2; *Statutes at Large,* XLVI, 918–28.

11 Harry Wiersema, "The River Control System," in Roscoe C. Martin (ed.), *TVA: The First Twenty Years* (Knoxville, 1956), 77–84; *Report of the Joint Committee Investigating the Tennessee Valley Authority,* Senate

Doc. 56, 76th Congress, 1st Session (1939), 137–43; *Additional Appropriations for Emergency Purposes*, 137–202.

12 *Additional Appropriations For Emergency Purposes*, 137–202.

13 *Ibid.*

14 *History of Appropriations Made by the Congress of the United States for the Tennessee Valley Authority*, Senate Doc. 35, 79th Congress, 1st Session (1945), 14.

15 *Tennessee River and Tributaries*, 497.

16 *Congressional Record*, 74th Congress, 1st Session (1935), 10898.

17 Wiersema, "The River Control System," in Martin (ed.), *TVA: The First Twenty Years*, 85.

18 Florence (Ala.) *Herald*, October 10, 1933.

19 Chattanooga *Times*, September 15, 1933.

20 Chattanooga *News*, September 28, 1933; Chattanooga *Times*, September 28, October 3, 28, 1933, March 5, 12, 1934; Knoxville *Journal*, December 3, 16, 1933; Rockwood (Tenn.) *Times*, March 29, May 31, 1934; Florence (Ala.) *Times*, June 27, 1934; Joint Committee to Investigate the Tennessee Valley Authority, Hearings, *Investigation of the Tennessee Valley Authority*, 75th Congress, 3rd Session (1938), 667.

21 New York *Times*, March 5, 12, 1934.

22 Florence (Ala.) *Times*, December 8, 1933.

23 Chattanooga *News*, March 30, 1934.

24 Chattanooga *Times*, December 18, 1933.

25 Herman Finer, *The TVA: Lessons for International Application* (Montreal, 1944), 181–83.

26 *History of Appropriations*, Senate Doc. 35, 79th Congress, 1st Session (1945), 1–27; Senate, Subcommittee of the Committee on Appropriations, Hearings, 1933–45; Lilienthal, *Journals*, I, 386–695.

27 Chattanooga *Times*, December 18, 1933.

28 Chattanooga *News*, January 17, March 5, 7, April 24, May 21, November 16, 1934; Chattanooga *Times*, March 3, 12, May 21, June 4, 5, October 31, 1934.

29 While the litigation was financed by Edison Electric Institute, the trade association for the utility industry, the firms concerned were seeking to block TVA's electrical generation program because they feared that increased hydroelectrical power would injure their businesses. An earlier effort had been made by these concerns to hamstring the Authority's program by arguing before the Alabama Public Service Commission that TVA was a threat to state regulation of utilities. This argument was later carried over when the firms brought suit against the Authority. This contention became moot when the legislatures of Alabama and Tennessee granted special rights to TVA to operate as a rate-regulatory body outside the jurisdiction of the state utility commissions. Joseph C. Swidler and Robert H. Marquis, "TVA in Court: A Study of TVA's Constitutional Litigation," *Iowa Law Review*, XXXII (January, 1947), 304; Elliott Roberts, *One River—Seven States: TVA-State Relations in the Development of the Tennessee River* (Knoxville, 1955), 66–78.

30 Swidler and Marquis, "TVA in Court," 304.

31 *Ibid.*, 304.

32 *Ashwander et al.* v. *Tennessee Valley Authority*, 9 F. Supp. 965 (N. D. Ala., 1935).

33 Swidler and Marquis, "TVA in Court," 307–308.

34 The fear of an adverse decision by the Supreme Court must have been uppermost in the Authority's thinking, for the attitude of the court toward

the Roosevelt program was decidedly unfriendly. Erik M. Eriksson and Trent H. Steele, *Constitutional Basis for Judging the New Deal* (Rosemead, California, 1936), 62–63; Lilienthal, *Journals,* I, 59.

35 *To Amend the Tennessee Valley Authority Act,* 303–307; *Congressional Record,* 74th Congress, 1st Session (1935), 7133–41, 7214–22, 10768–77.

36 *Congressional Record,* 74th Congress, 1st Session (1935), 10348, 10768–98; *To Amend the Tennessee Valley Authority Act,* 1–446.

37 *Congressional Record,* 74th Congress, 1st Session (1935), 7214, 7224–25, 7298–99, 7467, 11037–38.

38 Senator Norris' remarks when he introduced the proposed amendments on the Senate floor appear to lend credence to the view that Congress regarded the TVA primarily as a power project. Norris explained the need for rewriting the 1933 law in this way: "Queer as it may seem, Mr. President, while we debated the TVA Act for about twelve years, off and on, it was never once suggested, so far as I remember, that we should provide in the proposed act the depth for navigation. We did provide for navigation; that is the principal object of the original act; we provided that the river be made navigable, but nowhere did we say what its depth for navigation should be." *Congressional Record,* 74th Congress, 1st Session (1935), 7214.

39 *Statutes at Large,* XLIX, 1075.

40 Several congressmen charged that the Authority was not keeping Congress informed of its developmental program. The accusation had validity since funds used by the corporation were allocated to it by the President. Since Congress was not utilizing its power to appropriate as a means of supervising the Authority's activities, it had very little control over the agency. Apparently this loss of control over a governmental program in which huge sums were to be expended caused concern in the minds of many congressmen. Anti-TVA representatives supported the demand for a blueprint of the Authority's plans, probably because it offered an opportunity to throw an obstacle in the way of the bill's successful passage. *Congressional Record,* 74th Congress, 1st Session (1935), 10885–97.

41 *Statutes at Large,* XLIX, 1076.

42 See p. 137, note 38.

43 Swidler and Marquis, "TVA in Court," 300.

44 *Congressional Record,* 74th Congress, 1st Session (1935), 7134–35, 10768–83.

45 *To Amend the Tennessee Valley Authority Act,* 91–101.

46 *Tennessee River and Tributaries,* 13.

47 James S. Bowman, hydraulic engineer, TVA, to district engineer, U.S. Corps of Engineers Office, Nashville, Tennessee, September 1, 1934, quoted in "Transcript of Record," *Tennessee Electric Power Companies* v. *Tennessee Valley Authority* (7 vols.; Washington, 1938), VII, 4110; hereinafter cited as "Transcript of Records," TEP Case.

48 David E. Lilienthal, "Principles Governing Dam Building Program," Office Memorandum to TVA Board of Directors in minute files of Tennessee Valley Authority Board, Minute Entry Number 10–12–34a.

49 Speech of David E. Lilienthal before the Shelby County Young Democratic Club, October 20, 1934, in files of Tennessee Valley Authority Technical Library, Knoxville, Tennessee.

50 Birmingham *Age-Herald,* February 20, 1935.

51 While the Bock press statement indicates a strong interest in improving the upper and middle sections of the river for navigation, it must be remembered that this attitude on the part of TVA was of recent origin.

Two months before, Clifton T. Barker had testified in the Ashwander trial that the improvement of the river above Chattanooga was considered unfeasible from an economic standpoint. See testimony of Barker in "Transcript of Record," TEP Case, III, 1990.

52 During the period when the Authority was allocated its funds by the Chief Executive and before Congress began to assert greater financial control over the TVA, the agency was able to ignore to some extent the demands of local interests and valley congressmen. When urged to build more dams or projects in certain localities, TVA argued that construction should be an engineering decision, not a political one. According to Lilienthal's testimony before the joint committee which investigated the Authority in 1938, he seriously questioned the wisdom of an accelerated construction program. Lilienthal advanced the following reasons for not undertaking a hasty program: that the Authority lacked adequate engineering data about sites located by the Corps of Engineers prior to 1930, and, consequently, cost estimates for budgetary considerations were impossible until extensive surveys had been completed; that the TVA organization was new and already working at a rapid pace which, if accelerated, might result in reduced efficiency on the part of the Authority's staff; that an enlarged program of construction might force the agency to neglect some of its other purposes; and that he preferred to delay exceedingly large capital expenditures until a market for the TVA's electrical power could be found. Despite these serious considerations, Lilienthal recalled that he had been won over to an accelerated program by Arthur E. Morgan. Lilienthal also pointed out that "there were weighty considerations in favor of an accelerated program." *Investigation of the Tennessee Valley Authority*, Part II, 665–67.

53 Specific dams to be constructed were not mentioned. The budget request simply provided for at least one tributary dam and a main-river dam. The Chattanooga *Times* reported that these projects probably would be the Hiwassee and Aurora dams. Chief Executive, *The Budget for the Fiscal Year Ending June 30, 1936* (Washington, 1935), 710; Chattanooga *Times*, January 8, 1935.

54 The TVA's budget estimates are submitted to the Bureau of the Budget several months before the President sends his budget message to Congress in January of each session of Congress. Usually the TVA budget is sent to the Budget Bureau in September. John H. Clark, "Financial Administration," in Martin (ed.), *TVA: The First Twenty Years*, 64–66.

55 House, Subcommittee of the Committee on Appropriations, *Second Deficiency Appropriations Bill, Fiscal Year, 1935*, H. Rep. 1261 to accompany H. R. 8554, 74th Congress, 1st Session (1935), 11.

56 The appropriations bill drawn up by the House was not written out in an itemized manner. The TVA directors outlined their program for the House committee which considered each project proposed by the Authority. After hearing the director's testimony, the committee then recommended a lump sum for the agency's use. The committee expected the TVA to use the appropriation for those activities which had been given committee approval. The committee report to the House was also contractual in nature, for in it was revealed the purpose for which funds were to be expended. In this way the Authority was given some leeway in the use of its money, but at the same time it could not go beyond certain limits. Prior to 1935, such restrictions were unknown since the agency received its funds from the President.

57 *Congressional Record,* 75th Congress, 1st Session (1935), 9859.
58 Senate, Subcommittee of the Committee on Appropriations, Hearings, *Second Deficiency Appropriations Bill, Fiscal Year, 1935,* 74th Congress, 1st Session (1935), 1.
59 Senate, Subcommittee of the Committee on Appropriations, *Second Deficiency Appropriations Bill, Fiscal Year, 1935,* S. Rep. 1085 to accompany H. R. 8554, 74th Congress, 1st Session (1935), 11.
60 McKellar was not working alone in trying to write a bill which would specifically direct the TVA regarding expenditure of its funds. The McKellar amendment was given substantial support in the hearings by Senators Josiah W. Bailey and Robert R. Reynolds and Representative Zebulon Weaver of North Carolina. Senator Alben W. Barkley of Kentucky also argued strongly in favor of amending the House bill. The North Carolina congressmen were interested in securing money for the construction of the Hiwassee Dam, which would be located in western North Carolina and Senator Barkley was pressing for an early construction of the dam at Aurora Landing, a few miles south of the southern boundary of Kentucky. The possibility of cheap power to attract industry and the hope of federal funds to stimulate the economy of their states led these men to support McKellar.
61 *History of Appropriations Made by the Congress . . . for the Tennessee Valley Authority,* 15.
62 *Ibid.*
63 *Second Deficiency Appropriations Bill, Fiscal Year, 1935,* 11; House and Senate Conference Committee, *Second Deficiency Appropriations Bill, Fiscal Year, 1935,* H. Rep. No. 1715, 74th Congress, 1st Session (1935), 8; *History of Appropriations Made by the Congress . . . for the Tennessee Valley Authority,* 24.
64 *History of Appropriations Made by the Congress . . . for the Tennessee Valley Authority,* 16.
65 Tennessee Valley Authority, *Annual Reports* (Washington, D.C., 1935), 5; (1936), 109.
66 Swidler and Marquis, "TVA in Court," 308.
67 *Ashwander et al.* v. *Tennessee Valley Authority,* 297 U.S. 288 (1936).

Chapter 3

1 A project depth of nine feet has an additional two feet of over-depth. This allows vessels of nine-foot draft to operate in a nine-foot channel.
2 The Army Engineers had selected a site at mile 43 (Aurora site) which the Tennessee Valley Authority found unsuitable because of foundation conditions. A site was found at mile 22 where the Kentucky Dam was built. It should be pointed out that the Corps of Engineers based its recommendations on preliminary geological explorations. More intensive investigations of foundation conditions usually are undertaken after the decision to build has been made.
3 *Tennessee River and Tributaries,* 4, 42–52; TVA, *Annual Report* (1934), 42.
4 Charles H. Vivian, "Remaking the Tennessee Valley," *Compressed Air Magazine,* XXXIX (August, 1934), 4496.
5 Section 17 of the Tennessee Valley Authority Act authorized the construction of a dam on the Clinch River by the Secretary of War, the Secretary of the Interior (Bureau of Reclamation), or by "such engineer or engineers as he (the President) may designate." *Statutes at Large,* XLVIII, 67.

6 President, *Executive Order* No. 6162, June 8, 1933.
7 *Congressional Record,* 73rd Congress, 1st Session (1933), 2341.
8 Carl A. Bock to Board of Directors, June 30, 1934 (Memo), Minutes of Board of Directors, Tennessee Valley Authority, Knoxville, Tennessee.
9 Tennessee Valley Authority, *Design of Tennessee Valley Authority Projects: Civil and Structural Design,* Technical Report No. 24 (Washington, 1952), I, 149–58.
10 "Transcript of Record," TEP Case, III, 1952–55, 2235, 2242–43.
11 TVA, *Design of Tennessee Valley Authority Projects,* I, 17–19, 25–26.
12 Wiersema, "The River Control System," in Martin (ed.), *TVA: The First Twenty Years,* 85.
13 Contractor organizations usually include the cost of all construction machinery when bids are submitted on a project. Since only one dam generally is involved, the cost of machinery must be reflected in the contractor's construction estimate. The Tennessee Valley Authority was able to use expensive equipment at a series of projects and thus reduce costs at each project by successive use of equipment. The work force also became more efficient when it could be transferred from dam to dam rather than be laid off for periods of time. The logic of this practice was pointed out time and time again before appropriations committees when budget requests were being made.
14 *Investigation of the Tennessee Valley Authority,* 3227–29.
15 TVA, *Annual Report* (1936), 77–99.
16 By the end of the fiscal year 1936, 9-foot depth on the Tennessee existed from Paducah, Kentucky to the Gilbertsville Dam site, a distance of 22.5 miles. The next 237 miles upstream varied in depth from four to seven feet. At this point, the Wilson Dam provided 9-foot depth for 15 miles to the Wheeler Dam, which formed a navigable waterway 74 miles long. From the upper reaches of the Wheeler reservoir to the Hales Bar Dam, some 82 miles, only three to four feet of water were available at this time. The Hales Bar Dam provided a 33 mile stretch of 9-foot channel upstream to Chattanooga, 464 miles from Paducah. Above Chattanooga, depths of one to four feet were to be found for 193 miles to a point above Knoxville where the Tennessee is formed.
17 House Subcommittee of the Committee on Appropriations, Hearings, *Independent Offices Appropriations Bill, 1939,* 75th Congress, 2nd Session (1937), 925.
18 Tennessee Valley Authority, *Report to the Congress on the Unified Development of the Tennessee River System* (Knoxville, 1936), 13–56; hereinafter cited as TVA, *The Unified Plan.*
19 *Ibid.,* 20–71. A map showing the necessary dams to complete this project is shown on page 69 of *The Unified Plan.*
20 The House Military Affairs Committee devoted a considerable portion of its time in 1935 to a bill, proposed by Representative John E. Rankin of Mississippi, to extend the provisions of the TVA Act to the Tombigbee River. Arthur E. Morgan also reported the merits of such a proposition in his testimony before the committee. *To Amend the Tennessee Valley Authority Act,* 101–102, 167–99; TVA, *The Unified Plan,* 42.
21 Interview with Vanus P. Neely, Nashville, Tennessee, April 10, 1957.
22 TVA, *The Unified Plan,* 44.
23 "Ohio Valley Improvement Association Opposes TVA Control Over Ohio River Valley," *Waterways Journal,* L (April 11, 1936), 7; American Waterways Operators, Inc., *The Inland Waterways: Facts and Figures* (Wash-

ington, 1950), 407; Donald T. Wright, "Watershed Authorities," *Waterways Journal,* LXVII (August 15, 1953), 7.

24 The Wheeler, Norris, Pickwick, Guntersville, Chickamauga, and Hiwassee dams were under construction when the report was filed. The proposed dams were those at Gilbertsville, Kentucky, Watts Bar, Coulter Shoals, and Fontana. TVA, *The Unified Plan,* 24–25.

25 TVA, *The Unified Plan,* 45–46, 89–105.

26 "Transcript of Record," TEP Case, II, 1167–73, III, 1956–57, 1983–84, 1995–99; *Tennessee Electric Power Companies* v. *Tennessee Valley Authority,* 21 F. Supp. 847 (E. D. Tenn., 1938).

27 TVA, *Annual Report* (1938), 107–108, 405–406.

28 Swidler and Marquis, "TVA in Court," 312.

29 The engineers estimated the cost of a low-dam navigation project at $75,000,000. The TVA reported its net investment in navigation and flood control as of June 30, 1937, to be $148,079,176. *Tennessee River and Tributaries,* 4–5; TVA, *Annual Report* (1937), 103.

30 Swidler and Marquis, "TVA in Court," 314.

31 National Conservation Commission, *Report of the National Conservation Commission,* Senate Doc. 676, 60th Congress, 2nd Session (1909), 45.

32 According to the Corps of Engineers, a waterway improvement project is considered economically justifiable if the sum of the benefits and savings that will accrue to the public over a period of time from the use of the waterway is greater than the cost and maintenance of the improvement. Thomas A. Scott, *River and Harbor Improvements: How They are Initiated, Authorized, and Completed* (New York, 1938), 25–28; Major Rufus W. Putnam, the navigation expert who testified for the utilities, asserted that the cost of improving the Tennessee River for navigation, whether by the low-dam method or by means of high dams, was not economically justified. He declared that future traffic over a thirty-year growth period after the completion of a 9-foot channel would not exceed five million tons annually. Traffic savings on this tonnage, he reasoned, would be $3,200,000 a year. The minimum cost for providing a 9-foot waterway was estimated by the Corps of Engineers to be $75,000,000. If interest charges, operation, and maintenance costs were added to the original capital outlay, Putnam claimed that the cost of either plan of improvement would exceed the investment justified by estimated savings. He said that "with the low dam plan the cost exceeds the justifiable investment by about $39,400,000; with the TVA plan the cost exceeds the justifiable investment by $425,650,000," in "Transcript of Record," TEP Case, II, 116–67.

33 "Transcript of Record," TEP Case, II, 1151–89, 1391–95.

34 While utility spokesmen argued that wide lakes endangered river-craft, a key TVA witness, Colonel Lewis H. Watkins of the Corps of Engineers, testified that greater hazards existed to vessels on narrower channels since wind might force a barge or towboat to run aground before compensating action could be taken. *Ibid.,* II, 1534–57, 1598–1600.

35 *Ibid.,* II, 1550.

36 *Ibid.,* III, 1776–81, 1795–97, 1803.

37 *Tennessee Electric Power Companies* v. *Tennessee Valley Authority,* 21 F. Supp. 847 (E. D. Tenn., 1938).

38 *Tennessee Electric Power Companies* v. *Tennessee Valley Authority,* 306 U.S. 118 (1939).

39 Between 1933 and 1938, a total of fifty-seven suits had been brought against the Tennessee Valley Authority, questioning its constitutional basis. *Report*

of the Joint Committee Investigating the Tennessee Valley Authority, 66–67.

40 Hearings, *Investigation of Tennessee Valley Authority*, 103–107; Lilienthal, *Journals*, I, 39.

41 *Report of the Joint Committee Investigating the Tennessee Valley Authority*, 23, 25. The work of the Authority was divided among the three directors according to their interests and backgrounds. Arthur E. Morgan assumed the responsibility for construction, education, and land planning; Harcourt A. Morgan was to administer the agricultural and fertilizer operations and public relations of the Authority; David E. Lilienthal was charged with the responsibility of power operations, legal relations, and transportation. This division of authority gave Arthur E. Morgan the duty of building the channel while Lilienthal was responsible for promoting its use. Since the channel was of little use until 1938 this division had small effect on the overall navigation development.

42 New York *Times*, March 4, 1938; Lilienthal, *Journals*, I, 69–74.

43 Robert L. Duffus, *The Valley and Its People: A Portrait of TVA* (New York, 1946), 71–75.

44 *Ibid.*, 73.

45 *Report of the Joint Committee Investigating the Tennessee Valley Authority*, 237.

46 *Ibid.*, 259.

47 *Ibid.*, 275–77.

48 In a memorandum dated November, 1938, Arthur E. Morgan had proposed such a reorganization of the Authority. Morgan claimed that the power functions of the TVA should be separated from those of flood control and navigation because of the constant threat of using the water for power revenues at the expense of flood control and navigation. The long controversy in the board apparently had led Morgan to believe that "if the power side of the Authority happens to command a majority in the Board the opinions of the engineers responsible for flood control may be overridden." Therefore, division of the agency into distinct river control and power marketing organization seemed to Morgan to be the only positive way of preventing an eventual catastrophe. *Ibid.*, 27. The committee majority rejected Morgan's proposal. Hearings, *Investigation of the Tennessee Valley Authority*, 5027–36.

49 Finer, *The TVA: Lessons for International Application*, 150.

50 John Oliver, "Administrative Foundations," in Martin (ed.), *TVA: The First Twenty Years*, 39–49.

51 House Subcommittee of the Committee on Appropriations, Hearings, *Public Works Appropriations Bill, 1956*, 84th Congress, 1st Session (1955), 166–69.

52 Finer, *The TVA: Lessons for International Application*, 150.

53 Tennessee Valley Authority, *A Short History of the Tennessee Valley Authority, 1933–1956* (Knoxville, 1956), 3.

54 *Congressional Record*, 76th Congress, 1st Session (1939), 1190–93, 1583–98; 3rd Session (1940), 9696–97, 9715–19.

55 TVA, *Annual Report* (1941), 1–16; House Subcommittee of the Committee on Appropriations, Hearings, *Independent Offices Appropriations Bill, 1941*, 76th Congress, 3rd Session (1939), 1607–1896; Duffus, *The Valley and Its People*, 23–39, 136.

56 Chattanooga *Times*, March 26, 1939; New York *Times*, August 6, 1939; Tennessee Valley Authority, *Engineering Data: TVA Water Control Projects*, Technical Monograph No. 55, Vol. I (Knoxville, 1954), 1–15.

57 The construction of Kentucky Dam and Watts Bar Dam had already been initiated before the war emergency began. The third dam, located at Coulter Shoals and later renamed Fort Loudoun, had been planned and its exact location determined, but no construction had begun prior to July 8, 1940. Senate, Subcommittee of the Committee on Appropriations, Hearings, *Making an Additional Appropriation for TVA for Fiscal Year 1941: To Provide Facilities to Expedite the National Defense,* 76th Congress, 3rd Session (1940), 1–26; TVA, *Annual Report* (1941), 12–19; Wiersema, "The River Control System," in Martin (ed.), *TVA: The First Twenty Years,* 85–86.

58 These were the Kentucky, Watts Bar, and Fort Loudoun dams on the main river, and the Apalachia, Chatuge, Ocoee No. 3, Nottely, Fontana, and Douglass Dams on the tributaries of the Tennessee. The steam plant under construction was the Watts Bar project.

59 Wiersema, "The River Control System," in Martin (ed.), *TVA: The First Twenty Years,* 86.

60 TVA, *Engineering Data,* Technical Monograph No. 55, Vol. I (1954), 31–35.

61 Memphis *Commercial Appeal,* October 31, 1943.

62 "2500 Persons Gather for Opening River Terminal in Tennessee City," *Tennessee River Journal,* I (February, 1944), 1, 6.

63 The 1943 press announcements were quite premature. A slack-water channel was available throughout the length of the river, but above Chattanooga an 8-foot depth was not available until April, 1945. This depth was being used extensively, however, by river craft. Full project depth of eleven feet, which included two feet of overdepth, was not finally obtained until November, 1952. TVA, *Engineering Data,* Technical Monograph No. 55, Vol. I (1954), Pt. 5, p. 3; House Subcommittee of the Committee on Appropriations, Hearings, *Independent Offices Appropriations Bill, 1943,* 77th Congress, 2nd Session (1942), 851, 890–97; Senate Subcommittee of the Committee on Appropriations, Hearings, *Independent Offices Appropriations Bill, 1944,* 78th Congress, 1st Session (1943), 459–62.

64 "Kentucky Dam Opening Expected September 15," *Tennessee River Journal,* II (September, 1944), 5.

65 House Subcommittee of the Committee on Appropriations, Hearings, *Independent Offices Appropriations Bill, 1945,* 78th Congress, 2nd Session (November 7, 1943), 309.

66 New York *Times,* August 6, 1939.

67 Clifton T. Barker, "Developments in Tennessee River Navigation," *Waterways,* XVII (July, 1953), 13.

68 Interview with Howard G. King, Sheffield, Alabama, June 9, 1959.

69 House Subcommittee of the Committee on Appropriations, Hearings, *Independent Offices Appropriations Bill, 1939,* 75th Congress, 2nd Session (1937), 1068–75; Davidson, *The Tennessee,* II, 277–80; Donald T. Wright, "Paducah to Knoxville on the Tennessee River," *Waterways Journal,* LXVIII (April 24, 1954), 7–8.

70 Senate Subcommittee of the Committee on Appropriations, Hearings, *Independent Offices Appropriations Bill, 1946,* 79th Congress, 1st Session (1945), 115.

71 Louisville *Courier-Journal,* October 1, 1949.

72 Davidson, *The Tennessee,* II, 277.

73 Clifton T. Barker, "Navigation on the Tennessee River," *Engineering News-Record,* CXXXVI (February 21, 1946), 285.

74 TVA, *Annual Report* (1948), p. A 15, Schedule A.

Chapter 4

1 Knoxville *News-Sentinel,* August 22, 1943.
2 James P. Pope, "The Tennessee Waterway Moves On," an address to the Chattanooga Kiwanis Club, Chattanooga, Tennessee, June 30, 1942, in files of Tennessee Valley Authority Technical Library, Knoxville, Tennessee.
3 The above figure represents fixed assets in navigation facilities as of June 30, 1958. TVA, *Annual Report* (1958), Schedule "A," A17.
4 Roberts, *One River—Seven States,* 29.
5 This requirement stemmed from Congress' desire to set up a "yardstick" for utility rate regulation and its policy of making federal power projects self-supporting. The TVA charges its projects costs to only three objectives: navigation, flood control, and power generation. The value of each system is determined by the sum which would have been required to construct an alternative, or single-purpose, project which would have afforded benefits equal to those that have resulted from combining all three objectives into multiple-purpose development. A detailed account of TVA's allocation methods may be found in Joseph S. Ransmeier, *The Tennessee Valley Authority: A Case Study in the Economics of Multiple Purpose Stream Planning* (Nashville, 1942), 305–42.
6 *Statutes at Large,* XLVIII, 69.
7 *Regionalized Freight Rates: Barriers to National Productiveness,* House Doc. 137, 78th Congress, 1st Session (1943), vii; TVA, *Annual Report* (1934), 5; Lilienthal, *Journals,* I, 81, 150–51.
8 Roberts, *One River—Seven States,* 27–28.
9 *Ibid.*
10 Both the TVA and the Corps of Engineers assumed that a large amount of the freight on the river would be that diverted from the railroads because of cheaper water freight rates. *Tennessee River and Tributaries,* 85; Tennessee Valley Authority, *Prospective Commerce on the Tennessee River* (Knoxville, 1941), 17.
11 TVA, *Annual Report* (1951), 22.
12 The Authority prepared and submitted to the President the following three studies on the interterritorial freight-rate problem: *The Interterritorial Freight Rate Problem of the United States,* House Doc. 264, 75th Congress, 1st Session (1937); *Supplemental Phases of the Interterritorial Freight Rate Problem of the United States,* House Doc. 271, 76th Congress, 1st Session (1939); and *Regionalized Freight Rates: Barriers to National Productiveness,* House Doc. 137, 78th Congress, 1st Session (1943).
13 *The Interterritorial Freight Rate Problem of the United States,* House Doc. 264, 75th Congress, 1st Session (1937), xi.
14 David E. Lilienthal, *The Widening of Economic Opportunity Through TVA* (Washington, 1940), 9.
15 The ICC, after vigorous pressure by the Southern Governors' Conference and the TVA, issued an order in May, 1952, which provided for a revision of the class-rate structure. The story of the southern freight-rate fight is told in William H. Joubert, *Southern Freight Rates in Transition* (Gainesville, Florida, 1949), 287–388.
16 TVA, *Annual Report* (1936), 56.
17 David E. Lilienthal, "The Tennessee River Goes to Town," an address to the Rotary Club of Atlanta, Georgia, October 6, 1941, in files of Tennessee Valley Authority Technical Library, Knoxville, Tennessee.
18 Roberts, *One River—Seven States,* 23–24.

19 TVA, *Annual Reports* (1948–59), Exhibits II and III in appendixes of reports.
20 Roberts, *One River—Seven States,* 24.
21 TVA, *The Unified Plan,* 44.
22 TVA, *Annual Report* (1938), 20.
23 Tennessee Valley Authority, *Report and Recommendations Concerning Public Terminal Facilities for the Tennessee River System* (Knoxville, 1939), 1.
24 *Ibid.*
25 Roberts, *One River—Seven States,* 30.
26 Interview with Earl P. Carter, Chattanooga, Tennessee, August, 1957.
27 James P. Pope, "Tennessee River Terminal Development," an address at the organizational meeting of the Tennessee Valley Waterways Conference, Chattanooga, Tennessee, June 28, 1940, in files of Tennessee Valley Authority Technical Library, Knoxville, Tennessee.
28 "Program for the Meeting of the Executive Committee, Tennessee Valley Waterways Conference," Decatur, Alabama, December 20, 1940. Manuscript in possession of the author.
29 The state of Alabama had several years previously amended its constitution to permit the state to engage in the construction of the public docks at Mobile. This amendment had restricted future dock building in several respects. Total cost of dock construction was not to exceed $10,000,000, and this amount already had been consumed in the development of the Mobile facilities. Moreover, the amendment did not permit interstate cooperation. In brief, any attempt to form an interstate agreement would have required changing the Alabama constitution.
30 "Program for the Meeting of the Executive Committee, Tennessee Valley Waterways Conference."
31 *Ibid.;* John P. Ferris, TVA commerce department, to Earl P. Carter, president, Tennessee Valley Waterways Conference, September 12, 1940; Clifton T. Barker, chief, TVA river transportation division to Carter, January 7, 1941, Tennessee Valley Waterways Conference Manuscript Collection, in possession of the author.
32 Chattanooga *Times,* October 18, 1940.
33 Barker to Carter, April 16, June 17, 1941, Tennessee Valley Waterways Conference Manuscript Collection.
34 Ferris to Carter, September 12, 1940; Carter to Ferris, September 13, 1940, Tennessee Valley Waterways Conference Manuscript Collection; Chattanooga *Times,* October 18, 1940.
35 P. H. Wood to Governor Prentice Cooper, February 1, 1941; Arthur V. Snell to Cooper, February 3, 1941; Earl P. Carter to Cooper, February 5, 1941; Tom O. Duff to Cooper, February 5, 1941; P. H. Wood to State Representative James B. Ragon, Jr., February 5, 1941; Tom O. Duff to Ragon, February 5, 1941; Chattanooga Chamber of Commerce Waterways Committee to Ragon, February 5, 1941, Tennessee Valley Waterways Conference Manuscript Collection.
36 "Minutes of the meeting of the Chattanooga Chamber of Commerce Waterways Committee," February 24, 1941, Tennessee Valley Waterways Conference Manuscript Collection.
37 Roberts, *One River—Seven States,* 30.
38 "Minutes of the meeting of the Chattanooga Chamber of Commerce Waterways Committee," February 24, 1941, Tennessee Valley Waterways Conference Manuscript Collection.

39 Roberts, *One River—Seven States,* 30.
40 Barker to Carter, March 18, 1942, Tennessee Valley Waterways Conference Manuscript Collection.
41 *Ibid.*
42 Nashville *Tennessean,* May 3, 1942; E. P. Ericson, "River Transportation," in Martin (ed.), *TVA: The First Twenty Years,* 97.
43 Carter to Donald T. Wright, April 12, 1943; Wright to Fred A. Roberts, secretary, Knoxville Chamber of Commerce, April 9, 1943, Tennessee Valley Waterways Conference Manuscript Collection; *Independent Offices Appropriations Bill, 1944,* 377–515.
44 "Guntersville Dedication," *Tennessee River Journal,* I (November, 1943), 2; "2500 Persons Gather for Opening River Terminal in Tennessee City," *Tennessee River Journal,* I (February, 1944), 1, 6.
45 Tennessee Valley Authority, *Cheaper Transportation Via the Tennessee River* (Knoxville, 1946), 29–35.
46 "Provision and Management of Public-Use River Terminal" (Program Authorization No. 2, June, 1943), Minutes of Board of Directors, Tennessee Valley Authority, Knoxville, Tennessee.
47 Barker to Carter, February 14, 1941, Tennessee Valley Waterways Conference Manuscript Collection.
48 Interview with Clifton T. Barker, Knoxville, Tennessee, July 12, 1957; Tennessee Valley Authority, *Proposed Tennessee River Terminals at Knoxville, Chattanooga, Guntersville, and Decatur* (Knoxville, 1942).
49 TVA, *Annual Report* (1957), 23.
50 Interview with Clifton T. Barker, Knoxville, Tennessee, July 12, 1957; Interview with George B. Tully, Knoxville, Tennessee, February 2, 1963.
51 Roberts, *One River—Seven States,* 31.
52 Earl P. Carter, "The Need for a Consistent Federal Policy Toward Use of the Inland Waterway Resources of the U.S.," *Waterways Progress,* II (June, 1945), 6.
53 Ferris to Carter, March 3, 1945, Tennessee Valley Waterways Conference Manuscript Collection.
54 When freight moves from origin to destination over two or more railroads, a single joint rate and billing system is used to render greater convenience to the shipper. The railroads then divide the revenue obtained in accordance with a pre-arranged formula. The ICC Act permits similar arrangements between land and water carriers, which would result in a saving to the shipper of approximately 20 percent as compared with an all-rail rate.
55 Joint rates were in effect for the port of Knoxville from 1923 until 1936 even though virtually no waterborne freight was received or shipped from that city. Apparently, the prospect of future water movements led the railway companies to abolish these rates. U.S., Interstate Commerce Commission Docket No. 30774, *American Barge Line Company, et al.* v. *The Alabama Great Southern Railroad Company, et al.,* "Brief of the Intervener: Tennessee Valley Authority," May 1, 1954, 54–55; hereinafter cited as ICC Docket No. 30774, "Brief of the Intervener: TVA," May 1, 1954.
56 Ericson, "River Transportation," in Martin (ed.), *TVA: The First Twenty Years,* 106–107.
57 *Ibid.,* 105.
58 House Subcommittee of the Committee on Military Affairs, Hearings, *To Amend the Tennessee Valley Authority Act of 1933,* 76th Congress, 1st Session (1939), 236–37.

59 Chattanooga *Times,* February 24, March 19, 1939; Chattanooga *Free Press,* February 28, 1939; Memphis *Press-Scimitar,* March 16, 1939.
60 A thorough treatment of this problem has been done by the President's Water Resources Policy Commission, *Report of the President's Water Resources Policy Commission* (Washington, 1950), I, 421–40.
61 TVA, *Annual Report* (1941), 3; Interstate Commerce Commission, *Commercial Barge Lines, Inc., Extension—General Commodities, No. W-751 (Sub-No. 9),* CCLXXXV (1953), 349–68.
62 Ferris to Carter, March 3, 1945, Tennessee Valley Waterways Conference Manuscript Collection.
63 "Minutes of the Meeting of Waterways Committee," March 16, 1945, *ibid.*
64 Ferris to Chester C. Thompson, president, American Waterways Operators, Inc., April 30, 1945, Tennessee Valley Waterways Conference Manuscript Collection.
65 David E. Lilienthal, chairman, Tennessee Valley Authority, to Carter, June 14, June 28, 1946; Harcourt A. Morgan, vice-chairman, Tennessee Valley Authority, to Carter, July 9, 1946; Carter to Morgan, July 11, 1946, Tennessee Valley Waterways Conference Manuscript Collection.
66 Roberts, *One River—Seven States,* 36.
67 Ericson, "River Transportation," in Martin (ed.), *TVA: The First Twenty Years,* 106–107.
68 Ex-barge grain is grain transported outbound from a port by rail which has had a prior movement into that port by barge.
69 Ex-rail grain is grain transported outbound from a port by barge which has had a prior movement into that port by rail.
70 One of the three barge lines was the Arrow Transportation Company of Sheffield, Alabama. It is the largest carrier with headquarters in the valley region.
71 Roberts, *One River—Seven States,* 34.
72 Tennessee Valley Authority, *The Barge Grain Case: Its Significance to the Tennessee Valley and the Southeast* (Knoxville, 1951).
73 Roberts, *One River—Seven States,* 34.
74 *Ibid.*
75 Civil Action No. 961, Federal District Court for the Northern District of Alabama, *Arrow Transportation Company, et al.* v. *United States of America and Interstate Commerce Commission, et al.,* July 29, 1959.
76 *Ibid.,* 10.
77 *Ibid.,* 18.
78 Interview with George B. Tully, Knoxville, Tennessee, July 31, 1959.
79 The Corps of Engineers reported thirty-nine operators with a total barge capacity of 42,550 tons in 1930. *Tennessee River and Tributaries,* 34, 227–29.
80 Private carriers are those which use their own vessels or chartered vessels for carrying their own goods. Common carriers are those which offer their services to the general public for the transportation of freight, freight and passengers, or passengers alone, and usually have published freight and/or passenger rates. Contract carriers are those which contract to carry freight at rates determined by argeement and do not publish freight rate tariffs or have regular routes. According to the new provisions, some fifty-two carriers with a capacity of 1,391,234 tons were brought under ICC jurisdiction. Another 114 carriers with a capacity of 728,699 tons were exempted from ICC regulations for various reasons. Charles S. Morgan, *Problems in the Regulation of Domestic Transportation by Water: ICC Ex Parte No. 165* (Washington, 1946), 19–22, 359–65.

81 Daggett, *Principles of Inland Transportation*, 837.

82 Morgan, *Problems in the Regulation of Domestic Transportation By Water*, 134–35.

83 This procedure is followed in order to enable the ICC to determine whether or not additional competition would result in an unnecessary duplication of services and a subsequent division of revenues to such an extent that profitable operations by all concerned would be impossible. In short, the ICC, in addition to protecting the public interest, seeks to protect the carriers from each other as a result of "destructive competition." National Resources Planning Board, *Transportation and National Policy* (Washington, 1942), 451.

84 The ICC denied the following companies common carrier rights on the Tennessee River between 1943 and 1953: Arrow Transportation Company, Union Barge Lines, Upper Mississippi Towing Corporation, Central Barge Company, American Barge Lines, Commercial Barge Lines, Inc., Cumberland River Sand Company, Sioux City–New Orleans Barge Lines, Inc., and the Mississippi Valley Barge Lines. In four instances these orders have been reversed and extension of rights has been granted. See the following Interstate Commerce Commission reports: *Union Barge Line Corporation Applications for Certificate, Permit, and Exemptions, No. W-104*, CCL (1942), 249; *Tennessee Valley Sand and Gravel Company Common and Contract Carrier Application, No. W-114*, CCL (1942), 500; *Upper Mississippi Towing Corporation Common Carrier Applications, No. W-764*, CCLX (1943), 85; *Central Barge Company Applications, No. W-326*, CCLX (1944), 329; *American Barge Line Company Applications, No. W-552*, CCLX (1946), 783; *Cumberland River Sand Company, Incorporated, Common Carrier Application, No. W-534*, CCLX (1946), 734; *Mississippi Valley Barge Line Company et al. Merger, Finance Docket No. 15391*, CCLXV (1946), 53; *Commercial Barge Lines, Inc., Extension of Operations—Cincinnati, No. W-751 (Sub-No. 2)*, CCLXV (1948), 291; *Commercial Barge Lines, Inc., Extension—General Commodities, No. W-751 (Sub-No. 9)*, CCLXXXV (1953), 349; *Sioux City and New Orleans Barge Lines, Inc., Extension—Mississippi River System, No. W-431 (Sub-No. 1)*, CCLXXXV (1953), 463. Five of the above listed carriers are the largest carriers on the inland waterways. These five carriers hauled approximately 70 percent of the total tonnage of the Mississippi River and its tributaries in 1944. Interstate Commerce Commission, *Selected Financial and Operating Statistics from Annual Reports of Carriers by Water, 1944* (Washington, 1945), 10–15; hereinafter cited as *Selected Statistics of Carriers by Water, 1944*.

85 *Independent Offices Appropriations Bill, 1941*, 1631.

86 In 1956 seven common carriers had operating rights over some portions of the river. Only five of these, however, had rights to operate over the entire distance of the river. One of these carriers was in the passenger excursion business and may be eliminated, since its operations do not effect the situation. On the Ohio River in the same year, eight common carriers were in operation over the most heavily trafficked portion of that river. In this case, also, only five carriers had operating rights for the entire distance of the river. It should be remembered that in addition to the common carriers, a large number of private and contract carriers were operating on the Tennessee River. Some fifty-eight of these carriers were in operation in 1955, but many of them made only one or two trips on the river. Tennessee Valley Authority, *Barge Lines Which Operated on the Tennessee River:*

Calendar Year, 1956 (Knoxville, 1957); Tennessee Valley Authority, *Common Carriers of General Commodities on the Tennessee River and Interconnecting Inland Waterways* (Knoxville, 1955); Interstate Commerce Commission, *Transport Statistics in the United States: Carriers by Water, 1955* (Washington, 1956), Part 5, p. 39.

87 Under the provisions of the Dension Act of 1928, the Federal Barge Lines, operated by the Inland Waterways Corporation, was permitted to operate throughout the Mississippi River system, the Warrior River, and the Savannah River but was not allowed to operate on the Ohio. This limitation on its operations was put into the act at the request of Ohio Valley interests. Since the Tennessee was a tributary of the Ohio, it was, by virtue of its geographic position, excluded from the operating area of the Federal Barge Lines. Therefore, the extension of the service area of the government facility would have required congressional amendment of the Denison Act. A move in this direction was certain to arouse the opposition of both rail and water carriers in the Ohio and Tennessee valleys. This probably accounts for the hesitant position taken by the officials of the Inland Waterways Corporation. The TVA, accustomed to waging war against vested interests, obviously was willing to risk such a fight. Another obstacle may have dampened the hopes of both agencies. Even if successful legislative action had been taken, there yet remained the problem of ICC approval. Whether or not the commission would have permitted the Federal Barge Lines to operate on the Tennessee is a moot point. Knoxville *News-Sentinel,* July 10, 1941; Ferris to Carter, July 6, 1941; Carter to Ferris, July 18, 1941; Barker to Carter, March 19, 1942, Tennessee Valley Waterways Conference Manuscript Collection.

88 House Subcommittee of the Committee on Appropriations, Hearings, *Government Corporations Appropriations Bill, 1948,* 80th Congress, 1st Session (1947), 70–73; Nashville *Tennessean,* March 2, 1951; Interstate Commerce Commission, *Federal Barge Lines, Inc., Purchase, Etc., Finance Docket No. 18261,* CCLXXXV (1953), 439–49.

89 Although it was a costly operation, the Federal Barge Lines maintained a less-than-barge-load service for small shippers along the Mississippi and Warrior rivers. Extension of this service to the Tennessee would have enabled the TVA to solve one of its most difficult problems.

Chapter 5

1 American Waterways Operators, Inc., *Inland Waterways: Facts and Figures* (Washington, 1950), 9–10.

2 A very cogent and concise essay on towboat and barge improvements is that of Harry B. Dyer, "Modern Towboat and Barge Design," *Journal of the Waterways and Harbors Division of the American Society of Civil Engineers,* LXXXII (December, 1956), 1–9. Dyer lists seventeen improvements in towboats and eight changes in barge design and construction which have brought greater efficiency of operation to inland water craft and a subsequent reduction in transportation costs.

3 American Waterways Operators, Inc., *Inland Waterways: Facts and Figures,* 24.

4 *Ibid.,* 26.

5 Gilbert M. Dorland and George R. Bethurum, "Growth of Commerce: Tennessee and Cumberland Rivers," *Journal of the Waterways and Harbors Division of the American Society of Civil Engineers,* LXXXII (September, 1956), 4.

6 *Ibid.,* 5.

7 TVA, *Report and Recommendations Concerning Public Terminal Facilities for the Tennessee River System*, 2.

8 Tennessee Valley Authority, *Major Freight Landings on the Tennessee River System* (Knoxville, 1954); *Revisions to Major Freight Landings on the Tennessee River System* (Knoxville, 1955).

9 American Waterways Operators, Inc., *Inland Waterways: Facts and Figures*, 39. An excellent but somewhat out-of-date analysis of terminal improvements, trends in costs per ton of freight handled, and possible improvements in cargo-handling facilities may be found in Morgan, *Problems in the Regulation of Domestic Transportation by Water*, 292–310. Morgan reported that terminal costs per ton of freight on the Mississippi River system declined from $1.10 to $.46 between 1936 and 1944. More efficient handling of commodities by the use of mechanical devices, he reported, accounted for a portion of this reduction in costs.

10 American Waterways Operators, Inc., *New Dimensions in Transportation* (Washington, 1956), 35.

11 Bureau of the Census, *Statistical Abstract of the United States* (Washington, 1958), 566.

12 By multiplying the volume of traffic by the length of haul, one obtains the ton-mileage figures for the river. Ton-mileage figures more accurately reflect the transportation service which the stream is rendering than aggregate tonnage, since they take into account not only the volume of traffic but the length of haul as well. Department of War, Commercial Statistics: Water-Borne Commerce of the United States (*Annual Reports of the Chief of Engineers* [Washington, 1921–1951]), Part 2 (1921), 73; (1930). Department of the Army, "Waterways and Harbors: Gulf Coast, Mississippi River System, and Antilles," in Board of Engineers for Rivers and Harbors, *Waterborne Commerce of the United States* (Washington, 1957), ix.

13 Morgan, *Problems in the Regulation of Domestic Transportation By Water*, 243–44.

14 "National Summaries," in *Waterborne Commerce of the United States*, 11.

15 Morgan, *Problems in the Regulation of Domestic Transportation By Water*, 243–44.

16 ICC, *Transport Statistics in the United States: Carriers By Water, 1955*, Part 5, 39.

17 ICC, *Selected Statistics of Carriers By Water, 1944*, 10.

18 ICC, *Transport Statistics in the United States*, Part 5, p. 3.

19 The state of Illinois spent $20,000,000 in an attempt to canalize the Des Plaines and Illinois rivers before this project was turned over to the federal government. Daggett, *Principles of Inland Transportation*, 48–49.

20 Ray L. Wilbur and Arthur M. Hyde, *The Hoover Policies* (New York, 1937), 266.

21 For economical inland transportation, a 9-foot controlling depth is generally set as the standard channel. National Resources Planning Board, *Transportation and National Policy* (Washington, 1942), 51.

22 Chief of Engineers, *Annual Report* (1957), I, 30.

23 *Waterborne Commerce of the United States* (1957), Part 2, pp. 140–41, 159–60, Part 5, p. 22.

24 Full project width and depth throughout the channel were attained in November, 1952, with the completion of dredging activities below Kentucky Dam. TVA, *Annual Report* (1953), 20.

25 Vogel, "Role of the Civil Engineer in Multipurpose River Development," 435–37.

26 Ericson, "River Transportation," in Martin (ed.), *TVA: The First Twenty Years,* 99.
27 Knoxville *Journal,* December 30, 1933.
28 *Ibid.*
29 Stuart Chase, "TVA: The New Deal's Best Asset," *Nation,* CXLII (June 10, 1936), 739.
30 Chattanooga *Times,* September 20, 1933.
31 Almon E. Parkins, "The Tennessee Valley Project: Facts and Fancies," *Journal of the Tennessee Academy of Science,* VIII (October, 1933), 345–57; Fred J. Lewis, "An Engineer Looks at the Tennessee Valley Project," *Journal of the Tennessee Academy of Science,* IX (July, 1934), 167–76. Parkins was professor of economic geography at George Peabody College for Teachers, and Lewis was a member of the Civil Engineering Department at Vanderbilt University.
32 Tuscumbia (Ala.) *Times,* April 2, 1934.
33 Chattanooga *News,* October 28, 1933, May 8, 1934; Chattanooga *Times,* May 9, 1934.
34 Chairman Arthur E. Morgan's testimony before a Congressional committee in 1935 supports this conclusion. Morgan, when queried about the future prospects of navigation on the river by representatives who thought that future traffic would not justify the expense of providing a channel, made the astonishing statement, "I am not today arguing for the 9-foot channel. I am saying that Congress, in its wisdom has established [authorized] it, made it a part of our public policy." *To Amend the Tennessee Valley Authority Act,* 97.
35 *Waterborne Commerce of the United States* (1954), Part 2, ix; (1957), Part 2, p. 147.
36 TVA, *Annual Report* (1958), 22.
37 Ericson, "River Transportation," in Martin (ed.), *TVA: The First Twenty Years,* 99–101.
38 *Waterborne Commerce of the United States* (1957), Part 2, pp. 147–48.
39 TVA, *Annual Report* (1958), 54.
40 Waldorf V. Howard, *Authority in TVA Land* (Kansas City, Missouri, 1948), 52–73; Donald T. Wright, "1953 Tennessee Tonnage Equals 1960 Forecast," *Waterways Journal,* LXVIII (April 24, 1954), 4; Knoxville *Journal,* June 30, 1954.
41 Forest Crutchfield, "Paducah Outlook for 1935," *Waterways Journal,* XLVIII (December 29, 1934), 3; Forest Crutchfield, "Tennessee River," *Waterways Journal,* XLVIII (September 1, 1934), 14.
42 Nashville *Tennessean,* April 27, 1941; TVA, *Annual Report* (1941), 3.
43 Charles T. Taylor, "Transportation on the Tennessee," Sixth Federal Reserve District *Monthly Review,* XXXIV (February 29, 1949), 18.
44 *Tennessee River and Tributaries,* 230.
45 David E. Lilienthal, "Navigation on the Tennessee River: Its Effect Upon the Economic Future of the South," an address to the Southern Economic Association, Knoxville, Tennessee, November 5, 1937, in files of Tennessee Valley Authority Technical Library, Knoxville, Tennessee.
46 David E. Lilienthal, "Tenn. River Provides Big Trade Vein," *Tennessee River Journal,* I (May, 1944), 1.
47 Dorland and Bethurum, "Growth of Commerce: Tennessee and Cumberland Rivers," 5.
48 *Waterbone Commerce of the United States* (1957), Part 2, pp. 147–48.
49 *Ibid.*

50 TVA, *Annual Report* (1949), 13–14.

51 Tennessee Valley Authority, *Navigation in the Development of the Tennessee Valley* (Knoxville, 1949), 10.

52 ICC, *Selected Statistics of Carriers By Water, 1944,* p. 12.

53 ICC, *Transport Statistics in the United States,* Part 5, p. 12.

54 Interview with Howard G. King, Sheffield, Alabama, June 8, 1959.

55 *Tennessee River and Tributaries,* 226–29.

56 A list of boat operators, their equipment and services, with other pertinent information, may be found in House, Subcommittee of the Committee on Appropriations, Hearings, *Independent Offices Appropriations Bill, 1940,* 76th Congress, 1st Session (1938–1939), 1743–44.

57 TVA, *Annual Report* (1937), 5–11.

58 TVA, *Navigation Conditions on the Tennessee River,* 8–10. This document, which described channel conditions, river traffic, terminal facilities, and carrier service on the river in 1941, represents the TVA's endeavors to supply water-transportation firms and shippers with information about the merits of the improved river.

59 The towboat fleet remained constant in number, but increased towing capacity resulted from more powerful engines and greater operating efficiency provided by slack-water navigation. Therefore, the actual number of boats in operation is not a perfect index to the development of carrier facilities on the river.

60 TVA, *Navigation Conditions on the Tennessee River,* 13–15; Department of War, Board of Engineers for Rivers and Harbors, *Transportation Lines on the Mississippi River System and the Gulf Intracoastal Waterway, 1941* (Washington, 1941), 120–22; hereinafter cited as *Transportation Lines on the Mississippi River System.*

61 TVA, *Navigation Conditions on the Tennessee River,* 13–51. Comprehensive common-carrier service as used here means that barge-line companies will handle any size shipment offered by shippers at a nondiscriminatory freight rate. While many carriers are classified as common carriers, most do not accept less than barge-load lots; and, even though their tariffs imply that lesser loads will be accepted, the special rates granted on barge-load shipments effectively discourage movements of lesser proportions. This situation has constituted, in the past and at present, a major obstacle to the use of river transportation by small shippers. Taylor, "Transportation on the Tennessee," 18; Chattanooga *Times,* May 10, 1949; Interstate Commerce Commission, *Commercial Barge Lines, Inc., Extension—General Commodities, No. W-751 (Sub-No. 9),* CCLXXXV (1953), 356–57.

62 *Transportation Lines on the Mississippi River System,* 179–87, 270–72; District Engineer's Office, Corps of Engineers, *List of Commercial Operators Operating on the Tennessee River, 1956* (Nashville, 1956); District Engineer's Office, Corps of Engineers, *List of Commercial Operators Operating on the Tennessee River, 1959* (Nashville, 1959).

63 Ericson, "River Transportation," in Martin (ed.), *TVA: The First Twenty Years,* 101. Lengths of haul for 1957 were obtained from *Waterborne Commerce of the United States* (1957), Part 5, p. 22.

64 TVA, *Annual Report* (1955), 19.

65 "Tennessee River Aided 14 'Outside' States," *Waterways Journal,* LXIX (July 2, 1955), 15; District Engineer's Office, Corps of Engineers, *Freight Traffic, Tennessee River, 1954* (Nashville).

66 TVA, *Annual Report* (1954), 5–6. The building of inland waterway vessels and sea-going merchant ships at Decatur, Alabama, during the war helped

to swell the outbound tonnage. Tennessee Valley Authority, *Tennessee River Navigation* (Knoxville, 1953), 20.

67 To illustrate: In studying the economic feasibility of proportional rail-barge rates between the Tennessee Valley and the Gulf Coast, TVA decided that "the average all-rail first class rate from Chattanooga, Tennessee, to Vicksburg, Mississippi, Baton Rouge and New Orleans, Louisiana, is $.73, and a similar computation on the basis of an average water distance of 1,316 miles between these ports produces a constructive all-water first class rate of $.88. . . ." TVA, *Prospective Commerce on the Tennessee River*, 19.

68 M. C. Dupree, "The Importance of River Transportation to the Petroleum Industry," *Waterways Journal*, LXVII (April 18, 1953), 9.

69 About one half of the petroleum supplies move from Ohio and Mississippi river points where circuity is not a significant factor in the trade exchange. The result, of course, is a greater exchange of goods between the Tennessee region and these areas, where markets for Tennessee River products exist.

70 *Waterborne Commerce of the United States* (1957), Supplement to Part 5, pp. 3–8, 15–16, 37, 45.

71 Coal from the southern Appalachian fields commands a higher price from domestic consumers than coal from midwestern fields. It is preferred by domestic consumers because of its hardness, low ash and sulphur, and low clinkering action, and because it ignites and burns with greater ease. Consumer demand, therefore, is responsible for what appears to be a "carrying coal to Newcastle" situation.

72 District Engineer's Office, Corps of Engineers, *Freight Traffic, Tennessee River, 1958* (Nashville).

73 District Engineer's Office, Corps of Engineers, *A List of the Principal Ports on the Tennessee River, 1958* (Nashville, 1958); District Engineer's Office, Corps of Engineers, *Tonnage by Locks: Tennessee River, 1958* (Nashville, 1958).

74 In its 1941 traffic survey, the TVA estimated that approximately 8 percent of the total prospective tonnage would move through public-use terminals. TVA, *Prospective Commerce on the Tennessee*, 30.

75 Tennessee Valley Authority, *Tennessee River Public-Use Tonnage, 1942–56* (Knoxville, 1957).

76 TVA, *Prospective Commerce on the Tennessee River*, 23–27; District Engineer's Office, Corps of Engineers, *Freight Traffic, Tennessee River, 1945–58* (Nashville).

77 Chattanooga *Times*, May 10, 1949.

78 ICC, *Commercial Barge Lines, Inc., Extension—General Commodities, No. W-751 (Sub-No. 9)*, CCLXXXV (1953), 349–68.

79 *Ibid.*

80 The water-freight firm maintained that trailer-barge traffic could not be transported profitably unless it was allowed to extend its barge-load traffic operating rights over an extensive area of the inland waterways. It hoped to integrate barge-load and less-than-barge-load operations and by so doing to spread transportation costs to take care of the uneconomical trailer-barge traffic. *Ibid.*, 357.

81 *Ibid.*, 362–68.

82 "To Move Iron and Steel to South By Barge," *Waterways Journal*, LXVII (August 15, 1953), 8; "Forwarder Files Answer to Railroads' Protest," *Waterways Journal*, LXVII (November 21, 1953), 8; TVA, *Annual Report* (1957), 23.

83 L. A. Parish, executive assistant to the director of the Alabama State Docks Department, to author, June 21, 1960.

84 John V. Krutilla and Otto Eckstein, *Multiple Purpose River Development: Studies in Applied Economic Analysis* (Baltimore, 1958), 170–98.

85 L. A. Parish to author, June 21, 1960; Earl M. McGowin, director, Alabama State Docks Department, to author, April 27, 1960.

86 *Ibid.*

87 TVA, *Annual Report* (1957), 23; TVA, *Major Freight Landings on the Tennessee River System,* 1–25; Clifford A. Allen, *A Program for the People of Tennessee*, political pamphlet distributed by Allen for Governor Headquarters, Nashville, 1958.

Chapter 6

1 Canalization of the river was accomplished by the construction of nine high dams and locks between Paducah, Kentucky and Knoxville, Tennessee. All of the structures except the Wilson and the Hales Bar dams were built by the TVA.

2 Gordon R. Clapp, "The Tennessee Valley Authority," in Merrill Jensen (ed.), *Regionalism in America* (Madison, 1952), 320.

3 Senate, Subcommittee of the Committee on Public Works, Hearings, *Revenue Bond Financing by TVA,* 86th Congress, 1st Session (1959), 107.

4 J. Porter Taylor, director, TVA Division of Navigation, to author, September 4, 1964.

5 John V. Krutilla, "Industrial Development of the Tennessee River," (unpublished study in files of Government Relations and Economics Staff, Tennessee Valley Authority, Knoxville, 1955), 3–18.

6 Interstate Commerce Commission, *Grain in Multiple Car Shipments—River Crossings to the South,* "Statement of J. Porter Taylor," ICC I and S Docket No. 7656, April 4, 1962, p. 16.

7 J. Porter Taylor, "Navigation: A Tool in Industrial Development," speech before the Tennessee Valley Public Power Association, Nashville, Tennessee, April 17, 1958, in files of Tennessee Valley Authority Technical Library, Knoxville, Tennessee.

8 The Tennessee Eastman Corporation of Kingsport, Tennessee, has effectively bargained with rail carriers and secured concessions. The Eastman Corporation and the Aluminum Company of America own waterfront terminal sites but have not found it necessary to build such facilities. Information office, Tennessee Valley Authority, *River Traffic and Industrial Growth* (Knoxville, 1962), 15.

9 Krutilla, "Industrial Development of the Tennessee River," 11.

10 Rail carriers quote a special rate on a particular shipment or on a given commodity which moves or could move more economically by water between certain points. A blanket rate would apply to an entire section or area and to one or several commodities moving between territories which are close to a commercially navigable stream. A thorough discussion of railroad tactics used to prevent utilization of water transportation by shippers may be found in Senate, Subcommittee on Surface Transportation of the Committee on Interstate and Foreign Commerce, Hearings, *Problems of Railroads,* 85th Congress, 2nd Session (1958), 1205–17.

11 D. Phillip Locklin, *Economics of Transportation* (Rev. 3rd. ed.; Chicago, 1947), 195–99, 534–41.

12 Clifton T. Barker, "Barge Delivery of Coal to TVA Steam Plants," *Waterways,* XVI (January, 1953), 11.

13 *Ibid.*, 11–17.

14 John R. P. Friedmann, "Industrial Opportunities on the Tennessee River," (unpublished study in files of Government Relations and Economics Staff, Tennessee Valley Authority, Knoxville, 1954), 4–9.

15 John R. P. Friedmann, *The Spatial Structure of Economic Development in the Tennessee Valley* (Chicago, 1955), 134.

16 TVA, *River Traffic and Industrial Growth* (Knoxville, 1959), 6.

17 Barker, "Developments in Tennessee River Navigation," 32.

18 TVA, *River Traffic and Industrial Growth* (1962), 7–8.

19 Huntsville, Alabama is located eleven miles from the river's edge, but industrial development has occurred along the river adjacent to Huntsville. The use made of the river by these installations near Huntsville tends to make that city a river-oriented center, and it should be regarded as a port.

20 "Linkages may be of several kinds. They may consist, for example, of related technical processes: in the use of the same raw materials; in the employment of the same kind of skilled labor; in one industry using as its raw materials the finished products of another industry; or in an ancillary industry providing special services for the main industry." Friedmann, *The Spatial Structure of Economic Development in the Tennessee Valley,* 35.

21 TVA, *River Traffic and Industrial Growth* (1962), 8–9.

22 Friedmann, *The Spatial Structure of Economic Development in the Tennessee Valley,* 35.

23 The tri-cities are Florence, Sheffield, and Tuscumbia, Alabama.

24 TVA, *River Traffic and Industrial Growth* (1962), 8–12.

25 Taylor, "Navigation: A Tool in Industrial Development"; TVA, *Annual Report* (1958), 24. A recent appraisal of the importance of navigation to Chattanooga concluded: "The river is regarded as one of Chattanooga's most important assets in attracting new industry, both for the lower-cost transportation it provides and as a source of processing water. Most of the large plants locating here in recent years have been adjacent to the waterway." Chattanooga *Times,* June 23, 1959.

26 "Bowaters Offers Farmers Bigger Pulpwood Market," *Tennessee Conservationist,* XXII (December, 1956), 10–11; Ericson, "River Transportation," in Martin (ed.), *TVA: The First Twenty Years,* 100–101.

27 TVA, *River Traffic and Industrial Growth* (1962), 14.

28 Friedmann, *The Spatial Structure of Economic Development in the Tennessee Valley,* 42–43, 132–36.

29 York Willbern, *Cities and Riverfront Lands* (University, Alabama, 1947), 7–10.

30 Shelton, *The Decatur Story,* 2–7; Howard K. Menhenick, "Local Riverfront Development," *American City,* LXV (November, 1950), 85; Stefan H. Robock, "Industry Comes to the Tennessee Valley," an address to the Beta Gamma Sigma Fraternity, University of Tennessee Chapter, Knoxville, Tennessee, April 29, 1952, in files of Tennessee Valley Authority Technical Library, Knoxville, Tennessee; Commonwealth of Kentucky, Agricultural and Industrial Development Board, *The Chemical Century Comes to Calvert City* (Frankfort, Kentucky, 1953), 1–32; Huntsville (Ala.) *Times,* December 23, 1954.

31 Davidson, *The Tennessee,* II, 284.

32 TVA, *Annual Report* (1949), 14.

33 Clifton T. Barker, "Developments in Tennessee River Navigation," *Waterways,* XVII (August, 1953), 33; TVA, *River Traffic and Industrial Growth* (1962), 15.

34 *Revenue Bond Financing by TVA,* 106–107.
35 *Ibid.,* 108.
36 *Problems of Railroads,* 1163.
37 Taylor, "Navigation: A Tool in Industrial Development."
38 Robock, "Industry Comes to the Tennessee Valley."
39 "Tennessee Valley Governors Tell of Bright Future," *Tennessee Valley Industrialist,* I (January, 1946), 12–13; Thomas L. Bailey, "Balancing Agriculture with Industry," *Tennessee Valley Industrialist,* I (March, 1946), 14–15. Bailey was governor of Mississippi at the time this article was written.
40 An appraisal of TVA's agricultural program is Norman I. Wengert, *Valley of Tomorrow: The TVA and Agriculture* ("University of Tennessee Record: Extension Series," XXVIII [Knoxville, 1952]). Wengert argues that TVA's agricultural program has been too narrowly confined to its phosphatic fertilizer activities. He feels that many of the more serious problems of valley agriculture have been slighted as a result of TVA's preoccupation with the use of phosphate as a cure-all for agricultural problems of the valley farmer. Wengert, *Valley of Tomorrow,* 136–37. A rosier view of the results of TVA's agricultural program is presented by Leland G. Allbaugh, "Fertilizer-Munitions and Agriculture," in Roscoe C. Martin (ed.), *TVA: The First Twenty Years,* 171–74.
41 Allbaugh, "Fertilizer-Munitions and Agriculture," in Martin (ed.), *TVA: The First Twenty Years,* 172.
42 *Ibid.,* 172–73.
43 David E. Lilienthal, "Navigation on the Tennessee River: Its Effect Upon the Economic Future of the South," speech before the Southern Economic Association, Knoxville, Tennessee, November 5, 1937, in files of Tennessee Valley Authority Technical Library, Knoxville, Tennessee.
44 TVA, *Annual Report* (1937), 44–45; W. C. Lepper, "Refrigerator Barge Meets with Unusually Bad Luck," *Waterways Journal,* LXIX (August 20, 1955), 14.
45 Howard, *Authority in TVA Land,* 68.
46 *Southeastern Association of Railroad and Utilities Commissioners, et al.* v. *Atchison, Topeka and Sante Fe Railway Company, et al.,* Ford K. Edwards, "The Economy of the South," Exhibit 532, Interstate Commerce Commission Docket No. 31874 (1958), 38–47; hereinafter cited as Edwards, "The Economy of the South."
47 *Ibid.,* 13.
48 *Supra,* 42.
49 Edwards, "The Economy of the South," 8.
50 *Ibid.,* 13–24.
51 "Brief of the Intervener—TVA," ICC Docket No. 30774, May 1, 1954, p. 26.
52 Robert W. Williams, "Hall County and the Poultry Industry," *Georgia Business,* XV (October, 1955), 6.
53 "Barges and Broilers," *Broiler Industry,* XXII (May, 1959), 9.
54 The area of the South which could obtain substantial reductions on the price of grain barged from the Midwest includes the northern parts of Mississippi, Alabama, Georgia, the Western portion of South Carolina, extreme Western North Carolina, and Middle and Eastern Tennessee. Since, however, joint rail-barge rates have not been effected for the entire area, a much smaller region actually is benefitted. Only 39,000 miles of an area of 73,000 square miles receive Midwest grain at a reduced price be-

cause of lower transportation costs. TVA, *The Barge Grain Case: Its Significance to the Tennessee Valley and the Southeast,* 8–11.

55 "Barges and Broilers," 8.

56 District Engineer's Office, Corps of Engineers, *Tennessee River Waterborne Commerce, 1958* (Nashville, 1959), 1.

57 TVA, *Annual Report* (1961), 28.

58 "Barges and Broilers," 8.

59 *Ibid.*

60 Decatur (Ala.) *Daily,* May 28, 1959.

61 Edison H. Thomas, "No. 200 to Guntersville," *The L and N Employee Magazine,* XXXV (June, 1959), 7.

62 "Statement of J. Porter Taylor," ICC I and S Docket No. 7656, April 4, 1962, p. 16.

63 Thomas, "No. 200 to Guntersville," 8.

64 W. T. McAllister, "Labor Plus Water: Big Edge," *Broiler Industry,* XXII (June, 1959), 16.

65 Interstate Commerce Commission, ICC I and S Docket No. 7656, April 4, 1962, p. 16.

66 McAllister, "Labor Plus Water: Big Edge," 16.

67 "Barges and Broilers," 8.

68 Williams, "Hall County and the Poultry Industry," 6.

69 McAllister, "Labor Plus Water: Big Edge, " 16.

70 "Barges and Broilers," 9.

71 "Brief of the Intervener—TVA," Interstate Commerce Commission Docket No. 30774, May 1, 1954, p. 25.

72 Edwards, "The Economy of the South," 14.

73 "Brief of the Intervener—TVA," Interstate Commerce Commission Docket No. 30744, May 1, 1954, p. 26.

74 Decatur (Ala.) *Daily,* May 28, 1959.

BIBLIOGRAPHY

TENNESSEE VALLEY AUTHORITY

Unpublished Materials

Executive Order No. 6162, June 8, 1933, in minute files of Tennessee Valley Authority Board, Knoxville, Tennessee.

Carl A. Bock. Office Memorandum to Board of Directors (June 30, 1934), in minute files of Tennessee Valley Authority Board, Knoxville.

Lilienthal, David E. "Principles Governing Dam Building Program," Office Memorandum to Board of Directors (October 9, 1934), in minute files (Entry Number 10–12–34a) of Tennessee Valley Authority Board, Knoxville.

———. Speech before the Shelby County (Tennessee) Young Democratic Club, Memphis, Tennessee (October 20, 1934), in files of Tennessee Valley Authority Technical Library, Knoxville.

———. "Navigation on the Tennessee River: Its Effect Upon the Economic Future of the South." Speech before the Southern Economic Association, Knoxville (November 5, 1937), in files of Tennessee Valley Authority Technical Library, Knoxville.

Pope, James P. "Tennessee River Terminal Development." Speech before organizational meeting of the Tennessee Valley Waterways Conference, Chattanooga, Tennessee (June 28, 1940), in files of Tennessee Valley Authority Technical Library, Knoxville.

Lilienthal, David E. "The Tennessee River Goes to Town." Speech before Atlanta, Georgia, Rotary Club (October 6, 1941), in files of Tennessee Valley Authority Technical Library, Knoxville.

Pope, James P. "The Tennessee Waterway Moves On." Speech before Chattanooga, Tennessee, Kiwanis Club (June 30, 1942), in files of Tennessee Valley Authority Technical Library, Knoxville.

"Provision and Management of Public-Use River Terminal" (Program Authorization No. 2, June, 1943), in minute files of Tennessee Valley Authority Board, Knoxville.

Robock, Stefan H. "Industry Comes to the Tennessee Valley." Speech before the Beta Gamma Sigma Fraternity, University of Tennessee Chapter, Knoxville (April 29, 1952), in files of Tennessee Valley Authority Technical Library, Knoxville.

Friedmann, John R. P. "Industrial Opportunities on the Tennessee River," a study of water-front sites and industrial use of the Tennessee River, Knoxville, 1954, in files of Government Relations and Economics Staff, Tennessee Valley Authority, Knoxville.

Krutilla, John V. "Industrial Development of the Tennessee River," a study of the locational factors in the industrialization of the river and utilization of the river by industry, Knoxville, 1955, in files of Government Relations and Economics Staff, Tennessee Valley Authority, Knoxville.

Taylor, J. Porter. "Navigation: A Tool in Industrial Development." Speech before the Tennessee Valley Public Power Association, Nashville, Tennessee (April 17, 1958), in files of Tennessee Valley Authority Technical Library, Knoxville.

Published Materials

Board of Directors

Annual Reports, 1934–1958, Washington, D.C., 1934–1958.

Report to the Congress on the Unified Development of the Tennessee River System, Knoxville, 1936.

Commerce Department

Report and Recommendations Concerning Public Terminal Facilities for the Tennessee River System. Knoxville, 1939.

Navigation Conditions on the Tennessee River. Knoxville, 1941.

Prospective Commerce on the Tennessee River. Knoxville, 1941.

Proposed Tennessee River Terminals at Knoxville, Chattanooga, Guntersville, and Decatur. Knoxville, 1942.

Director of Information

Cheaper Transportation Via the Tennessee River. Knoxville, 1946.

Shelton, Barrett. *The Decatur Story.* Knoxville, 1949.

Tennessee River Navigation. Knoxville, 1953.

A Short History of the Tennessee Valley Authority, 1933–1956. Knoxville, 1956.

River Traffic and Industrial Growth. Knoxville, 1959.

River Traffic and Industrial Growth. Knoxville, 1962.

Division of Navigation and Local Flood Relations

Major Freight Landings on the Tennessee River System. Knoxville, 1954.

Common Carriers of General Commodities on the Tennessee River and Interconnecting Inland Waterways, December 31, 1955. Knoxville, 1955.

Revisions to Major Freight Landings on the Tennessee River System. Knoxville, 1955.

Tennessee River Navigation Costs and Benefits. Knoxville, 1956.

Barge Lines Which Operated on the Tennessee River: Calendar Year, 1956. Knoxville, 1957.

Tennessee River Public-Use Tonnage, 1942–56. Knoxville, 1957.

Division of Regional Studies

Navigation in the Development of the Tennessee Valley. Knoxville, 1949.

The Barge Grain Case: Its Significance to the Tennessee Valley and the Southeast. Knoxville, 1951.

Divisions of Engineering and Construction

Design of Tennessee Valley Authority Projects: Civil and Structural Design. 3 vols. Technical Report No. 24, Washington, D.C., 1952.

Engineering Data: TVA Water Control Projects. 2 vols. Technical Monograph No. 55, Knoxville, 1954.

OTHER UNPUBLISHED MATERIALS

Tennessee Valley Waterways Conference (1940–1946)

Correspondence of Officers and Members

Minutes of Meetings

Copies of Proposed Legislative Bills Concerning the Organization of a Tennessee River Terminal Authority

Program of Meetings

Miscellaneous Documents Pertaining to Terminals on the Tennessee River

Tennessee Valley Authority Reports of Proposed Terminal at Chattanooga, Tennessee

McGowin, Earl M., director, Alabama State Docks Department, to author, April 27, 1960.

Parish, L. A., executive assistant to the director of the Alabama State Docks Department, to author, June 21, 1960.

INTERVIEWS

Barker, Clifton T., Navigation Consultant, Division of Navigation and Local Flood Relations, Tennessee Valley Authority, Knoxville, July 12, 1957.

Carter, Earl P., former president of the Tennessee Valley Waterways Conference, Chattanooga, August, 1957.

King, Howard G., vice-president of Arrow Transportation Company, Sheffield, Alabama, June 9, 1959.

Neely, Vanus P., Navigation Supervisor, Corps of Engineers, Nashville, April 10, 1957, July, 1958, July, 1959.

Taylor, J. Porter, Director, Division of Navigation and Local Flood Control, Tennessee Valley Authority, Knoxville, July, 1959.

Tully, George B., Transportation Economist, Navigation Economics Branch, Tennessee Valley Authority, Knoxville, July 31, 1959.

GOVERNMENT PUBLICATIONS

General

Congressional Record, 57th Congress through 76th Congress (1903–1964).

United States Statutes at Large, XVI (1869–1871), XXVI (1889–1891), XXVIII (1893–1895), XXXIV (1905–1907), XXXVII (1911–1913), XL (1917–1919), XLVI (1929–1931), XLVIII (1933–1934), XLIX (1935–1936).

United States House of Representatives

Documents

Report on the Examination and Survey of the Tennessee River, House Executive Doc. 271, 40th Congress, 2nd Session (1868).

Tennessee River and Tributaries: North Carolina, Tennessee, Alabama, and Kentucky. House Doc. 328, 71st Congress, 2nd Session (1930).

Message from the President Requesting Legislation to Create a Tennessee Valley Authority, House Doc. 15, 73rd Congress, 1st Session (1933).

A History of Navigation on the Tennessee River System, House Doc. 254, 75th Congress, 1st Session (1937).

The Interterritorial Freight Rate Problem in the United States, House Doc. 264, 75th Congress, 1st Session (1937).

Supplemental Phases of the Interterritorial Freight Rate Problem of the United States, House Doc. 271, 76th Congress, 1st Session (1939).

Regionalized Freight Rates: Barriers to National Productiveness, House Doc. 137, 78th Congress, 1st Session (1943).

Hearings

Additional Appropriations for Emergency Purposes. Hearings before the Subcommittee of the Committee on Appropriations, 73rd Congress, 2nd Session (1934).

To Amend the Tennessee Valley Authority Act. Hearings before the Committee on Military Affairs on H.R. 6876, 6793, 6774, 4676, 2865, 74th Congress, 1st Session (1935).

To Amend the Tennessee Valley Authority Act of 1933. Hearings before the Subcommittee of the Committee on Military Affairs, 76th Congress, 1st Session (1939).

Independent Offices Appropriations Bill, 1939. Hearings before the Subcommittee of the Committee on Appropriations, 75th Congress, 2nd Session (1937).

Independent Offices Appropriations Bill, 1939. Hearings before the Subcommittee of the Committee on Appropriations, 76th Congress, 1st Session (1938–1939).

Independent Offices Appropriations Bill, 1939. Hearings before the Subcommittee of the Committee on Appropriations, 76th Congress, 3rd Session (1939).

Independent Offices Appropriations Bill, 1943. Hearings before the Subcommittee of the Committee on Appropriations, 77th Congress, 2nd Session (1942).

Independent Offices Appropriations Bill, 1945. Hearings before the Subcommittee of the Committee on Appropriations, 78th Congress, 2nd Session (1943).

Government Corporations Appropriations Bill, 1948. Hearings before the Subcommittee of the Committee on Appropriations, 80th Congress, 1st Session (1947).

Public Works Appropriations Bill, 1956. Hearings before the Subcommittee of the Committee on Appropriations, 84th Congress, 1st Session (1955).

Reports

House and Senate Conference Committee, *Second Deficiency Appropriations Bill, Fiscal Year, 1935*. H. Rep. 1715, 74th Congress, 1st Session (1935).

House Subcommittee of the Committee on Appropriations, *Second Deficiency Appropriations Bill, Fiscal Year, 1935*, H. Rep. 1261 to accompany H.R. 8554, 74th Congress, 1st Session (1935).

United States Senate

Documents

National Conservation Commission, *Report of the National Conservation Commission.* Senate Doc. 676, 60th Congress, 2nd Session (1909).
Joint Committee on the Investigation of the Tennessee Valley Authority, *Report of the Joint Committee Investigating the Tennessee Valley Authority,* Senate Doc. 56, 76th Congress, 1st Session (1939).
History of Appropriations Made by the Congress of the United States for the Tennessee Valley Authority: Also History of Funds for the Development of the Tennessee River, Senate Doc. 35, 79th Congress, 1st Session (1945).

Hearings

Second Deficiency Appropriations Bill, Fiscal Year, 1935. Hearings before the Subcommittee of the Committee on Appropriations, 74th Congress, 1st Session (1935).
Making an Additional Appropriation for TVA for Fiscal Year 1941: To Provide Facilities to Expedite the National Defense. Hearings before the Subcommittee of the Committee on Appropriations, 76th Congress, 3rd Session (1940).
Independent Offices Appropriations Bill, 1944. Hearings before the Subcommittee of the Committee on Appropriations, 78th Congress, 1st Session (1943).
Independent Offices Appropriations Bill, 1946. Hearings before the Subcommittee of the Committee on Appropriations, 79th Congress, 1st Session (1945).
Problems of Railroads. Hearings before the Subcommittee on Surface Transportation of the Committee on Interstate and Foreign Commerce, 85th Congress, 2nd Session (1958).
Revenue Bond Financing by TVA. Hearings before the Subcommittee of the Committee on Public Works, 86th Congress, 1st Session (1959).

Reports

Senate Subcommittee of the Committee on Appropriations, *Second Deficiency Appropriations Bill, Fiscal Year, 1935.* S. Rep. 1085 to accompany H.R. 8554, 74th Congress, 1st Session (1935).

Joint Committees

Hearings

Investigation of the Tennessee Valley Authority, Hearings before the Joint Committee to Investigate the Tennessee Valley Authority, 75th Congress, 3rd Session (1938).

Chief Executive

The Budget for the Fiscal Year Ending June 30, 1936. Washington, D.C., 1935.
Transportation and National Policy. National Resources Planning Board, Washington, D.C., 1942.
Report of the President's Water Resources Policy Commission. 3 vols. Washington, D.C., 1950.

Department of Commerce

Statistical Abstract of the United States. Bureau of the Census, Washington, D.C., 1958.

Department of the Treasury

Aids to Navigation Regulations. United States Coast Guard, Washington, D.C., 1953.

Department of War

Annual Reports of the Chief of Engineers. United States Army, Washington, D.C., 1876–1955.

Freight Traffic: Tennessee River, 1937–1958. Corps of Engineers, Nashville: District Engineer's Office, 1937–1959 (mimeographed).

Transportation Lines on the Mississippi River System and the Gulf Intracoastal Waterway, 1941. Board of Engineers for Rivers and Harbors, Washington, D.C., 1941.

Waterborne Commerce of the United States, Parts 2 and 5. Board of Engineers for Rivers and Harbors, Washington, D.C., 1954–1957.

List of Commercial Operators on the Tennessee River, 1956, 1959. Corps of Engineers, Nashville: District Engineer's Office 1956, 1959 (mimeographed).

A List of the Principal Ports on the Tennessee River, 1958. Corps of Engineers, Nashville: District Engineer's Office, 1958 (mimeographed).

Tonnage By Locks: Tennessee River, 1958. Corps of Engineers, Nashville: District Engineer's Office, 1958.

Tennessee River Waterborne Commerce, 1958. Corps of Engineers, United States Army, Nashville: District Engineer's Office, 1959.

Interstate Commerce Commission

Tennessee Valley Sand and Gravel Company Common and Contract Carrier Application, No. W-114. CCL, 1942.

Union Barge Line Corporation Applications for Certificate, Permit, and Exemptions, No. W-104. CCL, 1942.

Upper Mississippi Towing Corporation Common Carrier Applications, No. W-764. CCLX, 1943.

Central Barge Company Applications, No. W-326. CCLX, 1944.

American Barge Line Company Applications, No. W-552. CCLX, 1946.

Cumberland River Sand Company, Incorporated, Common Carrier Application, No. W-534. CCLX, 1946.

Mississippi Valley Barge Line Company et al. Merger, Finance Docket No. 15391. CCLXV, 1946.

Commercial Barge Lines, Inc., Extension of Operations—Cincinnati, No. W-751 (Sub-No. 2). CCLXV, 1948.

Commercial Barge Lines, Inc., Extension—General Commodities, No. W-751 (Sub-No. 9). CCLXXXV, 1953.

Federal Barge Lines, Inc., Purchase, Etc., Finance Docket No. 18261. CCLXXXV, 1953.

Sioux City and New Orleans Barge Lines, Inc., Extension—Mississippi River System, No. W-431 (Sub-No. 1). CCLXXXV, 1953.

Selected Financial and Operating Statistics from Annual Reports of Carriers by Water, 1944. Bureau of Transport Economics and Statistics, Washington, D.C., 1945.

Charles S. Morgan, *Problems in the Regulation of Domestic Transportation by Water: ICC Ex Parte No. 165.* Washington, D.C., 1946.

American Barge Line Company et al. v. *The Alabama Great Southern Railroad Company, et al.,* "Brief of the Intervener: Tennessee Valley Authority," ICC Docket No. 30774, 1954.

Transport Statistics in the United States: Carriers by Water, 1955. Bureau of Transport Economics and Statistics, Washington, D.C., 1956.

Southeastern Association of the Railroad and Utilities Commissioners, et al. v. *Atchison, Topeka and Santa Fe Railway Company, et al.*, Ford K. Edwards, "The Economy of the South," Exhibit 532, ICC Docket No. 31874, 1958.

Grain in Multiple Car Shipments—River Crossings to the South. "Statement of J. Porter Taylor," ICC I and S Docket No. 7656, April 4, 1962, p. 16.

LEGAL CASES

Ashwander et al. v. *Tennessee Valley Authority*. 9 Federal Supplement, 965 (Northern District of Alabama, 1935).

Tennessee Electric Power Companies v. *Tennessee Valley Authority*. "Transcript of Record," 7 vols. Washington, D.C.: Judd and Detweiler, Inc., Printers, 1938.

Tennessee Electric Power Companies v. *Tennessee Valley Authority*. 21 Federal Supplement 847 (Eastern District of Tennessee, 1938).

Tennessee Electric Power Companies v. *Tennessee Valley Authority*, 306 U.S. 118 (1939).

Arrow Transportation Company, et al. v. *United States of America and Interstate Commerce Commission, et al.* Civil Action No. 961 (Northern District of Alabama, 1959).

BOOKS

American Waterways Operators, Inc. *Inland Waterways: Facts and Figures*. Washington: American Waterways Operators, Inc., 1950.

American Waterways Operators, Inc. *New Dimensions in Transportation*. Washington: American Waterways Operators, Inc., 1956.

Campbell, Thomas J. *The Upper Tennessee*. Chattanooga: privately printed, 1932.

Daggett, Stuart. *Principles of Inland Transportation*. Rev. 3rd. ed. New York: Harper and Brothers, 1941.

Davidson, Donald. *The Tennessee*. 2 vols. New York: Rinehart and Company, Inc., 1946–1948.

Duffus, Robert L. *The Valley and Its People: A Portrait of TVA*. New York: Alfred A. Knopf, 1946.

Eriksson, Erik M. and Trent H. Steele. *Constitutional Basis for Judging the New Deal*. Rosemead, California: Rosemead Review Press, 1936.

Finer, Herman. *The TVA: Lessons for International Application*. Montreal: International Labour Office, 1944.

Folmsbee, Stanley J. *Sectionalism and Internal Improvements in Tennessee*. Knoxville: East Tennessee Historical Society, 1939.

Friedmann, John R. P. *The Spatial Structure of Economic Development in the Tennessee Valley*. Chicago: University of Chicago Press, 1955.

Hamer, Philip. *Tennessee: A History*. 4 vols. New York: American Historical Society, Inc., 1933.

Howard, Waldorf V. *Authority in TVA Land*. Kansas City, Missouri: Frank Glenn Publishing Company, Inc., 1948.

Hubbard, Preston J. *Origins of the TVA: The Muscle Shoals Controversy, 1920–1932*. Nashville, Vanderbilt University Press, 1961.

Jensen, Merrill (ed.). *Regionalism in America*. Madison, 1952.

Joubert, William H. *Southern Freight Rates in Transition*. Gainesville, Florida: University of Florida Press, 1949.

Krutilla, John V. and Otto Eckstein. *Multiple Purpose River Development:*

Studies in Applied Economic Analysis. Baltimore: Johns Hopkins Press, 1958.

Lilienthal, David E. *The Journals of David E. Lilienthal: The TVA Years, 1939–1945*. New York: Harper and Row, 1964.

Lilienthal, David E. *The Widening of Economic Opportunity Through TVA*. Washington: Government Printing Office, 1940.

Locklin, D. Philip. *Economics of Transportation*. Rev. 3rd. ed. Chicago: R. D. Irwin, Inc., 1947.

Martin, Roscoe C. (ed.). *TVA: The First Twenty Years*. Knoxville: University of Alabama and University of Tennessee Press, 1956.

Martin, William E. *Internal Improvements in Alabama*. ("Johns Hopkins University Studies in Historical and Political Science," Vol. XX.) Baltimore: Johns Hopkins University Press, 1902.

Ransmeier, Joseph S. *The Tennessee Valley Authority: A Case Study in the Economics of Multiple Purpose Stream Planning*. Nashville: Vanderbilt University Press, 1942.

Roberts, Elliott. *One River—Seven States: TVA-State Relation in the Development of the Tennessee River*. Knoxville: The Bureau of Public Administration of the University of Tennessee, 1955.

Scott, Thomas A. *River and Harbor Improvements: How They Are Initiated, Authorized, and Completed*. New York: Press of Joseph D. McGuire, 1938.

Wengert, Norman I. *Valley of Tomorrow: The TVA and Agriculture* ("University of Tennessee Record: Extension Series," XXVIII.) Knoxville: Bureau of Public Administration, University of Tennessee, 1952.

Wilbur, Ray L. and Arthur M. Hyde. *The Hoover Policies*. New York: Charles Scribners' Sons, 1937.

Willbern, York. *Cities and Riverfront Lands*. University, Alabama: University of Alabama Bureau of Public Administration, 1947.

MISCELLANEOUS

Commonwealth of Kentucky, Agricultural and Industrial Development Board. *The Chemical Century Comes to Calvert City*. Frankfort, Kentucky, 1953.

Allen, Clifford A. *A Program for the People of Tennessee*. Nashville: Allen for Governor Headquarters, 1958.

ARTICLES IN PERIODICALS

Bailey, Thomas L. "Balancing Agriculture with Industry," *Tennessee Valley Industrialist*, I (March, 1946), 14–15.

"Barges and Broilers," *Broiler Industry*, XXII (May, 1959), 8–10.

Barker, Clifton T. "Barge Delivery of Coal to TVA Steam Plants," *Waterways*, XVI (January, 1953), 11–17.

———. "Developments in Tennessee River Navigation," *Waterways*, XVII (July, 1953), 13–16, 32.

———. "Navigation on the Tennessee River," *Engineering News-Record*, CXXXVI, Part I (February 21, 1946), 285–88; Part II (March 7, 1946), 351–54.

"Bowaters Offers Farmers Bigger Pulpwood Market," *Tennessee Conservationist*, XXII (December, 1956), 10–11.

Carter, Earl P. "The Need for a Consistent Federal Policy Toward Use of the Inland Waterway Resources of the U.S.," *Waterways Progress*, II (June, 1945), 6, 8.

Chase, Stuart. "TVA: The New Deal's Best Asset," *Nation*, CXLII (June 10, 1936), 738–41.

Crutchfield, Forest. "Paducah Outlook for 1935," *Waterways Journal,* XLVIII (December 29, 1934), 3.

———. "Tennessee River," *Waterways Journal,* XLVIII (September 1, 1934), 14.

Dorland, Gilbert M., and George R. Bethurum. "Growth of Commerce: Tennessee and Cumberland Rivers," *Journal of the Waterways and Harbors Division of the American Society of Civil Engineers,* LXXXII (September, 1956), 1–17.

Dupree, M. C. "The Importance of River Transportation to the Petroleum Industry," *Waterways Journal,* LXVII (April 18, 1953), 9.

Dyer, Harry B. "Modern Towboat and Barge Design," *Journal of the Waterways and Harbors Division of the American Society of Civil Engineers,* LXXXII (December, 1956), 1–9.

"Forwarder Files Answer to Railroads' Protest," *Waterways Journal,* LXVII (November 21, 1953), 8.

"Guntersville Dedication," *Tennessee River Journal,* I (November, 1943), 2.

Henry, S. T. "No Present Need For Completion of Dam No. 3 on the Tennessee," *Engineering News-Record,* CXL (November 2, 1933), 537.

Holt, Albert C. "Economic and Social Beginnings of Tennessee," *Tennessee Historical Magazine,* VII (January, 1922), 297–98.

Hunger, M. F. "U.S. Coast Guard on the Tennessee River," *Tennessee River Journal,* II (September, 1944), 5.

"Kentucky Dam Opening Expected September 15," *Tennessee River Journal,* II (September, 1944), 5.

Lepper, W. C. "Refrigerator Barge Meets With Unusually Bad Luck," *Waterways Journal,* XLIX (August 20, 1955), 14.

Lewis, Fred J. "An Engineer Looks at the Tennessee Valley Project," *Journal of the Tennessee Academy of Science,* IX (July, 1934), 167–76.

Lilienthal, David E. "Tenn. River Provides Big Trade Vein," *Tennessee River Journal,* I (May, 1944), 1.

McAllister, W. T. "Labor Plus Water: Big Edge," *Broiler Industry,* XXII (June, 1959), 16.

Menhenick, Howard K. "Local Riverfront Development," *American City,* LXV (November, 1950), 83–85.

"Ohio Valley Improvement Association Opposes TVA Control Over Ohio River Valley," *Waterways Journal,* L (April 11, 1936), 7.

Parkins, Almon E. "The Tennessee Valley Project: Facts and Fancies," *Journal of the Tennessee Academy of Science,* VIII (October, 1933), 345–57.

Pritchett, Herman. "The Development of the Tennessee Valley Authority Act," *Tennessee Law Review,* XV (February, 1938), 128–41.

Swidler, Joseph C., and Robert H. Marquis. "TVA in Court: A Study of TVA's Constitutional Litigation," *Iowa Law Review,* XXXII (January, 1947), 296–326.

Taylor, Charles T. "Transportation on the Tennessee," Sixth Federal Reserve District (Atlanta, Georgia), *Monthly Review,* XXXIV (February 29, 1949), 13–19.

"Tennessee River Aided 14 'Outside' States," *Waterways Journal,* LXIX (July 2, 1955), 15.

"Tennessee Valley Governors Tell of Bright Future," *Tennessee Valley Industrialist,* I (January, 1946), 12–13.

Thomas, Edison H. "No. 200 to Guntersville," *The L and N Employee Magazine,* XXXV (June, 1959), 6–9.

"To Move Iron and Steel South by Barge," *Waterways Journal*, LXVII (August 15, 1953), 8.

"2500 Persons Gather for Opening River Terminal in Tennessee City," *Tennessee River Journal*, I (February, 1944), 1, 6.

Vivian, Charles H. "Remaking the Tennessee Valley," *Compressed Air Magazine*, XXXIX (August, 1934), 4487–4514.

Vogel, Herbert D. "Role of the Civil Engineer in Multipurpose River Development," *Civil Engineering*, XXVI (July, 1956), 435–437.

Wengert, Norman. "Antecedents of TVA: The Legislative History of Muscle Shoals," *Agricultural History*, XXVI (October, 1952), 141–47.

Williams, Robert W. "Hall County and the Poultry Industry." *Georgia Business*, XV (October, 1955), 6.

Wright, Donald T. "Paducah to Knoxville on the Tennessee River," *Waterways Journal*, LXVIII (April 24, 1954), 7–8.

———. "1953 Tennessee Tonnage Equals 1960 Forecast," *Waterways Journal*, LXVIII (April 24, 1954), 4.

———. "Watershed Authorities," *Waterways Journal*, LXVII (August 15, 1953), 7.

NEWSPAPERS

Birmingham *Age-Herald*, 1935.
Chattanooga *Free Press*, 1939.
Chattanooga *News*, 1933–1934.
Chattanooga *Times*, 1933–1935, 1939–1940, 1949, 1959.
Decatur (Ala.) *Daily*, 1959.
Florence (Ala.) *Herald*, 1933.
Knoxville *Journal*, 1933, 1954.
Louisville *Courier-Journal*, 1949.
Memphis *Commercial Appeal*, 1943.
Memphis *Press Scimitar*, 1939.
Nashville *Tennessean*, 1939, 1941–1942, 1951.
New York *Times*, 1932, 1934, 1938–1939.
Rockwood (Tenn.) *Times*, 1934.
Tuscumbia (Ala.) *Times*, 1934.

INDEX

DATE DUE